WORLD LITERATURE FOR THE
WRETCHED OF THE EARTH

World Literature for the Wretched of the Earth

Anticolonial Aesthetics, Postcolonial Politics

J. DANIEL ELAM

Fordham University Press
NEW YORK   2021

Copyright © 2021 Fordham University Press

All rights reserved. No part of this publication may be reproduced, stored in a retrieval system, or transmitted in any form or by any means—electronic, mechanical, photocopy, recording, or any other—except for brief quotations in printed reviews, without the prior permission of the publisher.

Fordham University Press has no responsibility for the persistence or accuracy of URLs for external or third-party Internet websites referred to in this publication and does not guarantee that any content on such websites is, or will remain, accurate or appropriate.

Fordham University Press also publishes its books in a variety of electronic formats. Some content that appears in print may not be available in electronic books.

Visit us online at www.fordhampress.com.

Library of Congress Cataloging-in-Publication Data available online at https://catalog.loc.gov.

Printed in the United States of America

23 22 21   5 4 3 2 1

First edition

Contents

	Preface	vi
	Introduction: Impossible Subjects	1
1	Lala Har Dayal's Imagination	19
2	B. R. Ambedkar's Sciences	44
3	M. K. Gandhi's Lost Debates	67
4	Bhagat Singh's Jail Notebook	92
	Epilogue: Stopping and Leaving	113
	Acknowledgments	131
	Notes	135
	Bibliography	169
	Index	189

Preface

In 1931, S. R. Ranganathan, an unknown literary scholar and statistician from India, published a curious manifesto: *The Five Laws of Library Science*. The manifesto, written shortly after Ranganathan's return to India from London—where he learned to despise, among other things, the Dewey decimal system and British bureaucracy—argues for reorganizing Indian libraries. Ranganathan believed that India's libraries, many of which had been established by the British, could promote radically egalitarian ideals if they followed five fundamental laws. The five laws appear on the first page of the book: "Books Are for Use. Every Reader His Book. Every Book Its Reader. Save the Time of the Reader. Library Is a Growing Organism." For Ranganathan, India's dearth of public libraries prevents the country's independence. A national library system, properly conceived, would be the catalyst for national sovereignty—but of an independent India that would fundamentally differ from the nations of Europe. Ranganathan was not simply a library scientist; he was a librarian-philosopher of democratic critique.

Of all the laws, the second law—"Every Reader His Book"—is the most important for a future egalitarian reading community. The second law is the only one to receive more than one chapter. Ranganathan devotes three chapters, including three didactic dialogues, to it.

As if to emphasize the radical egalitarianism the law creates, Ranganathan concludes the first chapter on the second law with a didactic dialogue in which several authorities come forward to suggest that the communities they oversee should be prevented from reading books.

The "Psychologist" argues that the mentally ill in his care should not be given books; a man representing blind people argues that braille is too expensive and therefore should be eliminated; an expert on the illiterate suggests primers are useless; and the "Jailor" argues that books should be banned from prisons because they incite anticolonial passions—"no books for damned murderers!" he proclaims, perhaps with Bhagat Singh in mind.[1]

The second law, emerging in human form as a woman, counters each of these claims individually and reiterates her claim that every reader should have access to books and to reading. Each authority figure first balks, then becomes curious, and then relinquishes his power to the second law. Having been collectively persuaded, they join hands:

> All sing in a chorus:
> There's room for all
> Let not the mean
> Or learned dean
> Restrict the books
> T' a favoured few
> We've Books for all.
> Books for the rich
> And Books for the poor
> Books for the man
> And Books for the dame.
> Books for the sick
> And Books for the fit
> Books for the blind
> And Books for the dumb.
> Books for the bungler
> And Books for the wrangler
> Books for the burgher
> And Books for the cotter.
> Books for the lettered
> And Books for the fettered
> We've Books for all
> For one and all.[2]

The authorities, thus reconciled with the second law, leave with books and without their former authority: The second law has made them readers. Ranganathan proclaims this to be the first step in the *digvijaya* of library science, or what he calls "the world-conquering expedition" of readers, beginning first with India and the United States: the relinquishing of one's authority to the collective exegesis of readership, "perpetual education," and "unlimited democracy."[3]

This is not exactly what the British Raj had in mind when they established anglophone libraries (and pedagogy) in British India in the mid-nineteenth century. In his "Minute on Indian Education" from 1835, T. B. Macaulay declared not only that "Western literature" was intrinsically superior, such that "a single shelf of a good European library was worth the whole native literature of India and Arabia,"[4] but also that the British should teach English literature in order to create "a class of interpreters between us and the millions we govern; a class of persons Indian in blood and colour, but English in tastes, in opinions, in morals and in intellect."[5] The establishment of "good European librar[ies]" across British India became the means for the British to extend their imperial project. British authorship was the mechanism of British colonial authority.[6]

Of course, Indian readers were more unpredictable and less impressionable to colonial mimicry than Macaulay imagined or hoped them to be. Their reading habits ranged beyond the standard English canon.[7] By the 1920s and 1930s, anticolonial thinkers were busy theorizing reading not merely as consumption but also as a properly anticolonial practice. Anti-imperial critique envisioned the reader not as a sociological figure or a consuming subject but rather as an ideal figure for ethical and political practices. This anticolonial theory of reading was not concerned with the consumption of literary texts per se; instead, it tried to envision the possibility that the act of reading might signify—that is, the possibility of egalitarian emancipation.

In the first decades of the twentieth century, many South Asian thinkers had made reading and critique a fundamental part of anticolonial self-cultivation in the pursuit of expertise and mastery. But there appear to be just as many anticolonial agitators who urged their readers to read simply for the sake of reading—that is, for its inconsequence.

A more vibrant form of anticolonial thought emerged in the 1920s and 1930s, and Ranganathan was its most pragmatic proponent. This form of anticolonial thought argued for reading and communal interpretation not to cultivate a form of mastery but to disavow mastery altogether. To remain a reader—and to remain a reader with others—were the goals of this anticolonial theory of reading. To put it another way, in the terms of the didactic poem of the second law: To relinquish one's authority in order to become a reader was the ideal of this anticolonial theory of reading. To become or remain a reader, and thus purposefully to divest oneself of authorial claims, was to fundamentally challenge the logic of the British Raj, which claimed to prize self-mastery as the precondition for national independence.

In Ranganathan's four-hundred-page book about books and their readers, the word "author" appears only once—in a footnote—and very few authors' names are to be found in the text, even as examples. Ranganathan was uninterested in authors. As he explains in his chapter on the third law ("Every Book Its Reader"), readers are the sole purpose of a library, and books without readers, even books by so-called important authors, should be discarded from a library. *The Five Laws of Library Science* asserts the centrality of the reader in an anticolonial library science. The emergence of readers, Ranganathan notes, marks the transition from despotic rule to democracy and freedom. His book is a manifesto fundamentally invested in the tyro rather than the tyrant.

In the case of British India, where the British author was the aesthetic extension of British authority, reconfiguring the hierarchical relation between the allegedly transcendent author and the multitude of readers was a form of imagining a postcolonial egalitarianism. To upend the colonial configuration of authority, anticolonial writers disavowed expertise and self-mastery, instead asserting a heteronomous collectivity formed through practices of reading. As an anticolonial practice, reading could mark modes of refusal, nonproductivity, inconsequence, inexpertise, and nonauthority. In direct contrast to the values of British liberalism, these recalcitrant ideals were perfect for envisioning a radical egalitarianism rooted in communal reading and collective textual criticism.

Instead, anticolonial thinkers took up reading to perpetually refuse the expertise, and therefore sovereignty, that the British Raj would ostensibly recognize as deserving of national independence. Rather than becoming the "mimic men" T. B. Macaulay had imagined in his famous "Minute on Indian Education" in 1835, antiauthoritarian anticolonialism became a different menace, revealing the hierarchical and anti-egalitarian norms at the heart of British liberalism and the European nation-state. Envisioned in this way, anticolonial thought becomes more radically about retaining the promise of postcolonial antiauthoritarianism rather than the mere attainment of national independence.

Ranganathan offers Macaulay's "Minute" as the opposite of his readerly vision. Macaulay's bookshelf of British authors, he argues, simply reproduces British authority in British India by way of "mimic men" in the absence of the British.[8] According to Ranganathan, the class of elite Indian men the British Raj produced were "filters" (Macaulay's word was "interpreters"), but who had failed to distribute the education, and therefore the power, that they had been allegedly granted.

What begins as a minor critique of Macaulay's "Minute" becomes an anticolonial proclamation:

> If Macaulay's filter has proved a snare, ere long it will divert its course and keep clear of this clog in the "filter." The Second Law will not take a defeat. It must win ultimately. That is our faith. With the world opinion backing it, it may win even at no distant date. If they are shrewd business men, the "English-educated" Indians should greet it with an olive branch and volunteer their services in its holy war on lingering ignorance. Then only, they will gain any respect in the eyes of the world and then only can they survive amidst the forces that will be set free on the day that the Second Law plants its flag on Indian soil and puts the BOOKS in the hands of ALL, even as it has done on other soils.[9]

Readers form the centerpiece of Ranganathan's cosmopolitan anticolonial library science, and the cultivation of egalitarianism by way of readerly communities stands at the heart of Ranganathan's project. The future flag of India is marked not by new authority but, using Russia and the United States as models, by the idea "books in the hands of all": a truly egalitarian practice of reading and a radically antiauthorial and antiauthor belief in readers.

Ranganathan's philosophy of readerly egalitarianism borders on the absurd. Using a map of Tompkins County, New York, Ranganathan imagines a reading community designed around a set of concentric circles beginning at a centrally located library in the town of Ithaca and moving outward in increasingly larger circles; he imagines that outpost libraries would be located in each quadrant, and books would circulate among all the libraries.[10] This geographic model, he demonstrates, aligns with the "internal repose" produced by the communal discussion of shared texts, which prepares readers for democratic society.[11] The psychical circles of "internal repose," like Ithaca's geographic ones, move constantly from "facts (nadir)" to "fundamental/universal laws (zenith)" and back.[12] Ranganathan's point is not to dismiss facts—which are necessary for his proposed psychical process—but rather to insist on the importance of democratic and egalitarian institutions that create individuals who can resist authoritarianism. The circles, Ranganathan argues, foreground the nonteleology of a properly ethical library science: in the communities of upstate New York—as in the individual—mastery, expertise, and authority are never attained; books circulate and "fundamental and universal laws" shift under the weight of new "facts."[13]

Taken out of its historical context, a lengthy treatise on the ethico-political possibilities of library science might seem strange. But British India in the 1920s and 1930s was hectic with radical utopian proposals, anticolonial manifestos, and radical democratic critiques—not unlike other countries in the years just after World War I. Ranganathan was in good company. He was not alone in bringing home, after the war, a pastiche of Victorian optimism and shell-shocked pessimism. With adjustments and additions appropriate for the pessimistic utopianism of the moment, manuals of nineteenth-century liberal self-cultivation and self-care reappeared (like Herbert Spencer's and John Stuart Blackie's, but also, and more popular, Giuseppe Mazzini's proto-fascist *Duties of Man*), as did radical proposals for the reorganization of society, which were circulated heavily in the literary centers of British India, especially in Lahore, Delhi, Lucknow, Bombay, Madras, and Calcutta. The library became the locus of anticolonial activity (and, not unrelatedly, colonial surveillance) not simply because Indian anticolonial agitators were studying to become the future authorities of a postcolonial nation. Rather, for many anticolonial thinkers, the library became the location of a global egalitarian culture because it promoted a revolutionary inconsequentialism in the face of the imperial demand for practical knowledge.

Reading or critique, in this formula, was a practice of egalitarian antiauthoritarianism precisely because it urged readers to refuse the calls of authorship, and, relatedly, authority. To remain a reader—and to remain a reader with others—was precisely the goal of this anticolonial theory of reading. To become or remain a reader, and thus purposefully divest oneself of authorial claims, was to fundamentally challenge the logic of the British Raj, which claimed to prize self-mastery as the alleged proof necessary for national independence. To become or to remain a reader, and thus perpetually abjure self-mastery, also challenged the logic of European fascism (not far removed from the logic of British imperialism), which prized purity as the assurance of national homogeneity.

The radical importance of this anticolonial theory of reading and criticism, in my interpretation, is that it prizes practices of communal and egalitarian critique—a celebration of unknowingness *ad infinitum*—as the model by which a truly antiauthoritarian anticolonial politics might be attained. In this sense, although Ranganathan and his colleagues openly advocated Indian independence from British rule, they endeavored to imagine, quite seriously, a nation founded less on authoritative national sovereignty and more on egalitarian readerly internationalism—a flag of books, in the hands of all.

Anticolonial thinkers theorized practices of reading that perpetually refuse the self-mastery, and therefore sovereignty, that the British Raj would ostensibly recognize as deserving of national independence. Envisioned in this way, anticolonial thought becomes about retaining the promise of postcolonial, radically egalitarian antiauthoritarianism rather than merely attaining national independence. An anticolonial theory of reading, along with the concomitant refusal of liberal self-mastery, was a fitting response to the horrors European liberalism created around the world.

Ranganathan's lengthy manifesto is one of many such manifestos in South Asian political writing in the 1920s and 1930s that, on the one hand, imagine the relation between authorship and authority and, on the other, imagine anticolonialism as antiauthoritarianism. Anticolonial thinkers across the political spectrum not only argued for the importance of communal criticism against individual authorship but also went to great lengths to refuse their own authority and expertise. M. K. Gandhi, most famously, attempted to "reduce [himself] to zero" only to be challenged by the revolutionary activist Bhagat Singh for being too much of an author to properly act on behalf of the masses. Bhagat Singh's jail notebook attests to his own experiments to reduce himself to a "reader," even as postcolonial hagiographers have declared both men "masters" and "fathers" of modern India.[14]

The radicalism of the worldwide interwar period was quickly overshadowed not only by the horrors of fascism but also by the dull pragmatism required to transform newly independent colonies into postcolonial nation-states. By the 1940s, and certainly in the wake of the horrific partition of 1947, interwar antiauthoritarian ideals dwindled into the joylessness of establishing India and Pakistan as nations and aligning them with the norms introduced by the United Nations. In the course of becoming properly sovereign, the radical aesthetics that had undergirded South Asian anticolonialism were ignored in favor of state building. After Indian independence in 1947, Ranganathan played a central role in establishing India's national library system; he was the primary figure behind the Public Libraries Act of 1948. Although the act required Indian libraries to be free and open to the public (in accordance with the second law), the act also created gatekeepers and library masters—those same authorities that the second law had once converted into readers. Lost was that original anticolonial recalcitrance.

But to return to Ranganathan's utopian library is to imagine a vibrantly "bibliomigrant" world in which the circulation of aesthetic ideas could be made common and egalitarian: reading was revolutionary.[15] The library, with its endless collection of books—an infinitely "growing organism," as per Ranganathan's fifth law—was one way of theorizing anticolonial reading and communal discussion, acts that remained perpetually incomplete. It represents an anticolonial politics that does not seek dominance and mastery but rather attempts to remain a perpetual novice, in the service of a world after colonial rule.

WORLD LITERATURE FOR THE
WRETCHED OF THE EARTH

Introduction: Impossible Subjects

> *Each generation must discover its mission in relative opacity, either to fulfill it or betray it.*
>
> —FRANTZ FANON, WRETCHED OF THE EARTH

On his deathbed in the United States—a "country of lynchers"—Frantz Fanon frantically dictated *The Wretched of the Earth* (*Les Damnés de la Terre*) to his wife, Josie. He was dying rapidly from leukemia and had secretly flown to Bethesda, Maryland, for treatment under the name Omar Ibrahim. He lived long enough to proofread, with silent disappointment, Jean-Paul Sartre's commissioned preface, but he never saw his book in print. The same day French police raided presses to halt the book's circulation in Paris, on December 6, 1961, Fanon died in Bethesda. Fanon's makeshift homeland, Algeria, gained independence in 1962. (Martinique, Fanon's birthplace, is still under French rule.)[1]

Sartre's introduction, though certainly an important celebrity and political endorsement in 1961, has overshadowed subsequent analyses of Fanon's text. In a philosophical maneuver that Fanon had described in *Black Skin, White Masks* (*Peau noire, masques blancs*, 1952), Sartre understood white French men to be the book's primary, if not exclusive, audience.[2] If Fanon was addressing the colonizer at all, it was because Fanon knew that the colonizer, having become monstrous, was eavesdropping anyway. For Fanon, the process of national independence requires concern for its means without knowing its ends (or worse: fearing that its ends will produce colonizers but with new faces). Sartre saw in Fanon's cautious analysis a confident "dialectic" march toward "the history of man" (. . . *une autre histoire. Celle de l'homme*).[3] Consequently, where Fanon's concern with violence is analytic, tentative, and anxious, Sartre's is masochistically bloodthirsty. Where Fanon considered violence (in an abstract form) the treacherous means to an end, Alice Cherki writes, Sartre called for *actual* crime and murder.[4] We rightly cringe, then, when Sartre proclaims, "Fanon speaks out loud and clear. We Europeans, we can hear him."[5]

Almost but not quite. Certainly Sartre speaks so loudly and clearly in the first 20 pages of the book that Fanon is barely audible for the remaining 250. Hannah Arendt, writing in the context of U.S. student protests and Civil Rights movements, certainly couldn't hear Fanon's equivocation over Sartre's bravado. Arendt's attempt to rescue political action from "violence" does not align with Fanon's anticolonial concerns, but it is certainly closer than the Fanon she presents—which she admits in a footnote while condemning Fanon as "irresponsible" and "grandiose" in the body of the text.[6]

It is too easy to condemn Sartre for poor reading comprehension.[7] Instead, we might celebrate Fanon's ability to speak to his fellow anticolonial comrades while remaining largely unintelligible to his colonizer. We can delineate a set of interlocking theories that Fanon's anticolonial partial unintelligibility describes. First, *The Wretched of the Earth* is a document of *unknowing*. Fanon remains cautious about the politics of a postcolonial world to come. Second, it is also a document of unknowability. Even when it speaks in perfect French, the French cannot understand (another condition Fanon had diagnosed in *Black Skin, White Masks*). Third, by remaining unknowing and unknowable to colonial logics, it posits the basis of a collectivity on the condition of its unknowability.[8] In the conclusion, Fanon demands that the "wretched" form the mass that will endeavor to "create a new man" on the basis of their wretchedness.

Anticolonialism is a mission in relative opacity. By offering us an anticolonial politics of unknowing, unintelligibility, and collective unrecognizability, Fanon makes it possible to imagine the reformulation of anticolonialism that, while in the full view of the colonizer, nevertheless remains entirely beyond its imaginative purview. This mission is not entirely opaque, but *relatively* so: It is still capacious enough to incorporate those who are willing to participate in its anonymous egalitarianism. To borrow a particularly moving description from Hannah Arendt, "If men [sic] wish to be free, it is precisely sovereignty they must relinquish," in favor of "infinite improbabilities."[9] Anticolonialism thrives not in seeking recognition or self-mastery in order to demonstrate sovereignty, but in relinquishing that possibility in favor of a radically (and likely impossible) democratic ethos of antiauthoritarianism.

Politics can only be "the art of the possible" for those whose lives are secured by the state, or, in other words, only for those can confidently know that they will live to see the "possible" attained. Those whose lives are not guaranteed by the state, or those whose lives the state actively expects to end, cannot afford the luxury of such politics. The "wretched of the earth" require, instead, a politics of the impossible. This politics requires imagining and foregrounding, in the face of imminent or certain death, a politics not accountable to regimes of "success," "sustainability," or "attainability," but rather to "the meantime": the time being, the passing moment, and the present.

This is an unsustainable and inconsequential politics. It is a radical politics of the present. *The Wretched of the Earth* was prophetic not in the sense that it predicted a world after colonialism. More often than not, Fanon concedes that there will likely never be a world "after colonialism." National independence would only be a brief interruption of a majoritarian continuity, ceaselessly replicating the same colonial logics of hierarchy and oppression. The book's conclusion is a call to abandon Europe, its mad rush toward total slaughter, the pressures of its Cold War dichotomies and binaries, and its demand that the "Third World" be interpellated on "First World" and "Second World" terms. It is perhaps a vision for a utopian future, but it is a future that Fanon, whose health was deteriorating rapidly, knew he would not live to see. Despair and nihilism are insufficient for an anticolonial politics, but they guard against the equally unsatisfactory politics of optimism and hope.[10] Anticolonialism is, in this final instance, a project of locating fleeting moments of egalitarian politics in the relative opacity of an unguaranteed future.

Fanon's is one of many forms of anticolonialism that demonstrate that the philosophical project of radical egalitarianism emerged not from within Europe, but as a response to the horrors of its oppressive rule around the world. Conscripted to participate in a world they had not chosen, anticolonial and exiled thinkers nevertheless endeavored to imagine that world otherwise. David Scott has shown how these future postcolonial worlds were both romantically emancipatory and mired in deep tragedy.[11] For Scott, postcolonial studies, as the benefactor of these anticolonial imagined futures, has erred toward the romantic; as a correction, Scott argues that postcolonial futures must recuperate tragedy as the genre of the anticolonial imagination.

A vision of a postcolonial future, both alluring *and* grievous, stands at the center of most anticolonial thought. But it was a future that many anticolonial thinkers knew they would never inhabit. Anticolonial thought was written in exile, on deathbeds, in abjection, or in the face of "declined experience."[12] Anti-imperial thinkers did not simply write narratives of romance or tragedy. They sought vocabulary that could properly capture both the grandiose utopianism and self-effacing acquiescence necessary to imagine a world that they would not live to see. They attempted to create a language sufficient to imagine political collectivities motivated by the very fact of their current impossibility. They invented aesthetic forms necessary to imagine a worldwide egalitarianism rooted in the unlikelihood of any future at all.[13]

Anticolonialism thus operates at a seemingly paradoxical nexus: the incertitude of its own fulfillment and the refusal to betray the mission of emancipatory politics. The project of antiauthoritarian anticolonial thought, as we will discuss in the following pages, is to operate in conditions of relative opacity in two senses. First, anticolonial thought propounds theories of action in relative opacity, sufficient to form collectivities, but without getting recognized by the colonial state. Second, anticolonialism is an attempt to articulate a world that has yet to exist, which will likely never exist, and to do so without knowing it in advance. The anticolonial thinkers in this book embrace this condition of unknowing and non-futurity. Instead of trying to seek recognition or authority, anticolonial thinkers foreground relative opacity by celebrating the impossibility of their task and practicing forms of relinquishment, disavowal, and non-productivity necessary for anti-imperial survival in the compromised present.

In order to recuperate the anticolonial aesthetic vision conducive for its postcolonial egalitarian practice, this book reconceives of anticolonial thought as not merely political philosophy or aesthetic experimentation, but as both: that is to say, as critique. Critique and criticism, too, are practices of authorial or authoritative relinquishment. The critic-reader in this long tradition is "the figure in the carpet" whose readerly egalitarianism stays rooted in a pluralistic ontology that is "multitudinous beyond imagination, tangled, muddy, painful and perplexed."[14]

In this sense, I argue, the aesthetics of anticolonial thought are best illuminated by situating them in conversation with a practice occurring simultaneously on the fringes of or in exile from Europe: comparative philology. Although it is saddled with a reputation for being myopically pedantic, comparative philology in the 1920s and 1930s was experimenting with its methodology, its scope, and its political commitments. Philology, "the art of reading slowly" (or, literally, "the love of words"),[15] had held a fairly central role in the humanities through the nineteenth century.[16] Writing in exile or in secret, German Jewish philologists wrote for a literary world that might survive fascism, even if they would not. They imagined reading practices conducive for an egalitarian world, rid of its murderous drive for purity, defined instead by hospitality, heterogeneity, and improvisational assemblage.

Though the two bodies of work appear at first glance to be unrelated, they share more than mere contemporaneity. The thinkers in this book drew on philological scholarship to craft their anticolonial theory. More importantly, comparative philology and anticolonial political thought were both committed to envisioning a new "world" in response to, and from underneath, the horrors of fascism and colonialism, that a future "literature" was to imagine, inherit, and create. By reading philological criticism and anticolonial thought together—and as texts that offer a conjoined aesthetic and political theory—I illuminate a shared concern for radical humanism, egalitarianism, and worldliness.

This book therefore demonstrates how an anti-authoritarian practice of close reading, and the concomitant disavowal of authorial mastery, reshapes and reconfigures our current debates around critique and practices of radical politics. In contrast to previous studies of anticolonial writing that have focused on revolutionary outcomes and therefore prize national independence, sovereignty, and authority, I argue that anticolonial writing offers a political aesthetics centered on a commitment to "inconsequence" as a way of refusing future mastery and expertise. Drawing on this unacknowledged strain of anticolonial philosophy, this book offers an alternative theory of literary and political critique that inherits and reshapes the double intellectual afterlife of comparativism and postcolonial studies. In this vein, I suggest we foreground comparative philology and anticolonial thinkers as impossible subjects: a perpetually un-masterable discipline in the first instance, and philosophers committed to perpetual disavowal and relinquishment in the second.

The forms of anticolonial and philological thought presented in this book argue for reading and communal criticism *not* in order to cultivate a form of mastery, but precisely to disavow mastery altogether. These thinkers urged readers to read for its own sake—that is, for inconsequence.[17] Reading, in this formula, was a practice of egalitarian antiauthoritarianism precisely because it urged readers to refuse the calls of authorship, and, relatedly, authority. To remain a reader—and to remain a reader with others—was precisely the goal of this theory of reading. To become or remain a reader, and thus purposefully divest oneself of authorial claims, was to fundamentally challenge the logic of the British Empire and European fascism, which claimed to prize self-mastery as the alleged proof necessary for national independence.[18]

By foregrounding an anticolonialism not organized around the telos of its alleged realization, we recuperate an anti-nihilist non-futurity. These thinkers did not languish in the easy rejection of a postcolonial future, and they were not convinced that any predictable future was necessarily secured. It is possible to call this body of thought, in its most humble form, "a politics of the meantime," or a politics for those stuck in "the waiting room of history."[19] What anticolonial practices could take care of people whose anonymous deaths would certainly precede utopia? But in grander terms, this is a radical politics of the present, or what Kama Maclean has called a "politics of impatience":[20] Unable to sit and wait for a formal revolution to occur, these thinkers imagined ways of enacting it in the present in minor, unintelligible, and illegible ways.

Framed by Fanon's call to "create a new man" in the conclusion to *The Wretched of the Earth* and Erich Auerbach's call for a philology conducive for a new (but impossible) world, this book focuses primarily on South Asian anticolonial thought as a nexus of a global imagination available in the 1920s and 1930s. The figures presented in this book represent the wide range of anti-imperial critique between World War I and World War II.

World War I was the catalyst for the "crisis of the European Man" (so-named by Edmund Husserl in 1935) and the related demand, then, to rethink political and ethical possibilities around the world. Metaphysical and transcendental assurances could no longer be the basis of ethical and political claims. Stefanos Geroulanos has shown how the response to transcendental certitude produced new modes of non-humanist and illiberal philosophies.[21] The proliferation of ethical and political writing, in the 1920s and early 1930s, represented an often desperate but also optimistic attempt to reimagine a new world and a new human (and, relatedly, new aesthetic forms). To be sure, political philosophy from this period spanned the political spectrum and included radically egalitarian utopianism (cooperative mutual aid) as well as nationalist socialism (fascism).

This "crisis," however, was hardly endemic to Europe, even if its most notorious European forms now overshadow other, more minor contemporaneous offerings. In a new and shell-shocked world, writers promoted their own ideas about what was to be done, or what could now be done. On an emphatically global scale, philosophers and thinkers suggested ways of being with others in the world.

For a variety of reasons, it was in this brief period that it was possible to imagine a world without British rule, but not possible enough to begin sorting out the tedious details of the post-independent nation-state. It was possible, even, to imagine that the nation-state needn't—and shouldn't—be the only form of political collectivity.[22] To the extent that these were reasons to be optimistic, they were also cause for pessimism.

The British might leave, but there were plenty of local leaders keen to take their exact place. A colonized territory might become independent, but there were plenty of nationalists eager to blindly replicate Europe's disastrously xenophobic forms: national borders, cultural homogeneity, and defensive sovereignty. Consequently, anticolonial thinkers in this period allowed themselves the freedom to imagine wildly implausible postcolonial worlds. For the thinkers here, I hope to demonstrate, the very concepts of anticolonialism, freedom, egalitarianism, and political belonging could be repeatedly rethought and reimagined.

Lala Har Dayal, B. R. Ambedkar, M. K. Gandhi, and Bhagat Singh are the primary subjects in the chapters that follow. They are, of course, only four of many anticolonial thinkers whose political experimentation included minor gestures and practices of antiauthoritarianism. Although I will argue that they are theorists of minor, untraceable, and ephemeral acts, they are themselves hardly minor figures. Lala Har Dayal was one of the founders of the California- and Punjab-based *Ghadr* Party, which advocated for armed mutiny against the British Raj in the 1910s. B. R. Ambedkar is a leading figure of Dalit (formerly "untouchable") and anti-caste activism in the twentieth century, and he remains widely celebrated across India. As the leading national and global face of the Indian independence movement from the 1920s until his death, M. K. Gandhi espoused theories of "non-violence" that have been taken up by multiple civil rights activists. Bhagat Singh was one of the central figures in the Hindustan Socialist Republican Army in Punjab and an anticolonial martyr whose hanging, at 23, made him a regional and national hero.

These theorists wrote extensively about anticolonialism *as* antiauthoritarianism and global egalitarianism (rather than anticolonial figures working in more nationalist or xenophobic idioms). All four thinkers documented—extensively if not exhaustively—their various political and aesthetic experimentations, one of which was serious engagement with reading and critique as an anticolonial practice. These thinkers were self-consciously in conversation with many other people who were likely theorizing similar practices, whose voices appear in their theories. I regret that there are many activists whose voices do not appear in these pages, especially the women whom these men considered colleagues, adversaries, and friends.[23]

Yet it is precisely because these four men figure so prominently and "heroically" in postcolonial discussions of anticolonial activism—in both academic scholarship as well as in popular discourse—that they make especially rich theorists of their own antiauthoritarian insignificance. More so than other anticolonial figures, these men are considered experts of political and social theory, masters of various philosophical traditions, and authoritative leaders for an independent Indian nation. Alternatively, they are heroic assassins, brave bomb throwers, and daring fasters. To be sure, these are fair descriptions. But they fail to account for the ways in which these four figures were theorizing other acts of anticolonialism that have since been relegated to the dustbin of acts deemed improperly political (reading, moving-going), unrecognizably resistant (studying, eating), and insufficiently heroic (fumbling, failing).

These thinkers, very much aware of the *possible* consequences of their *recognizably* political actions, attempted to imagine, simultaneously, *impossibility* and *inconsequentiality* as rubrics for antiauthoritarian projects. Despite their significant disagreements, the thinkers presented here share a common theoretical belief: that the true practice of anticolonialism must be uninhibited by the telos of its realization. In Bhagat Singh's Bolshevik-inspired terms, this was permanent revolution. In M. K. Gandhi's renunciatory terms, this was infinite relinquishment. Lala Har Dayal imagined a revolution that was propelled forward as it looked backward at the horrors of history. B. R. Ambedkar took his intellectual inheritance of sociology and philology and pushed them to their breaking point in order to realize a human subject that would be fundamentally incapable of caste.

Departing from a clean history of ideas, and on behalf of an anti-canon of literary thought, our discussion in the pages that follow will trace disorderly histories, promiscuous modes of thought, impossible transformations, and improvisational adjacencies.[24] These are the methods, we will find, necessary to imagine a world "haunted by its own incertitude";[25] to act on behalf of "inconstructable questions";[26] and to remain "immune to the inducements of either hegemony or canonicity."[27] In the first instance, the reading practices discussed here are practices that seek to *evade* recognition rather than demand it. The goals of these collective practices are, variously: unrecognizability, indecipherability, unintelligibility, untraceability, and untranslatability in the face of an authority or an authorial/authorizing institution. In the second instance, these practices are attempts at "irrelevance," "inconsequence," "insufficiency," or the foregrounding of one's own in-expertise, anti-sovereignty, and unknowing. Leela Gandhi has dubbed similar practices trials in "moral imperfectionism" and non-renunciatory asceticism.[28] We will be interested instead in theories of collective practices invested in the fleeting moment, rather than practices of self-cultivation. In other words, what are the possibilities of a "self" relinquished to total unknowability and infinite risk? Aesthetically speaking, that is to say, a certain strain of anticolonialism has imagined the possibility of no "self" at all, but an anonymous, interpenetrating, multitudinous collectivity.

Scholars who dismiss anticolonial thought often do so along the lines that it allegedly produces dull practicality motivated by half-baked utopianism (or vice versa). Those who have engaged anticolonial thought more seriously but patronizingly have found it to be "improperly political," too fraught with ethical and moral prerogatives to be of use.[29] More vibrantly, though not without some defensiveness, scholars have argued that anticolonial thinkers provide us with robust and mature theories of violence, mastery, asceticism, equality, unconditionality, solidarity, utopianism, liberalism, modernity, freedom, democracy, cosmopolitanism, decolonization, and universalism.[30] Fewer scholars have overtly celebrated the aesthetics of anticolonial thought, but we often fall prey to justifying its canonicity by rendering it roughly equivalent to European forms.

In other words, in response to assertions that anticolonialism was too aesthetic to be political or too political to be aesthetic, we have retreated to two unappealing dead-ends: on the one hand, sacrificing the aesthetics of anticolonialism to the "joylessness of a utilitarian dispensation,"[31] or, on the other, replicating the very aesthetic hierarchies, canons, and authorities—even if with new faces—anticolonial thought had attempted to undermine. Some anticolonial thinkers have finally been allowed to produce political philosophy; the occasional anticolonial writer has finally been granted the status of "literary," or at least having written well. Nearly absent altogether, however, is the acknowledgment that many anticolonial thinkers unequivocally *refused* to think politics and aesthetics as separate. This suggests, to my mind, a disconcerting indifference to the fairly unambiguous claims of the writers themselves, especially those foregrounded in this book.[32] To this end, they prefigure contemporary attempts to think the human beyond the unit of the "individual." This is what Kandice Chuh has beautifully described as "illiberal humanisms," which foreground "relationality and entanglement rather than individuality and autochthony."[33] Let us take anticolonial critics at their word. To recuperate anticolonial theory in its fullest sense requires us to consider anticolonial thought as *critique*.

I mean "critique" here in the sense of its more capacious German genealogy (*Kritik*), therefore more or less synonymous with "criticism," and certainly indebted here to Walter Benjamin's lifelong cultivation of the term. Recall that Benjamin attempted to develop a form of aesthetic criticism suitable for political action in the present. Benjamin's sense of criticism was the product of an idiosyncratic alchemy: Kant tempered by Schegel and Goethe; Schegel and Goethe catalyzed by Marx; Marx pushed to crisis by Brecht.³⁴ In short, Benjaminian criticism is a recalcitrance against Enlightenment assurance (Kant's *Aufklarung*) in favor of enchantment and wonder (Weber's *Entzauberung der Welt*), but nevertheless compelled (contra Goethe and Schegel) by the emergency of the worldly political present (Schmitt's *Ausnahmezustand*). It is not a practice, therefore, of Kantian critical "maturity" but one of experience (*Erlebnis*) and encounter, too fleeting and ephemeral to "mature" at all. A re-enchanted, immature critique relies on imagination ("to read what has never been written") to imagine radical, pessimistic but utopian, politics ("a revolutionary chance to fight for the oppressed past"), which is fleeting (a memory that "flashes up at a moment of danger").³⁵ It is, additionally, a practice of self-erasure and of enabling "the masses" to cultivate, *as masses*, a form of aesthetic-political critique. Correctly so, Philip Weinstein has described this as "unknowing."³⁶ Benjamin's practice of criticism is, if not impossible, infeasible; that Benjamin continued to hone his techniques attests less to a practice of mastery and more to a practice of in-expertise: an attempt to become *even more* immature, *even more* enchanted, *even more* utopian, often to the embarrassment of his colleagues.

Benjamin began his graduate work in philology but switched to philosophy, and then attempted to combine both in his work on German tragedy. In an essay on "The Theory of Criticism," Benjamin wrote that philosophy aspires for unity, but philology aspires to be awed.³⁷ In response to Adorno's criticism that his work was too naïve, Benjamin begins to trace the contours of a philological critical orientation: "a 'wide-eyed presentation of the facts'" characterizes "the true philological attitude." Philology "magically fixates the reader" on a text, "whose exorcism is reserved for philosophy."³⁸ In an earlier essay on Goethe's *Elective Affinities*, Benjamin asserts the need for a critique that "stops short, however—as if in awe of the work, but equally from respect for the truth."³⁹ Where the critic stops, regimes of mastery continue. For Benjamin, critique grasps beauty in "the impossibility of unveiling," rather than the alleged benefits of discovering what is "underneath."⁴⁰ In contrast, recall the brutality with which the French demanded an "Algeria unveiled," in Fanon's detailed account.⁴¹ Where the critic revels in unknowing, the expert is driven murderously mad by the alleged "secret" being withheld from him. The expert defines unknown and anonymous others by the his inability to "possess" (and to penetrate) them. The critic, in contrast, stops in naïve awe before unknown and unpossessable others. Stopping short, in awe: These are the prerequisites for an immature critique, necessary for an inexpert project.

Erich Auerbach's monumental *Mimesis*, written in Istanbul and in exile from Nazi Germany, is the most famous example of naïve philological awe. A fragmentary collection of close readings, from Homer to Virginia Woolf, *Mimesis* stages multiple attempts to grasp "the representation of reality in Western literature." This subtitle alone should alert us to the impossibility of Auerbach's task.

In his introduction to the fiftieth anniversary of the English edition of *Mimesis*, Edward Said notes that "A great part of Auerbach's charm as a critic is that, far from seeming heavy-handed and pedantic, he exudes a sense of searching and discovery, the joys and uncertainties of which he shares unassumingly with his reader."[42] In other words, *Mimesis* is a fragmentary and partial text whose authorial presence and expertise is displaced in favor of a readerly sensibility. The book's methodology, as well as its aesthetic and political commitments, were implicit and often experimental. By foregrounding imperfection and insufficiency as the necessary critical sensibility, Auerbach wrote aesthetic theory for a world defined by its impossibility.

Let us imagine then that critique and criticism, properly reconceived, are methods of reading that remain relatively opaque. In "a paper read at a school," Virginia Woolf offers a question—how should one read a book?—which she refuses to answer. For Woolf, there is no correct way to read a book except to allow the text to impress upon you—that is, to experience no other sensation than momentary immersion and ecstasy.[43] "To read is to be elsewhere," Michel de Certeau reminds us; Roland Barthes finds himself being cruised in a poorly lit park (by both the text and the police). Upon reading, Marcel Proust finds himself thrown into his childhood, "beside the fire in the dining-room, in my bedroom, in the depths of the armchair with its crocheted head-rest, or on fine afternoons, beneath the nut bushes and hawthorns in the park, where every breath from the boundless fields came from so far off to play silently at my side, holding mutely out to my distracted nostrils the scent of the clover and the sainfoin to which my weary eyes would sometimes be raised," an incommunicable experience at the heart of uncounted, inconsequential afternoons.[44]

"We must remain readers," Woolf urges her audience. Walter Benjamin recalls the "fragile threads of a net in which I had once become tangled when learning to read" in his Berlin childhood.[45] Reading is not only to enter into a pact with the text, but to become entangled with an anonymous collectivity of others.[46] Criticism, in Pascale Casanova's reading of Henry James, "is to be sought not above and beyond the carpet itself, but by looking at it from another point of view."[47] To read is to become impure with the impression of others, in Adam Zachary Newton's deeply moving account: to find that *je est un autre*.[48] Critique as unknowing anonymity safeguards the experience of anonymous collective textual encounter by rendering enigmatic the very thing it claims to render intelligible. Critique as "open secret" announces and circumscribes the unintelligibility of this readerly collectivity.[49]

"Reading" thus names a revived genealogy of critique and criticism that foregrounds its own authoritative limits and insists instead on its own incompletion, in-expertise, and often its own implausibility.[50] This model of criticism works along minor networks: It is rooted in gestures, experiments, fragments, and practices that think at the boundaries of illegibility and unintelligibility. Configured this way, this practice of critique, imbued with minoritarian urgency, will certainly push us past the confines of self-satisfied critical authority that has "run out of steam," in Bruno Latour's words.[51]

This mode of criticism aligns with the scholarly practices of comparative philology occurring in response to the increasing force of fascism in Europe in the 1920s and 1930s. Foregrounding practices of impurity, anti-mastery, and the formulation of heteronomous critical practices stood in direct opposition to fascism, totalitarianism, and Nazism, which sought to produce collectivities on the bases of purity, mastery, domination, and homogeneity. In response, comparative philologists reveled in impurity (translation, commensurability), anti-mastery (the perpetual insufficiency of one's knowledge), and heterogeneity (comparison).[52] This required thinking (to borrow terms from more recent critics) equivalence *without* substitutability, equivalence *because of* inequality, "equivalences which do not unify,"[53] and "comparison that is common but not unified."[54]

Early twentieth-century philology theorized practices of reading as ways of retaining heterogeneity, perpetual inexpertise, and impurity in the face of fascist national homogenization and cultural purification. By foregrounding the philologist critic as perpetually insufficient—there were always more books to read, more languages to learn—philology envisioned a community of interdependent readers. In direct contrast to the goals of European fascism, these scholarly practices were necessary for retaining a commitment to other readers and critics, as well as a deference to those readers and critics, even when their lives were not assured.

The name of his scholarly endeavor—comparative philology—not only augers an unachievable task, but barricades against the temptations of scholarly expertise and mastery. Comparative philology (or, later, comparative literature), by way of a grammatical impossibility, names not an object of study but rather a method of study, an orientation toward reading, and an orientation toward authority.[55] Despite occasional halfhearted suggestions that comparative literature become a project of scholarly collaboration, most early theorists of comparativism asserted instead a celebratory resignation: The sum total of individual scholarship would never come close to comparing *all* literature—or even defining what "literature" is. Philology, in this sense, names an orientation toward reading and critique rather than a method. The critic would need to read with what Edward Said would later call "worldliness": a historical situatedness that moved slowly, appreciatively, and expansively across a perpetually unfinished reading list.[56] (We will discuss many perpetually unfinished reading lists in this book.) As an orientation toward authority, comparativism signals a deferential practice: not simply to the authors it heralds as "literary," but also to fellow critics. Literary criticism in this mode is a drive toward irrelevance and in-expertise.[57]

Comparativism requires a particular type of critic. Marcel Detienne calls this critic "a singular-plural being" who self-consciously chooses, experiments, and takes risks when they identify "the comparable."[58] The comparativists' goal is not to produce their subjects (texts, people, histories, and practices) as necessarily discrete, but rather perpetually intertwined and intertwining. We might therefore say that, following Detienne, assembling the comparable is an act of egalitarian illiberal critique: It is a struggle, even if inconsequential, against the forces of isolation, autonomy, insuperable difference, and incommensurability. It is therefore a "microconfiguration of politics" and an attempt to "engender other kinds of equality."[59] These stakes were especially high for thinkers like Auerbach who wrote about reading for his "friends": friends who were likely dead, friends who could not be known in advance, and friends whose "love" of reading might produce a fleeting moment of community otherwise destroyed by hate.[60]

Edward Said was the most imaginative benefactor of this conjoined genealogy of anticolonial thought and philological scholarship.[61] "True philological reading is active," Said writes, and it is "in search of freedom, enlightenment, more agency, and certainly not their opposites." The process of philological close reading was "a lifelong attentiveness to the words and rhetorics by which language is used by human beings who exist in history," not by authorial presences divined to live beyond it.[62] In other words, Said envisioned his commitment to reading and becoming a reader as fundamental practice of democratic and humanistic criticism, itself an intimately political practice: "all of it occurring in the world, on the ground of daily life and history and hopes, and the search for knowledge and justice, and then perhaps also for liberation."[63] To "live one's life philologically," in Sheldon Pollock's re-formulation, is to cultivate a properly egalitarian political and ethical critique.[64] This philology-as-a-way-of-life is an orientation toward a perpetually incomplete knowledge of a perpetually unknowable world.[65] Comparative philology thus heralds a critically imaginative, intersubjective, cohabitation with others in the world.

I suggest we recuperate a comparativist model of criticism conducive for the world it ideally seeks to bring into view: a world of radical equivalence marked by the impossibility of its total knowability. It is an impossible subject, finding affinities and affiliations between texts in mere relative opacity, still open to the errantry of contact and not yet foreclosed by the knowability of a world in its totality.[66]

These projects are, simply, impossible. Certainly, these projects are unsustainable; none of the projects here produced, even in their most practical forms, any satisfactory results. This is precisely the point. These anticolonial practices are interested in envisioning a nonteleological egalitarianism: one that might be tentatively staged in the present; one that might occur in a future that will not be reached; one that might occur fleetingly, ephemerally, unremarkably. To be unknown and unknowable, to abstain and be inconsequential, to relinquish and to disavow: Such projects demand that we reconsider our impulse toward evaluation on the grounds of political "recognition," "success" (or "failure"), "sustainability," and "consequentiality." These are precisely the imperious prescripts of liberal colonial rule, which promised national independence in return for the proof of liberal "maturity," properly demonstrated in the form of autonomous, self-knowing individuals.[67] Nevertheless, it is historically inaccurate and theoretically inadequate to suggest that anticolonial thought was either "for" or "against" liberalism.[68] While remaining firmly against liberalism's imperial effects, anticolonial thought posited liberalism as a still open question. Allow me to put this slightly differently, in two ways that will appear in the pages that follow. First, as Ambedkar and Gandhi will ask: How might liberalism be rendered impossible? Or, second, as Har Dayal and Bhagat Singh will ask: How might liberalism be put in the service of an impossible politics?

It should be clear that, to the extent that this book is about critique as a reading practice, it is not interested in attending to any demonstrable act of reading *per se*. In my analysis of anti-imperial critique, "reading" names the critical practice of both unknowability and unknowing. Critique imagines what reading *should* be, not what it is. Those interested in the elucidation of reading practices in the early twentieth century should consult outstanding resources elsewhere. This project does not concern itself with the concomitant concerns of reading as an empirical practice, though it has benefited greatly from projects that do. Questions of literacy, concerns about translation, the history of reading, debates about English versus South Asian "vernaculars," and descriptions of institutions (libraries, schools, and so on), are beyond the scope of this book.[69]

The "reader" is most notably absent precisely because the anticolonial thought explicated in the following pages has, in my analysis, theorized that subject position as necessarily unintelligible, unrecognizable, and unanswerable to the colonial desire to render its subjects identifiable and knowable. "Actual" readers and reading are not only irrelevant to this book but run counter to the anticolonial logics that I am attempting to follow over the course of the next chapters. The importance of reading in the analyses here, however, is that it is more invested in the political possibilities (and impossibilities) of an act that "leaves no traces."[70] This was not merely a celebration of the ephemeral and non-authorial, but often a matter of survival.

At first glance, it might seem impossible to reconcile my theoretical claim of anticolonial inconsequentiality with the historical fact that anticolonial thinkers themselves were quite busy making demands on, or against, the British Raj; throwing bombs; and imagining a postcolonial nation.[71] To my mind, these acts are not incompatible. It is possible to make demands on the state while attending to, with equal commitment, the finite lives of friends. To think consequence and inconsequence together, to imagine a future and to imagine no future at once, or to demand recognition and to value secrecy: These are not paradoxical practices for people whose lives have been deemed irrelevant.

To think these as "paradoxical" is to reproduce a pernicious logic whereby "politics" connotes action, masculinity, asceticism, and mastery, and "aesthetics" connotes inaction, effeminacy, indulgence, and dilettantism. Current defenses of the humanities rely on these binaries: Proper reading is "good for us" because it will make us better citizens or cosmopolitan subjects, even if it is unpleasant; improper reading is "bad" because it is useless, or even indulgent and insufficiently ascetic.[72] This defense of the humanities additionally relies on consequential values to-be-accrued, the imperious demand that criticism be instrumentalizable, and that subjects render themselves recognizable.

In response, this book foregrounds the pleasures of critique. It follows anticolonial thinkers for whom "reading" described enjoyable practices, abundant personal libraries, frivolous demands, and expansive sociality. These practices cherish inconsequentiality and "minor gestures" over "grand historical noise."[73] To the extent that these theorized practices are ascetic, they are far from the extra-worldly, self-denying, and pious practices that are generally associated with asceticism.

Anticolonialism and philology, in the 1920s and 1930s, understood their object of transformation to be nothing less than the *world*. Bhagat Singh, in conversation with leftist radicals in the United States and Europe, imagined a "universal brotherhood."[74] Ambedkar believed that universal contaminated contaminability—heralded alternatively as "fraternity" or "fellowship" (*maitra*)—was a necessarily worldwide mission. Har Dayal settled for no utopia smaller than a "World-State" of friendship. Gandhi sought to rebuild the world from its minor philosophies—aestheticism, vegetarianism, Theosophy—even if in a makeshift vocabulary.[75] Benjamin's critic could not rest until all the dead had been rescued from the enemy.[76] Fanon demanded the *end* of the world. Auerbach theorized a worldly philology conducive for *Weltliteratur*—not simply "world literature," but rather a worldly literature, a literature worthy of worldliness—whose "philological home is earth."[77]

The only certainty that any of these thinkers possessed about this "world," however, was that it was uncertain and, moreover, likely impossible. Bhagat Singh's "universal brotherhood" demanded "chaos" and assured death. Ambedkar's "fellowship" was produced by a commitment to shared suffering, which necessarily stalls abandoning the world as it is. Gandhi's philosophies were rooted in perpetual failure and loss. The citizens of Har Dayal's "World-State" were the descendants of the present, but they inherited an impossible past. Fanon offered the world an invitation to be his "comrades," knowing that his invitation would be misunderstood. The actualization of a true "world literature," Auerbach wrote, would mark the end of the world.

Philology and anticolonialism offer these utopian projects by theorizing ways of "reading" that favor the novice over the expert and the untraceable over the recognizable. With the "world" as its demand, reading names an impossible political theory determined to, in Barbara Johnson's evocative phrase, "encounter unexpected otherness."[78]

"Reading," theorized in this way, is an egalitarian affective relationship (*philia*, friendship) in relative opacity.[79] It is dependent, deferential, impure, and fleeting. This, in turn, requires that we speak in the name of collectivities defined by their unknowability, limitlessness, discontinuity, and heterogeneity (and certainly not their opposites). To remain a reader with anonymous others is to speak as a "we" with deference rather than presumption. To speak as "we" is to speak as a totality while "willingly renouncing any claims to sum it up or to possess it."[80] To speak as a "we" is an invitation to commit to this worldly, potentially infinite, relation.[81] To accept or to offer this invitation is a risk: We cannot know who else has offered or accepted, or who might offer or accept without our knowledge (or our existence). This is an antiauthoritarian political act, but it is also a "fiction" that demands our imaginative—political and aesthetic—commitment.[82]

"Reading" names the practices of collective unknowing and unknowability that anticolonialism and philology theorize for an antiauthoritarian and egalitarian world. What we will discuss in this book, therefore, are theories of "world literature" in their most necessary and impossible forms. Thinking "world literature" this way restores the aesthetic and political claims implicit in the agglutinative neologism, *Weltliteratur.* B. Venkat Mani's succinct definition of *Weltliteratur* offers a crucial insight to conceiving the importance of the agglutinative neologism: It is the name that makes possible critical claims to literature as self-consciously "historically conditioned, culturally determined, and politically charged."[83] In this sense, "world literature" does not name a list of texts, but rather a critical orientation toward a political and aesthetic world that may never be known in its totality. Framed differently, to borrow Aniket Jaaware's formulation: Instead of thinking "world literature" as an *in*stitution, we might recuperate a "world literature" of *de*stitution (and of de-institution): a world literature for the wretched of the earth.[84]

"World literature," as only a utilizable and institutionalizable program (or a list of texts), not only produces an unsatisfactory object of analysis but also reproduces the very logic of imperial control that an antiauthoritarian "world literature" would presumably want to avoid.[85] Auerbach identified this paradox: If a literary world were to be completely known and entirely mastered, "the idea of world literature would simultaneously be realized and destroyed."[86] In response, he proposed philological critique of inexpert "beginnings"—starting points (*Ansatzpunkte*), points of departure (*Ausgangspunkte*), or starting moments (*Ansatzphänomen*)—rather than ends or conclusions. These starting points "urgently" hinted at grand synthetic literary analyses that were unfinishable, and reveled in their perpetual insufficiency.[87]

This emphasis on the ineluctable contingency of beginnings, and on the refusal to predicate analyses on the possibility of their conclusion, is necessary for utopian projects. If the future egalitarian utopia we imagine is built only from our expertise in the knowable present, then we will assure the continuity of domination. If we decide, instead, that we may depart from the present for an unknowable future, without knowing how we might get there, we might finally find ourselves with others in an egalitarian, and likely fleeting, utopia.[88] Put differently: We must begin a mission in relative opacity, without guarantee of fulfilling it: Such are the conjoined utopian politics of philology and anticolonialism.

The anticolonial aesthetics under analysis here were (and are) intended for a postcolonial politics in the immediate present, without regard to its sustainability or its consequentiality. Anticolonialism imagined a future *after* colonialism, too, to be sure; but we might recuperate the experiments of a minor anticolonial practice to rupture, if only for a moment, the continuous colonial present. To imagine this, to borrow Didier Eribon's formulation, is to tentatively assert:

> the idea of an "us" that is at once impossible and inevitable, and which breaks up as it forms; of a life of "rupture" and "discontinuity" within a majoritarian world formed by the "continuous"; of a morality [and politics] as aesthetic—that is to say, common self-creation and reorganization, always reformulating, for which it would be vain to want to eventually make whole, closed, or complete.[89]

The results of such a minor politics "may not be spectacular . . . perhaps they are limited to modest contributions through books, partial or unfinished gestures, barely perceptible movements. But the effects are profound."[90]

Taken together, comparative philology and anticolonial thought offer us a model of "nonemphatic revelatory" critique in the service of a world we will not live to see.[91] In the meantime, we require emancipatory commitments that operate in "the indeterminate and the contingent . . . between what has passed and what lies ahead."[92] Both nihilism and hope are insufficient responses to tragic times, and they foreclose commitment to politics in the immediate present. We might endeavor, as Auerbach implores us at the end of *Mimesis*, "to emphasize the random occurrence, to exploit it not in the service of a planned continuity of action, but rather in and of itself."[93] It is a modest politics presented as aesthetic critique. To only connect, one might as well begin.

1 / Lala Har Dayal's Imagination

The Long Life of Revolution

In 1938, the Ghadr ("mutiny") Party published a curious pamphlet in Punjabi from San Francisco.[1] The famous studio portrait of anticolonial leader Bhagat Singh takes up most of the cover. Above the photograph is the title *baraabari de arth* ("The Meaning of Equality") and the author's name, Lala Har Dayal. Though Bhagat Singh and Lala Har Dayal never met, the juxtaposition of the two figures is simultaneously logical and provocative. It confirms the productive and powerful promiscuity of both men's anticolonial agitation and political afterlives.

In the early 1910s, the Ghadr Party had posed a significant threat to British rule in India. Its newspaper, *Hindustan Ghadr* (or sometimes only *Ghadr*), openly advocated rebellion and mutiny. The British Criminal Intelligence Department (C.I.D.) worked hard to prevent its global circulation, but by 1914, the expansive organization included active members in Vancouver, Mexico City, London, Paris, Cape Town, Lahore, Singapore, and Tokyo. In his role as the organization's founder and master propagandist (*pracharak*) Lala Har Dayal wrote essays on revolution, the 1857 Mutiny, pedagogy, and political philosophy.

Har Dayal left the United States in 1914 for Berlin. Under new leadership in early 1915, some members of the Ghadr Party returned to India with mutiny in mind. Among them was University of California, Berkeley engineering undergraduate Kartar Singh Sarabha, an active student leader in the Ghadr Party. The mutinous collective was caught at Lahore and the nineteen-year-old was hanged. Even if the Ghadr's *ghadr* was a failure, the organization nevertheless rekindled many Punjabis' anticolonial imagination. Kartar Singh Sarabha's hanging, the Jallianwala Bagh Massacre in Amritsar in 1919, and general dissatisfaction with M. K. Gandhi's nonviolence movement set the conditions for a resurgence of anticolonial agitation, especially in Punjab.

In response, a group of young men, inspired by Kartar Singh Sarabha's martyrdom (and the Irish Republican Army), founded the Hindustan Republican Army, which, by 1928, became the Hindustan Socialist Republican Army (HSRA).[2] Under the leadership of Chandrashekhar Azad and Bhagat Singh, the HSRA staged a number of political agitations and published articles, pamphlets, and manifestos. They sought to avenge the death of Punjabi leader Lala Lajpat Rai; Bhagat Singh was caught after setting off a smoke-bomb in the Central Legislative Assembly in Delhi while proclaiming *inqilab zindabad*: long live revolution.

By his own accounts and those of his many hagiographers, Bhagat Singh both fulfills and exceeds the trajectory supposedly initiated by Punjabi migrant laborers in California (who traced their anticolonial lineage back to the 1857 Indian Mutiny). It is as though, by way of Kartar Singh Sarabha, the Ghadr's failed *ghadr* was thus redeemed, seventeen years later, by an equally young Bhagat Singh. Both Bhagat Singh and Har Dayal have posed significant challenges to the narrow—and often competing—genealogies that have sought to claim them: nonviolent Indian anticolonialism, postcolonial Marxism, proto-Naxalism, proto-Maoism, and multiple variations on "revolutionary" that remain actively debated today.[3]

Time Out of Joint

A rigid classification of Indian anticolonialism's political stances and afterlives, in any event, does a disservice to the rich and expansive reach of its imagination, especially in the years between World War I and World War II. Anticolonial writers aligned with a wide range of political stances, many of them perhaps contradictory. The most productive strains of anticolonial thought reflected an open engagement with multiple ethical and political questions. The juxtaposition of Har Dayal and Bhagat Singh on the cover of *baraabari de arth* is a testament to this productive openness.

Nevertheless, and at first glance, the *baraabari de arth* pamphlet seems like a product of time out of joint: By 1938, the once revolutionary Har Dayal had applied for amnesty to return to India and was living in Philadelphia. Publishing a tract honoring Bhagat Singh printed illicitly while writing official recantations would have been a bold move.⁴ A second visit to Har Dayal's scattered archives, however, reveals a more curious trajectory. Har Dayal had written an essay in English entitled "The Meaning of Equality." But he had published it as a Ghadr Party pamphlet in the early 1910s (as an addendum to "The Social Conquest of the Hindu Race," which had been published in the Calcutta-based *Modern Review* in 1909).⁵ In his absence, the essay was translated into Punjabi and republished to memorialize the young anticolonial martyr.

There is nothing unusual about this in the context of global anticolonial print publics, which promoted cultures of reprinting and reproduction in order to achieve an ever-expanding network of readers. As Isabel Hofmeyr has beautifully shown in the case of M. K. Gandhi's writings, such cultures of recitation and reproduction produce a time out of joint with print capitalism's empty homogenous time.⁶ Even still, the 1938 *baraabari de arth* is a jarring alignment of two revolutionaries, such that the young Bhagat Singh—who "bade fair to oust Mr. Gandhi as the foremost political figure of the day"—is made, by way of juxtaposition, to look back on Har Dayal—the "most dangerous" of "all the Indian agitators"—active twenty years earlier.⁷

That the specter of an actively revolutionary Har Dayal haunts Bhagat Singh (which in turn re-animates a quiet Har Dayal),⁸ I suggest, illuminates the non-familial affiliations that helped make Indian anticolonialism such a vibrant and philosophically generous political force.⁹ Such affiliations highlight the globally dispersed genealogies of anticolonial thought. Anticolonial thinkers and writers stressed, rather than suppressed, these lineages of political thought. They appeared in textual juxtapositions, citations, imaginative translations, and creative misreadings. That anticolonialism foregrounded its philosophical ancestry while often constructing a future postcolonial utopia should alert us to its Janus-faced quality: at once looking forward and backward.

But more than this, these affiliations highlight the global communities of reading that Har Dayal, and certain strains of anticolonialism alongside him, sought to enact. I trace Har Dayal's anticolonial critique in two interconnected ways. First, I am interested in tracing his lifelong practice of reading nineteenth-century philosophy as an anticolonial practice in and of itself. This is to say that, for Har Dayal, the very act of reading was itself an anticolonial practice. Throughout his many published essays, but also in his extensive correspondence, Har Dayal modeled and described the process of reading as a proper anticolonial practice—and as a practice for the cultivation of the properly anticolonial self. Critique in this first sense was thus fully part of the formation of anticolonial selfhood.

Second, I am interested in tracing Har Dayal's reading practice, especially as it relates to nineteenth-century philosophy and philosophical fiction, as the formation of a proper anticolonial philosophy. In other words, Har Dayal models his own anticolonial vision on the juxtaposition his reading practice creates between (at least for the sake of this chapter) Herbert Spencer and William Morris, two men who would otherwise hardly share a unifying vision. In Har Dayal's reading practice, however, the two writers are taken together and used to create a properly anticolonial utopian "imagination" for his "World-State."

I rely heavily on *Hints for Self Culture,* which argues for reading as an anticolonial practice (especially "egalitarian reading groups"), as well as his private correspondence, where he not only keeps extensive notes about his own reading practices (which he marks as anticolonial, political, and occasionally ascetic) and creates reading lists for others to read along with him. Especially in *Hints,* Har Dayal constantly disavows his own authority in favor of other philosophers, and disavows his interpretations in favor of the future readers' interpretations. I understand this as a life-long commitment to reading (which includes, for Har Dayal: reading alone, reading together, and refusing authority).

This chapter ends with a brief meditation on the "history of imagination" as a tentatively suggested protocol for reading anticolonial thought in the present (and against the grain of history). A focus on reading and the practice of critique moves us away from the frustratingly simplistic view that a history of ideas must be a history of influences (a narrative that often privileges the European "origin" of a philosophical encounter). On the contrary, a focus on reading reveals the perpetually complicated maneuvers of interpretation that allow for the philosophical productivity of anticolonial thought.

In 1934, having completed his Ph.D. at the University of London, and after nearly fifteen years of relative silence, Har Dayal published *Hints for Self-Culture*, dedicated to Young Rationalists—perhaps with Bhagat Singh in mind.[10] The "little book" offers "short hints" for personal development along four axes: intellectual, physical, aesthetic, and ethical.[11] Like many self-culture guides of the late nineteenth and early twentieth centuries, the book features maxims towards the production of a healthy subject and consequently robust society.

Hints for Self-Culture is a long treatise on the multiple forms of required knowledge, which fall neatly into eighteen categories: science, history, psychology, economics, philosophy, sociology, languages, comparative religion, exercise, diet, art, architecture, sculpture, painting, music, dancing, oratory, and poetry. The final section, "Ethical Culture," is a reflection, building on this required knowledge, of the "Five Concentric Circles" of ethical and political action.

Har Dayal pleaded with his editors at Watts & Co. not to distribute the book in India, but the company was too pleased with its success to halt its circulation. In response, Har Dayal wrote to the India Office for their pardon, and the India Office declared the work "safe" along the lines that it was not political, but rather "theoretical, carefully."[12] This decision, though fortunate for Har Dayal, is a curious misjudgment by the colonial bureaucrats and censors. It suggests, however, that the British Raj operated on a conception of "the political" that meant, quite narrowly, a direct engagement with the state. Even if such a conception of "the political" was still relatively vacuous, it allowed colonial censors to determine the breadth and reach of the state into public affect. In this sense, sedition laws covered speech and text that could produce certain political sentiments, as well. Sedition, in other words, involved a complicated interplay of textual and social practices.[13] Determining this in advance was a considerably difficult task.[14] One censor worried about its "attack on Capitalism on Communist lines," but perhaps because *Hints for Self-Culture* participated in a popular genre of "self-culture" books, or perhaps because it was merely "philosophical propaganda," it was determined that the book was harmless.[15]

This decision not only suggests a curious misjudgment on the part of the censors, but also offers insight into the particular relegation, by contemporary political philosophy, of postcolonial studies to what Leela Gandhi has called "the rudimentary schoolroom of ethics."[16] Anticolonial writing, produced in affective, ethical, or aesthetic registers, allegedly fails to address properly political concerns. Even in otherwise sympathetic critical anarcho-utopian political philosophy, anticolonial and postcolonial theory is seen as failing to address "today's real enemy," or is seen as simply too particular to address new, universal and global concerns.[17] In response, some contemporary postcolonial critics have been quick to recuperate anticolonial thought as actively and equally political. The censor's analysis prefigures contemporary recuperations of anticolonial thought. In both present academic cases, however, as well as in the C.I.D.'s judgment, aesthetic and ethical thought is ignored or flattened, and thus rendered inessential to anticolonial or postcolonial writing.

On the contrary, in the supposed guise of the "carefully theoretical," anticolonial thought actually pushes us closer to the critical offerings of an avowedly anarchistic tradition (and therefore the often unacknowledged inheritance of postcolonial theory). It is thus neither merely philosophical nor myopically political. Instead, many strains of anticolonial thought demonstrate the need to realign political, ethical, aesthetic, and philosophical concerns as a way to envision a new world. To surrender any of these mutually supporting concerns to the other is to fundamentally misjudge the contribution of much of anticolonial thought.

In "The Indian Peasant," for example, published by Ghadr in 1913, Har Dayal urged friendship with the downtrodden and untouchable castes as a way to achieve unity.[18] The pamphlet offers a resounding critique of learned ideas of Brahmins and instead advocates the development of an "imagination" that extends beyond the boundaries of identity and attempts to imagine injustice outside of one's own experience. "Where we stop, humanity begins," he writes of the current limits of imagination. In order to achieve actual political equality (as opposed to "political activity," available only to elites), Har Dayal writes, "We must change the national psychology. . . . New modes of thought must be implanted into the minds of the people." Because traditional Indian stories praise kings and wealth, "the imagination of our children is poisoned from the source." For Har Dayal, this requires a new aesthetic, and one emerging from the underside of the project of national independence:

> The sweepers and the scavengers . . . Who will give them a voice? Who will be their poet? Who will write a Ramayana and a Mahabharata for them? India waits for her true Poet. . . . Let the Peasantry begin to speak of its burden of grief, and all poets and poetasters would be hushed into shame. The real epic of India remains to be written.

In the vein of Walt Whitman or William James, Har Dayal refuses an authorial position in favor of a multitude of authorial voices (none of which would, in his description, belong to him). In order for actual political revolution to occur, Har Dayal writes, one must fundamentally change the orientation of one's imagination and one's aesthetic frames: One must relinquish an authorial position to the non-authorities of India's peasantry. That "the real epic of India remains to be written," suggests an anti-authorial stance against the Indian literary tradition; the passive voice, moreover, removes the author from any sense of subject position and opens up the possibility of new form of non-authorial writing.

Instead, we receive the anticolonial agitator as an imaginative figure, a figure who reads voraciously and with hopes that reading could create new imaginations or future worlds. We should understand "imagination" as a way of accounting for promiscuity as the basis of anticolonial thought. This, of course, requires a different reading strategy than ones usually afforded to anticolonial thinkers and writers.

Reading envisions a theory of politics for a world that does not yet exist. It requires a radical realignment of politics, aesthetics, and ethics, and not only as discrete elements. Moreover, it requires an imaginative stance that reorients the moment of revolution to a time both beyond and before the present. This is a revolution in perpetuity—*inqilab zinda-bad* in Bhagat Singh's formulation—from the past, but for a world yet to come, and one that will remain tethered to (or enacted in) the present. In other words, anticolonial reading is revolutionary and must be *dangerous*: Guns and paper, in Har Dayal's account, are both weapons: "Lectures are delivered Books are printed. People say progress is being made and thus assure their own minds. We wish to prove that at present two things are wanted for progress. What are these? Papers and Arms—the paper *Ghadr* and guns!"[19]

Most scholarship on the Ghadr Party has alternately glorified and chided its violence instead of paying attention to its literary imagination, which the Party considered as dangerous as its bombs—the pen and the sword being equally mighty (as some of Ghadr's poetry, discussed later, expounds upon). The extensive documentation of Anglophone and vernacular reading practices in British C.I.D. files attests to the fact that the British Raj *and* Ghadr Party found reading a very dangerous thing, though for different reasons.

In the case of Har Dayal's *Hints for Self-Culture*, reading is a radical self-making process toward the creation of a future utopian project. In Har Dayal's hands, however, such a project requires a doubling-back of history; a political project which torques the present back onto its impossible pasts. The insurgent, impossible political theory thus offered in *Hints for Self-Culture* participates in a long and dispersed lineage of anticolonial and postcolonial thought.

Like the curious Ghadr pamphlet, *Hints for Self-Culture* not only posits a future postcolonial utopia that looks backward, it also demands a radical politics of the present that looks backward and forward at once. *Hints for Self-Culture* does this in two significant moves, in ways that the bulk of this chapter will explore. First, Har Dayal returns to nineteenth-century writers Herbert Spencer and William Morris in order to produce a radical self-making project for the present. Second, Har Dayal offers a utopian vision of a future "World-State," which, as the product of radical self-making, is a radical *world*-making project that repeatedly glances backwards. At each of these stages, a palimpsestic utopia emerges, with the figures of the past not fully erased but having morphed into something of use though only partially recognizable.

Ghadr di gunj

Har Dayal was born in Delhi in 1884. He attended Oxford University on a Bodleian Scholarship, but renounced his degree and left Oxford for London. He became a central part of the India House collective, under the leadership of Shyamji Krishnavarma, and moved with the organization from London to Paris in 1909. He left a year later for Martinique, Algiers, and, by 1911, the United States. From 1911 to 1914, he lectured at the University of California, Berkeley and Stanford University, toured the U.S. West Coast with prominent anarchists and leftists, and founded the Ghadr Party.

The British Criminal Intelligence Department (C.I.D.) worked hard to find reasons to convince the United States to deport Har Dayal, and by early 1914 he had been arrested under trumped-up charges. He posted bail and fled to Europe. From Berlin, he worked with the Indian Committee of National Independence, under the leadership of Virendranath Chattopadhyaya ("Chatto") and most likely funded by the German government.

The Ghadr Party played a major, if still underappreciated, role in Indian independence. Their publications, especially the *Hindustan Ghadr* and its poetry collection, *Ghadr di Gunj* (*Echoes of Mutiny*), reached audiences well beyond the reach of British surveillance. Similarly, Chatto's Committee in Berlin produced a significant amount of writing against the British that circulated widely by way of collectives across Europe, the United States, and the British Empire. More important, however, are the Ghadr Party's multiple overlapping concerns: from uniting the precarious diasporic labor force along the U.S. west coast to promoting pan-Islamism, internationalism, and cosmopolitanism across the world. The Ghadr Party was founded in part to recreate the 1857 Mutiny and organized a variety of actions with revolution in mind. Their newspapers and publications reflected its propaganda mission and remain the primary traces of an organization the British failed to fully grasp in their surveillance archive. The Party also organized and trained young men in armed revolt, smuggled weapons to and around the British Empire, and supported its members' livelihoods materially and emotionally.

In an attempt to render the Ghadr Party properly "political" in a narrow sense, scholars ignore the ethical, philosophical, and aesthetic contributions of the organization's writers—or perhaps they surrender them to the practicality of active revolution.[20] Placed solely under a rubric of the properly political, the Ghadr Party's often ephemeral actions were largely failures. Many of its publications articulated both a political and ethical critique of British (and American) imperialism. An analysis focused solely on political action renders irrelevant the proliferation of poetry and artwork that the Ghadr Party produced, and those works appear to have had the boldest afterlives in Punjabi anticolonialism through the 1930s.

Moreover, such a focus divides its members' biographies into two halves, wherein the Ghadr half becomes properly revolutionary and the post-Ghadr half becomes improperly theological, bureaucratic, or philosophical. In the case of Lala Har Dayal, this involves rendering his later graduate work and *Hints for Self-Culture* tangential to his vision for Ghadr. It ignores the similarities between his early pedagogical writings (1909–12), or even the slightly more aggressive "Indian Peasant" (1913), and his interest in education and aesthetics in *Hints*. Admittedly, by the time he published *Hints for Self-Culture* in 1934, Har Dayal had publicly renounced his revolutionary past and requested amnesty from the British Raj in order to return to India (he officially received it only posthumously). With the exception of *baraabari de arth*, there appear to be no signs that he had any interest in active revolution. I do not mean to suggest that his recantations were disingenuous, but by privileging active political agitation at the expense of quiet philosophical reflection, we ignore important theoretical strains present in Har Dayal's work. These ideas and reflections are political in the sense that they posit, in the imagined absence of a colonial state, processes of education, self-care, and societal development toward a future utopian world.

This focus also ignores the curious afterlives of revolution that the Ghadr Party attempted to both employ and create for itself. *Ghadr di Gunj (Echoes of Mutiny)*, first published in 1914 from San Francisco, was an attempt to aestheticize the 1857 Indian War of Independence by way of religious (predominately Sikh) poetry.[21] Although Har Dayal and the Ghadr Party worked for an active revolution, they also worked toward a language for the politics they wanted to enact: *echoes* of mutiny and an "Esperanto of Revolution."[22] *Ghadr di Gunj* should alert us not only to a concern for the poetics of revolution, but also to an imagination of the past that Har Dayal and the Ghadr Party sought to enact in their present. The echoes in *Ghadr di Gunj* (which are far from quiet reverberations) remind the illicit pamphlet reader that the horrors of 1857 create the revolutionary present.

Ghadr di Gunj is a loud reminder of the horrors of 1857 and a call to action to pick up the pen and the sword. In a pamphlet, written by Har Dayal in 1911 but circulated with *Ghadr di Gunj*, the agitator calls for a similar historical orientation:

> When we look back down the long blood-red avenues of our history, what pride, what hope stirs us . . . ! When we read the stirring history of those days [the Mutiny of 1857], whether in the calumnious pages of *feringhi* [white foreign] writers or in the more truthful and inspiring narrative which the loving imagination of a patriot has recently woven out of the records of the past . . . we must indeed be base and degraded wretches if our hearts are not thrilled with quenchless hopes for the future, if we are not urged on to further battle by restless visions of our near triumph rising out of the blood and ashes of their failures.[23]

Here, Har Dayal elaborates a vision of "echoes of mutiny" that propel political action into a vision for a hopeful future the ashes. It is worth noting Har Dayal's insistence on "the loving imagination of a patriot"—presumably V. D. Savarkar, whose inflammatory *The History of the Indian War of Independence* had been published in 1909—as the moment of historical authority. This combines, once again, two aspects of Har Dayal's critical and reading practice we have been discussing. First, it illustrates his refusal to become an authority and insistence on citing and quoting others. Second, it urges his own readers to read: that is, to read others with him ("when *we* read . . .").

"I live quietly and am engaged in reading and writing."

A continued focus on Ghadr's recorded actions and political positions will only continue to offer a masculine, muscled version of anticolonial action—in other words, a politically retrograde vision of what political action should look like.[24] Reading, critique, and self-reflection are thus consigned to be the useless supplement of anticolonial action, lacking the virility and force of bomb-throwing and assassinations. This focus is foolish even on crudely empirical level: The Ghadr Party enacted exactly one attempt at a *ghadr* in 1914, staged by no more than one hundred men of its one-hundred-page mailing list,[25] and this was an absolute failure. But more harmful is the recuperation of Ghadr actions as properly gendered—masculinist, virile, productive, action-oriented. In her otherwise excellent essay on Ghadr's use of *gurudwaras* as meeting sites for anticolonial action, Seema Sohi replays a tired line about the "masculinity" of "proper" anticolonial action while ignoring the *gurudwara* as the imagined initial location of reading groups, in Har Dayal's political vision.[26] Har Dayal's and, consequently, Ghadr's vision for gendered participation and action was considerably more expansive than this type of inquiry reveals. A focus on a mutinous reading thus stands a critical distance from the colonial/anticolonial masculine/feminine binaries, which remain as critically impractical as they were at the time.

Har Dayal insisted on a readerly orientation throughout his life, and actively cultivated one throughout his travels. His first biographer/hagiographer, Dharmavira, regularly noted Har Dayal's reading practices, but failed to make sense of them:

> Har Dayal was a moving library and had all his knowledge instantly available. Practically on each page of the book we find so many references and quotations, that we are amazed at the learning, memory, industry, and judgment of this genius. We cannot forget what he has said about himself: "I am very inquisitive. I am interested in everything that was, is and shall be."[27]

Har Dayal's insatiable interest in reading has been overlooked, or has been used to illustrate Har Dayal's global scholarly authority, which the agitator repeatedly disavowed. Har Dayal's reading practice was an attempt to reduce himself to the egalitarian dispensation of the reading community. "It is said that whenever Har Dayal took up a book it took possession of him and he practically lost himself in it,"[28] Dharmavira writes without appreciating this radical gesture.

On the contrary, quiet reading was foundational to Har Dayal's anticolonial vision well before *Hints for Self-Culture*. After leaving the India House collective in London in 1907, Har Dayal traveled to Paris, Algiers, and Honolulu. In his many letters back to his colleagues and friends in London, Har Dayal described his days reading at libraries in each town (most of which were unsatisfactory in their holdings).[29] Early on, Har Dayal was invested in reading practices that could properly correspond to anticolonial sentiment and education. In a letter to Madame Rana in 1910, Har Dayal provides one of the initial sketches of his critique (that he would craft and re-craft throughout his life). It is worth quoting at length:

> You should look well after Ranji, for a young man's character is formed between the age of 15 and 20. You should teach him to be simple....
>
> Further, from now banish all novels and dramas from his studies. *No novel, no drama.* After 22, he can read them. For novels and dramas corrupt the mind at this age. The books to be read at this age should be the following—
>
> Books of adventure and travel.

Biographies of Great Men.
Books of Natural History and Science written in popular form for boys.
Books of Morals.
Histories written in popular style.
Descriptions of different countries.
On the contrary, novels and dramas give no useful *information*, while they corrupt the mind.
For a man's character—his "penchant"—is formed between 15 and 22. He can become serious and earnest or frivolous and lax during these years. And the books that we read in youth influence our character immensely.[30]

Har Dayal repeatedly dismissed literature and fiction throughout his writing career, especially for young men and women. I think this was largely because currently existing literature failed to offer the proper imagination necessary for a postcolonial world, as we have previously discussed. Nevertheless, we should note here how Har Dayal's vision for proper anticolonial activity always involved extensive reading, as well as an expansive love of reading.

Har Dayal's interest in reading was clearest in his essays on pedagogy for *Modern Review* (some of which Ambedkar would read as he studied Buddhism).[31] Reading, in these essays, set the possibility for new forms of association and affiliation. Reading and critique was to be done in groups—which is to say, as Har Dayal would later in *Hints for Self-Culture*, that the sensibility conducive to anticolonial philosophy was a perpetual state of interpretation as a form of sociality with others. Reading and critique, in Har Dayal's account, named forms of non-filial association and communal, egalitarian analysis and conversation. "Man cannot live and grow alone.... Association brings home to a man the duties that he owes to others, and thus supplies the one condition essential to moral development. For him who comes into real contact with all types and ranks of men, human brotherhood remains no empty phase, but becomes a living creed ennobling and elevating his every day conduct," Har Dayal wrote in "Our Educational Problem" in 1908.[32]

Har Dayal's devotion to reading extended to his proposals for various projects he was never able to complete. From 1908 to 1934, Har Dayal's correspondence includes proposals for translating European philosophy into Hindi and Urdu, for writing primers in vernacular languages for philosophical development, and for writing pamphlets on "reading lists" for autodidactic men and women. Like *Hints for Self-Culture*, which are hints: "not exhaustive, but only selective,"[33] each list was accompanied by a self-effacing caveat, as in this example from a 1925 letter to his nephew: "I am rather diffident in suggesting a course of study for your energetic friend, but I think that the following books will be useful . . ."[34]

Especially in the context of anticolonial thought, I think we should read this interest in long reading lists and translation—into Hindi, Urdu, or, in some cases, English, as well as "modernization" attempts to render an ancient text appropriate for contemporary audiences—as a commitment to reading insofar as it seeks to relinquish authority in favor of making new fellow readers. Har Dayal clarifies this in *Hints for Self-Culture*: "It is great fun being a polyglot. You can then read many books and journals, receive foreign visitors in your home, translate letters and circulars for your favourite social and political movements, and render such other service as only a clever polyglot can give."[35] This focus on the *service* of translation is particularly revealing of his commitment to readership and reading practices rather than authorial control.

Hints for Self-Culture

Twenty significant years fall between *Ghadr di Gunj* and *Hints for Self-Culture*. Har Dayal left the United States for Berlin, Constantinople, Stockholm, and finally London. He had all but abandoned active political agitation; many of his contemporaries and biographers view his troubling *Forty-Four Months in Germany and Turkey* as his *volte-face*.[36] Many rural Punjabis who had not already crossed the black waters for farms in eastern California found themselves on battlefronts in western Europe. Writing home in 1915–17, these subaltern soldiers offered news of European generosity in conditions of abundance and messages of their own sacrifices in conditions of extreme paucity.[37]

In *Hints for Self-Culture*, the supposedly antithetical ethics of "generosity" and "self-sacrifice" often appear to emerge from a single imaginative sense of the globe. "Sacrifice can end the cruelty of the rich and the apathy of the poor. . . . Give yourself to the world!" Har Dayal proclaims in the crescendo to *Hints for Self-Culture*'s conclusion. "Welcome all to your home and your heart . . . all men and women and children without distinction for race or colour. Eat and drink with all."[38]

The book thus participates in a vibrant global conversation among ethical and philosophical thinkers that spanned the years between World War I and World War II (as well as a popular and apparently successful literary genre). Indeed, the book's introduction offers its context: "Your lot is cast in these sad times of turmoil and tribulation. Mankind anxiously asks if there is a way out of the gloom and horror of today into light and life."[39] This was a not uncommon sentiment. Many contemporaneous writers voiced a utopian vision nevertheless emerging from the horrors of World War I. Interwar utopian pessimism often suggested new ways of living that were marked with economic and philosophical uncertainty, cosmopolitan anxiety, and a partial and provisional openness.[40]

At the same time, the book also participates in a considerably older genre of self-cultivation handbooks, many with similar axes of self-culture: intellectual, physical, aesthetic, and ethical. At various points across the political spectrum, popular writers promoted a range of bodily practices toward the eventual cultivation of a better society: Working on the self was, by metonymic extension, working on society. This included liberal thinkers like John Stuart Blackie (*Blackie's Self Culture*, 1891), as well as proto-fascist/republican thinkers such as Giuseppe Mazzini (*Duties of Man*, 1860). Like other self-cultivation guides, Har Dayal's *Hints for Self-Culture* features maxims that range from the mundane (avoid bittersweet foods, chew thirty-two times per bite, always smile) to the grandly altruistic (learn and promote Esperanto, aid the elderly and disabled, study all thinkers who have served humanity). Har Dayal's work, however, ends with the development of World-State, a utopian community "with the Earth as its territorial basis. One State, one Flag, one Language, one Ethics, one Ideal, one Love, and one Life: that is our goal."[41]

The book thus offers a curious juxtaposition of very different times. It offers a particularly interwar vision of hospitality and sacrifice in the name of a new global utopia; at the same time, it does so by reaching back to the nineteenth century and wresting from it a predominately Victorian liberal model of self-cultivation toward a practice of radical self-making and global world-making. The result is a book that feels both vibrantly interwar and curiously *fin-de-siècle*, reflecting a moment where political possibilities had not yet settled into rigid political parties. Yet in 1934, these sensibilities had already begun, in the face of European fascism, to dim in popular consciousness. *Hints for Self-Culture* suggests the possibility, even during the emergence of fixed political identities and projects, of returning to a moment where one's political thought could still be "in motion" or reflect an ever-changing set of "promiscuous alliances."[42]

In other words, in its strange lack of contemporaneity, *Hints for Self-Culture* offers its own echoes of mutiny: of history reasserting itself in the present.[43] The book opens with a dedication "To A Young Fellow-Rationalist": "You stand between the past and the future: the world is yours to enjoy, to organize, and to reconstruct."[44] Another possible clue for this torqueing back to the past occurs early in the book, in Har Dayal's very long analysis of history,[45] which he concludes:

> I hold that history is a medley.... The march of Humanity has been irregular, disorderly, and haphazard. It has not been in a straight line, or in a circle, or in a spiral, or in any curve of a definite shape. It has been an up-and-down, down-and-up, forward-and-backward, right-to-left, left-to-right lawless and chaotic movement.[46]

As the central historical anchor for an ethical and political guide, this is a provocative claim, curiously aligned with Vico.[47] At first glance, it stands in stark contrast to the realization of World-State as the end result of a universal progressive march. On the other hand, it suggests that an orientation to the past and future that operates simultaneously. "Your daily life is History: what else is it . . . ? As you choose, so will History be made," Har Dayal notes a few pages later.[48] There is a curious jumble of tenses here, and it suggests Har Dayal's ethical philosophy of history relies in a constant "forward-to-backward" movement where the past, present, and future are all made at once and are interdependent.

If *Hints for Self-Culture* torques back to the nineteenth century for its post–World War I future utopian vision, it is because the present, like the future, is made of echoes of past mutinies, and those echoes refuse to go unheard. *Ghadr di Gunj*, echoing 1857, reasserts itself in *Hints for Self-Culture* as an additional echo of the aborted mutiny of 1914. Speaking in the same first-person plural like the texts of *Ghadr di Gunj*, Har Dayal suggests, is to speak history itself: "You can speak of yourself as 'We,' if you love History. When you speak, you are the mouthpiece of History. . . . The present has its roots in the past."[49] Even if the mutinous "we" has become a philosophical "we," the radical recuperation of revolutionary pasts is brought to the present, to form its roots. In the guise of the "carefully theoretical," Har Dayal's revolutionary vision emerges in both quieter and more grandiose forms: pedagogy and self-care underneath the state, and World-State beyond it. On our way there, allow me a slight detour, back once more to the mid-nineteenth century.

Herbert Spencer: Anticolonialist

Six years before the 1857 Mutiny, Herbert Spencer published *Social Statics*, his first major work of philosophical inquiry. In a grandly optimistic tone, the book offers an ethical guide based on the initial claim that "every man may claim the fullest liberty to exercise his faculties compatible with the possession of like liberty by every other man": the law of equal freedom.[50]

Spencer's popularity and public influence in the late nineteenth century is matched only by the obscurity into which he fell following World War I. His work influenced Emile Durkheim, Henri Bergson, and William James; and yet, by the mid-1920s, new popular philosophers were quick to dismiss his thought as irredeemably liberal, simplistic, and a parody of philosophy proper. He was most famous for promoting Social Darwinism (though the term is not his own) and Lamarckian evolutionary theory. Spencer's writings reflect a general Victorian optimism, a late nineteenth-century *laissez-faire* sensibility, and a vibrant moral and scientific relativism.[51]

Shruti Kapila and Harald Fischer-Tiné have written about Spencer's popularity among Indian anticolonialists in the early 1900s and 1910s, especially Shyamji Krishnavarma, who led the India House collective in London.[52] Krishnavarma offered scholarships in Spencer's honor, and occasionally offered paeans to the philosopher in his periodical, *Indian Sociologist*. Perhaps due to the promiscuousness of his thought, Spencer made a fine anticolonial thinker who offered a critique of empire from within it. Imperialism, for Spencer, increased the size of the state and diminished the capacities of the individuals it ruled. It thus produced a regression from industrial force to militaristic force, and made possible the "rebarbarization" of modern society.

Spencer's critique of imperialism, admittedly, had more to do with a distaste for the state rather than an appreciation of anticolonialism. Nevertheless, Krishnavarma and Har Dayal put him to use in their writings before the war.[53] As Kapila has noted, in Har Dayal's early interpretation of Spencer, the young agitator used the nineteenth-century philosopher's critique of the state to illustrate the double alienation of "the Hindu Race" under foreign rule. Though he is not formally cited, Herbert Spencer lurks behind "The Meaning of Equality" (*baraabari de arth*): Equality, for Har Dayal, is determined in the first instance by "the non-subjugation of one person's will to another's. The right to freedom of thought and action is one of the most dearly cherished possessions of man."[54] Equality, in other words, was engendered primarily by access to freedom. Har Dayal's equality, contra Spencer's, involves equal distribution of both political *and* economic power.[55]

Like the curious trajectory of Har Dayal's *baraabari de arth*, which was repurposed to honor the martyr of youthful anticolonialism, Herbert Spencer's *Social Statics* was republished in 1892 in altered form. Missing from the second edition was Chapter XIX, a politely titled chapter: "The

Right to Ignore the State." In this missing chapter, which was replaced by an addendum more aggressively titled "Man Versus the State," Spencer suggests the possibility to "withdraw" from the state when it fails to act ethically: A person can operate *underneath* the state to determine her morality, ethical protocols, and modes of association (friendship, loyalty, and family).

Which edition did Har Dayal read in London? Could we speculate, perhaps, that he encountered the later version in 1907, which led him to sculpt Herbert Spencer's heterogeneous afterlife into a direct critique of the imperial state? Might this mean that, by 1934, Har Dayal had discovered the quiet missing chapter originally published in 1851: the chapter that humbly offers, in contradistinction to the book in its absence, "the right to *ignore* the state"?

In other words, what I mean to suggest here (even if framed in pure speculation) is that Herbert Spencer's ghost (if not Herbert Spencer himself, who apparently moved in the opposite direction) shifts its focus from a direct engagement *against* the state to something considerably quieter: the possibility of enacting modes of freedom and ethical behavior *underneath* the state or in the absence of a concern for it altogether.[56] The right to ignore the state makes possible a range of ethical practices—friendship, fugitive egalitarianism, and self-care—that a direct engagement with the state forecloses. Such is the trajectory that Har Dayal creates for the philosopher by way of a peculiar reading practice. Spencer's direct agitation against the expanding state aligns with the Ghadr Party's actively revolutionary mission; Spencer's quieter practice of ignoring the state informs the practices of the self that form the utopian World-State of the future.

Indeed, most of the practices that Har Dayal advocates in *Hints for Self-Culture* are practices of ignoring the state, rather than addressing it. Most of the book's "intellectual culture" suggestions concern an autodidactic approach to history, philosophy, and aesthetics. At the beginning of *Hints for Self-Culture*, Har Dayal offers a lengthy description of how one should read historical and philosophical texts (which is worth quoting at length):

> In the never-ending struggle for Knowledge, you should work regularly and methodically. Devote a certain portion of your time daily to study or experiment. You feed the body several times a day: don't starve the Mind. Keep a diary, in which you should note the titles of new books. Get new and second-hand catalogues from the booksellers. Hunt for cheap second-hand books in the shops. Own a private library, however small. Take pride in the books that adorn

your home. With every book you buy, you add a millimeter to your mental stature. Borrow books from the public libraries and from your friends: don't forget to return them, otherwise your studies will be like a rainfall on a sloping roof.... It is a good plan to form a small group, in which each member reads a new book and then offers a paper on it, with copious quotations from the original. Such cooperative study is necessary, as your spare time is unfortunately limited. Life itself is short, far too short, for the lover of Knowledge.... We are old before we have discovered that we know very little indeed. Make haste to learn. J. R. Green, the famous historian, wrote: "I know what men will say of me, 'He died learning.'" Let men say the same of you, and it may be, it may be, that you will perhaps get the chance of continuing to learn after your farewell to this short life.[57]

We might identify three components of Har Dayal's anticolonial critique in this crucial paragraph. First, he argues that learning and reading require quotidian practice. Second, he continues his insistence on association and affiliation in this selection, with a focus on cooperative reading and learning (like certain tentative proposals for comparative philological projects in the shadow of world literature). Finally, a properly anticolonial self-culture values life learning and related relinquishment of authority or expertise—indeed, Har Dayal's ideal final realization is that one *lacks* knowledge. Taken together, and in the context of this quietly anticolonial text, these three key imperatives form the basis of what we have identified as anticolonial critique.

World-State

Having established the required educational grounds for the construction of an ethical self-culture (and a philosophy of history to ground that), Har Dayal shifts to the final section, "Ethical Culture." Har Dayal's ethical self-cultivation is fundamentally a process of self-care in the context of others: "Character is developed in a social milieu," he instructs his reader.[58] Because ethical culture is practiced socially, the ethical character realizes that ethics cannot be an Ideal, but rather is an individually practiced and historically specific mode of action. Friendship, therefore, forms the foundation for ethical practice: "The highest use of Friendship lies in the mutual encouragement and inspiration for the development of Personality.... Thus can Friendship be the handmaid of Ethics."[59]

This is a curious collectivity-forging practice, and it alerts us to a particular concept of the self that exceeds the boundaries of Marxist, anarchist, and socialist schema. Under the auspices of anticolonial critique, reading and collective critique became ways to reimagine social practices beyond the reach of the state—to claim, even if ephemerally, the possibility of "ignoring" the state. For many anticolonial thinkers, the power (and perhaps allure) of offering new modes of self-making was the self's metonymic relationship to the possibilities of a new state. As we will discuss in Chapter 3, M. K. Gandhi's ascetic practices—"experiments with truth"—suggest a relationship between the anti-authoritative self and collective egalitarianism. Har Dayal's model of friendship as a mode of self-culture, in some ways similar to Gandhi's (*Hind Swaraj* appears in a list of suggested reading), suggests an orientation outward rather than inward; friendship becomes, in this model, an "improvisational politics appropriate to communicative, sociable utopianism," to borrow Leela Gandhi's definition.[60]

Har Dayal's practice of friendship, explicated in a later section in *Hints*, is the creation of an aggressively non-filial, xenophilic community: "cultivate the society of foreigners and strangers . . . Build up your world-fellowship."[61]

Friendship falls not merely under the rubrics of ethical practice, but in Har Dayal's analysis, it emerges as a "political" stance. Not only does his "friendship" operate as a practice of self-culture and self-care, but it also illuminates and secures the metonymic relationship between the self and a global utopian project.

Friendship and self-cultivation is in the service of the "Five Concentric Circles" beyond the self. The first circle is "the Family," which Har Dayal describes as a single life-partner one maintains; the second circle, "the Relatives," includes siblings and parents. The third circle is "the Municipality," which is territorially and historically defined, and the fourth circle is "the Nation," which is marked by its geographical continuity and relative ethnic homogeneity. Together, these four circles are in service to the fifth circle, the "World-State," the universal ethical, social, and political utopia rooted in "the universal sacrament of friendship."[62]

World-State is admittedly a strange name for an ethics conjured under the sign of an affective relationship beyond the reach of the state. "World-State" operates with a curious relationship to "politics." Smuggled in, perhaps, in the "carefully theoretical" absence of the state, friendship fully recreates the vision for what a state ought to be (or not be). In Har Dayal's analysis World-State emerges from friendship and yet remains tethered to such intimate practices. The precise mechanics of World-State go undefined because its guiding principles—liberty, equality, and fraternity—

require an acceptance of World-State as perpetually contingent.[63] (We will see these principles again in our discussion of Ambedkar.)

In contradistinction to other popular interwar conceptions of internationalist states—also called "World-State"—Har Dayal's vision offers a considerably smaller government, and one that suggests a critically anarcho-utopian vision for community care and support. Aldous Huxley, H. G Wells, and George Orwell, among others, offered "World-State" as a dystopian future under a domineering (often communist) world order.[64] Har Dayal, on the other hand, foregrounds the intimacy of World-State: "It makes all feel that men and women are not Many, but One. . . . That One is Humanity, the World-State, in which all shall live and move and have their being."[65] Even though its name suggests the presence of a state apparatus, Har Dayal aligns it with "Humanity," a more appropriate extension of friendship, community, sacrifice, and hospitality.

Under Har Dayal's optimistic analysis, the future utopia of "World-State," veering from the International, offers an affective orientation for the dismal, interwar present. Concomitantly, Herbert Spencer's isolationist libertarianism in the past becomes a micropolitical anticolonialism for the present. World-State, in this sense, is a Janus-faced project: "It is blessed today as the harbinger of joy and peace, and it will be blessed tomorrow," Har Dayal proclaims.[66] (Twenty-two years earlier, in the spirit of direct state agitation, Har Dayal had offered the exploding bomb as the "harbinger of hope,"[67] a curious echo of mutiny still present in 1934.)

And thus he triumphantly concludes:

> Work thus, and wait for the World-State. It shall come, not today and not tomorrow, but in its own good time. But if you live in the light of its Ideal now and here, you are already a citizen of that State. You belong to it. You may be born in the present nation-state, but you are not of it. Your heart is elsewhere. . . . Your children and grandchildren will rejoice in the light and warmth of the Sun that shall illumine the Earth in the days to come, the serene and spacious World-State, one and indivisible.[68]

Once again, Har Dayal's past and future turn on the axis of the present. It is not merely that the past is put into service for the present, but that the future is as well. It is a backwards-glancing future, where the children of the future praise their ancestors of the present. The two epigraphs at the bottom of the final page are from nineteenth-century figures: socialist William Morris and poet Arthur Hugh Clough, and they serve to doubly suggest this configuration of anticolonial utopian time.[69] Concurrently (and literally so), the present is made to be not of itself; an anticolonial utopian time is perpetually "elsewhere": the past and future—and yet, nevertheless, firmly and resolutely active in the contingent present. Har Dayal's revolutionary time demands a commitment to past, present, and future utopias that stretch in multiple directions across time, and multitudinous affective directions across the present. Pedagogy, self-care, friendship, hospitality, and sacrifice are not only imagined with these directions in mind, but are fundamentally made possible by affiliations in times seemingly out of joint with the present.

Under the possibility of such disjointed time, it seems only fitting that Bhagat Singh's handsome, cosmopolitan portrait repurposes an aging Har Dayal's *baraabari de arth* in 1938. Har Dayal's lifelong commitment to pedagogy, his repeated belief in the political power of adolescence,[70] and his dedication of World-State to "children and grandchildren" suggest an investment in youth, newness, and immaturity. It is not altogether surprising, then, that Har Dayal's revolutionary afterlife is often tied, and intimately so, with Bhagat Singh and the Hindustan Socialist Republican Army (HSRA). In 1929, the HSRA declared that revolution was the only solution to the oppression of Indian colonialism, and that "the youths of our nation have realized this truth."[71]

In other words, perhaps the productively promiscuous afterlives of the multiple Har Dayals—the actively political and the carefully theoretical to suggest two—have not been so badly abused. Having been declared a youthful rebel, a Marxist, a republican, a socialist, an anarchist, and a nationalist, Har Dayal's ghost can only agree. As his writings indicate, one's own afterlives are difficult things to manage. Nevertheless, in the spirit of radical anticolonial utopian time, we, with him, might appreciate the simultaneous reaching back to lost pasts while stretching forward toward unreachable utopias. Such an abandoning of one's self to the wantonness of one's afterlives suggests a continued commitment to hospitality and sacrifice to extreme and radical points. It suggests, in doubling back, a dedication not only to youthfulness but to a politics of active immaturity: one where the present operates to bring about a future utopia, which remains tethered to the immature politics of its own past: the first-person plural present across the echoes of revolt.

Toward a History of Imagination

In 1915, Jack London published a semi-autobiographical novel, *The Little Lady of the Big House*, to tepid response and sales. The plot focuses on a physically and sexually virile woman, Paula, and the love triangle that emerges around her. Early in the novel, Paula hosts a dinner party with a curious guest:

> "And the Hindoo, there—who's he?" [asks Graham.]
> "That's Dar Hyal.... He's a revolutionist, of sorts. He's dabbled in our universities, studied in France, Italy, Switzerland, is a political refugee from India, and he's hitched his wagon to two stars: one, a new synthetic system of philosophy; the other, rebellion against the tyranny of British rule in India. He advocates individual terrorism and direct mass action. That's why his paper, *Kadar*, or *Badar*, or something like that, was suppressed here in California, and why he narrowly escaped being deported; and that's why he's up here just now, devoting himself to formulating his philosophy" [answers Paula].[72]

Dar Hyal is charming; he dances with Paula briefly and defends the merits of his "blastic" synthetic philosophy, an updated philosophy based on his reading of Herbert Spencer.

Despite the curious fictional cameo, London has offered a correction to Har Dayal's biographers: Even here, he is both a philosopher and revolutionary; *The Little Lady of the Big House* marks in fiction an out-of-joint biography (doubled by the spoonerism of Har Dayal's name).

Drawing, then, from fiction, pamphlets, poetry, newsletters, and ethical manuals, we might finally arrive at an account of anticolonialism that can properly account for the wide expanse of its imagination—an imagination not easily contained by simple biography or historical fact. On the contrary, this approach to Har Dayal reveals a substantially more complex relationship between reading, writing, anticolonial action, and the proper "time" of anticolonialism itself.

Har Dayal's anticolonialism is critique in the vein we have been discussing because, like the "echoes of mutiny," it is an anticolonialism organized around its proliferation.[73] "Echoes" (*gunj*) serves as the proper metaphor for our inquiry here, insofar as it situates insurgent thought around the continued proliferation and circulation of anticolonial thought rather than its origins (which are always displaced, either to the past or to the future, or simply vague). This is a process of reception instead of production.

We have also been discussing Har Dayal's palimpsestic utopian vision, which is at once a product of mid-nineteenth-century thought, *fin-de-siècle* radicalism, and interwar optimism (itself a quiet form of utopian pessimism). In the "elsewhere" of the radical present, a curious and insurgent political thought temporarily congeals in careful "hints." Such hints, which are "not exhaustive, but only suggestive," offer an imagination of non-authorial collectivities. This, in turn, requires a circuitous view of historical action and a hopeful vision for the future rooted (and perpetually tethered to) in the dismal present and the lost possibilities of the past.

The investments of this chapter, then, rely on anticolonial books and pamphlets out of joint with their time: forgotten texts imaginatively repurposed, obsolete philosophies reimagined, and utopian futures practiced in the present. Such texts, which may sit uneasily in their own time, foreground their imagined affective communities and philosophical genealogies. These genealogies illuminate the scale of the anticolonial imagination.

I use "imagination" here instead of "ideas" in order to highlight an unruly unit of political and aesthetic action. This is, perhaps, to take Har Dayal at his own word: to suggest a new "imagination" (like that of the Indian Peasant), which offers new aesthetic and ethical protocols. I want to suggest here that the protocols of reading demanded by Har Dayal's quieter works align closer with a history of percepts. His ethical and political suggestions are not quite ideas; they are hints. The torqueing of the present back onto the past, and the future back onto the present, suggest here something not quite (but also more than) "histories of [ideas'] uses in argument," to borrow Quentin Skinner's formula.[74] Rather, Har Dayal's work hints at a history of imagination's uses in affect: not only as a call-to-arms in the stalled Ghadr poetry of 1914, but as a resuscitation of antiquated philosophy for a fundamentally new conjuncture. In other words, Har Dayal's use of Herbert Spencer, as I have suggested, is less about using the Victorian philosopher's ideas in a new argument, but rather reading nineteenth-century liberal philosophy (with, perhaps, Spencer's bearded visage) to fulfill its utopian possibilities in the revolutionary present. If Shyamji Krishnavarma *used* Spencer for anticolonial thought, Har Dayal makes Spencer *become* an anticolonialist. Similarly, under Har Dayal's pen, "World-State" is not an idea, but rather a practice for the present: an affective and imaginative stance rooted in the crises of global war and the horrors of late-Raj rule.

Borrowing Har Dayal's own term, "imagination" (used especially in "The Indian Peasant"), we might do best to understand the trajectory of Har Dayal's anticolonialism as one offered by way of critique—as an appeal, in this instance, to the more imaginative, less historically linear, constructions of an anticolonial worldly orientation. This stance, with its insistence on time out of joint, offers a different model of anticolonial agitation than one simply aimed at armed revolt and national independence (two things Har Dayal advocated for, to be sure). The model of anticolonial critique that emerges from closer attention to Har Dayal's scattered archives reveals an insistence on imagining the 1857 mutiny and the youth politics of the future (say, Bhagat Singh) in the same fictive moment. Har Dayal's anticolonialism did not proceed linearly; his term, "imagination," then here allows us to construct an alternative critical history of anticolonialism that stretches both forward and backward—from 1915 to 1857, and then to 1851 (but also 1892), and to 1938—which is precisely why the material afterlives of his *baraabari de arth* seem so haunting.

In other words, the aesthetic critique that Har Dayal offered was twofold: In the first instance, he demanded that a fundamental anticolonial practice *was*, in fact, reading. His long lists of reading suggestions (always tentatively offered—hints, suggestions, preliminary offerings) were implicitly and explicitly offered as practices of anticolonial self-cultivation. Anticolonial agitation, for Har Dayal, *was* reading. By reading, by marking his reading practices in his writing, he was attempting to cultivate a critical sensibility in order to be a proper, though non-instrumentalizable, anticolonial politics. In the second instance, Har Dayal offers a practice whereby reading texts out of order and out of joint produces an altogether new imaginative political theory. This anticolonial critic aligns with Timothy Brennan's description of the philological critic, which he describes as "curious, anti-utilitarian, imaginatively driven, idealistic . . . , drawn to ideas for their own sake, polymorphous in his or her intellectual wanderings and experiments."[75]

This is seen clearest, as I have shown, in Har Dayal's imaginative approach to the study of history. History is to be read out of order and with no eras or epochs in mind (they are for nations and religions, which the World-State will not possess). "If History is to be studied in a scientific and cosmopolitan spirit," Har Dayal writes, "a new era must be employed for reckoning dates and periods of time,"[76] and in order to understand the "topsy-turvy" motions of history. In other words, Har Dayal's critical intervention involves a re-mixing of history by way of a reading practice. Thus, 1857 *can* appear next to 1914; and the children of the World-State can look back onto their past (our present) as ushering their present (our impossible future—though, if we are proper "young rationalists," perhaps our present).

If we restrict our attention to Har Dayal's and the Ghadr Party's only occasional insistence on mutiny, we retrieve a dangerously flat account of the types of anticolonial action the group promoted. A continued focus on physical violence, coupled with a continued privileging of the masculinist authority of anticolonial polemical writing—both indebted to a mostly non-imaginative empiricism—produces, if not an entirely teleological account of anticolonial thought, certainly a unidirectional, future-oriented, anticolonial sensibility. We risk ignoring the actual impact of the afterlives of the Ghadr Party had in Punjab, which were aesthetic, philosophical, and literary in their orientation.[77]

A closer focus on anticolonial critique offers, in contrast, a more long-term practice of nonemphatic critique that the Ghadr Party and its members attempted to envision for themselves and their readership. It offers a more democratic and global view of political action, whereby reading communities could extend ever-outward, with a focus on reflection, interpretation, and friendship. It reveals the admittedly more conceptually difficult and yet more accurate afterlives of Ghadr Party after its failed *ghadr*, from 1914 to the present. A closer focus on anticolonial critique also reveals a more imaginatively productive anticolonial orientation: Looking to the past and the future at the same time, critique envisions a long history of passive engagement that listens for the *ghadr di gunj*.

A focus on Har Dayal's reading and texts out of time—as well as the proliferation of his texts beyond his control—reveals that Har Dayal's commitment to anticolonial practice continued well beyond the failed mutiny of 1914, contrary to what historians of the Ghadr Party have consistently implied. It does not render Har Dayal's later work "merely" philosophical.

In early 1934, just before the publication of *Hints for Self-Culture*, Har Dayal wrote to his friend, popular writer Van Wyck Brooks, in Philadelphia:

> I am not very much troubled or depressed by the world situation, as I look beyond it, as St. Augustine described the City of God, when the old Empire was falling in ruins about him. I look forward to a new Socialist order of international politics, which must succeed this rotten system of nationalism + capitalism. . . . But there's something new over there. Don't you think so?[78]

"Over there" was both Russia (though with a lengthy caveat) and "the future." In this spirit, we might do more to return to interwar anticolonial thought; not only to recuperate its ideas (though those are important, too), but to recuperate its imagination and its orientation to a new world, ghosted by the old and already haunted by the future.

2 / B. R. Ambedkar's Sciences

Curriculum Vitae

In receipt of a scholarship offered to him by the Maharaja of Baroda, a twenty-two-year-old B. R. Ambedkar arrived at Columbia University in 1913. Under the guidance of John Dewey, James Shotwell, Edwin Seligman, and James Harvey Robinson, Ambedkar finished his Master's degree in 1915 and his PhD in sociology in 1927. (He studied in London between the two degrees.)

At the time, Ambedkar's arrival in Morningside Heights in 1913 went mostly unnoticed, in stark contrast to the concurrent celebration of the 1913–14 University Visiting Professor, Henri Bergson. The philosopher was greeted in New York by Columbia University's head librarian, who presented him with a bibliography of scholarship produced by American academics: "A contribution to the bibliography of Henri Bergson," listing 496 entries. His lectures at Columbia were so popular that, James Shotwell writes, "the largest hall in the university was crowded to overflowing" and "a whole philosophical literature appeared."[1] The following academic year, 1914–15, John Dewey and Franz Boas co-taught a class, perhaps on "comparative ethics," that was overenrolled with graduate students from both anthropology and sociology.[2] In 1916, James Harvey Robinson and Charles Beard clashed with the University over what they identified as "academic freedom": the right of faculty to openly criticize U.S. foreign policy.[3]

In short, Ambedkar arrived in New York at an intellectually exuberant time. Ambedkar might have attended Bergson's lectures, and it seems likely that he took Dewey's and Boas's co-taught seminar. He also took classes in the history of socialism, European industrialization, the French Revolution, and statistics. He took a class with noted Indologist A. V. W. Jackson, who had recently overseen a magisterial nine-volume project on Indian history.[4] In 1916, shortly before his departure from New York, Ambedkar presented his own work in front of Alexander Goldenweiser's anthropology seminar. In one of his many excellent analyses of Ambedkar's political thought, Jesús Francisco Chaírez-Garza has written about how Ambedkar's relationship to Boas, Goldenweiser, and the anthropology department at Columbia laid the intellectual groundwork for his lifelong commitment to sociological thought and caste politics.[5]

Ambedkar returned to India in the 1920s, where he worked as an activist against caste oppression, a lawyer, and a political critic. Although the term is not his, Ambedkar is associated with the shift from the non-caste-Hindu identity "Untouchable" to the more provocative identity "Dalit" (literally, "ground-down") that would catalyze a number of Dalit rights movements during and after his lifetime.[6] In this chapter, we will discuss significant moments in Ambedkar's career, including his protest at Mahad in 1927 and the publication of *Annihilation of Caste* in 1936. Throughout the 1930s and 1940s, Ambedkar fought with Gandhi about the eradication of caste, most notably around the 1932 Poona Pact (discussed in Chapter 3). In addition to his work on caste, he wrote extensively on minority rights, social democracy, and nationalism. After Indian Independence in 1947, Ambedkar drafted the Indian Constitution and then watched in disappointment as the Constituent Assembly rejected most of his contributions. He resigned from public office in 1951 and focused his studies on Buddhism. Shortly before his death in 1956, Ambedkar converted to Navayana Buddhism, a doctrine he composed from his analysis of Pali Buddhist texts (discussed in the conclusion of this book).

Rather than catalogue Ambedkar's activities at Columbia or delineate the influences that the University had on the future Dalit activist, this chapter hopes to capture this heady conjuncture by retaining its sprawling intellectual promiscuities and disciplinary infidelities. What emerges, therefore, is an academic conversation that Ambedkar would articulate and render politically potent in his activism twenty to thirty years later. Ambedkar's political writings from the 1930s to the 1950s retain the vibrant assemblage of sociology, philology, and philosophy of the American academy in the 1910s. Under the rubrics of "critique," Ambedkar makes this assemblage the basis of a radically antiauthoritarian political philosophy, simultaneously anticolonial and anti-casteist.

To the extent that the figures in this book theorized anticolonial practices that involve renunciation or relinquishment, those practices were extremely varied, always experimental, and never straightforwardly ascetic. Still, there is obvious discomfort in placing Ambedkar under the same rubrics as the other thinkers here, especially Gandhi. (Recall Ambedkar's famous response when Gandhi asked him to relinquish his devotion to anti-caste politics in favor of the Indian nation: "Gandhiji, I have no homeland.")[7] Ambedkar did theorize asceticism and suffering in his reformulation of Buddhism, but that is not what we are discussing here. Ambedkarite relinquishment, in the discussion here, is not necessarily concerned with personal divestment, but with a certain *fin-de-siècle* sociological disavowal of the assurances otherwise secured for a liberal subject. Framed differently: Ambedkar's antiauthoritarian critique vitalizes a strain of *fin-de-siècle* sociological-philological criticism committed to the dismissal of the exceptionality of the autonomous individual, and, relatedly, to the imagination of an illiberal humanism as the model of egalitarian sociability and politics.

In this chapter, I hope to track how Ambedkar mobilizes the curious assemblage of early twentieth-century academic disciplines for an antiauthoritarian critique immune to the allures of liberalism and its alleged benefits: autonomy, self-mastery, and identitarian expertise. In the first instance, this critique relied on philological sources to reveal the anxiety, madness, arbitrariness, and therefore the total irrelevance, of authority. In the second instance, this critique reinvigorated the radical empiricism of early sociological critique in order to theorize new forms of what Aniket Jaaware has pointedly called "sociability."[8] Finally, by combining late nineteenth-century philology with early twentieth-century sociology, Ambedkar's critique imagines a political subject on the basis of the chaos of cell biology: perpetually contagious, heterogenous, and incapable of self-authorization or individual autonomy. This "sociophilic" subject would render caste unimaginable and would be the basis for an illiberal antiauthoritarianism.

"Man, an Imperfect Librarian"

A long-overdue academic interest in Ambedkar, which has produced outstanding work, has been understandably overwhelmed by the amount of material that surrounds the thinker.[9] His collected writings, assiduously edited by Vasant Moon under the auspices of the Government of Maharashtra, take up seventeen volumes, two of which have been subsequently divided into multiple parts to account for the breadth of Ambedkar's work.

This is made even more overwhelming by anecdotes, from his former colleagues and assistants, that at the end of his life his personal library contained 50,000 books. "It is well known that the late Dr. Ambedkar was a bibliophile," S.R. Dongerkery notes in an essay in honor of the anti-caste activist. "Dr. Ambedkar's hobbies are books, gardening, and dogs, in the descending order of attachment," Kartar Singh wrote. "He revels in reading books. . . . He is a voracious reader. . . . His devotion to books is so great that he studies late into the early hours of the morning every night." Toward the end of his life, Ambedkar acknowledged the possible losses his extensive reading had incurred: "I am a difficult man. . . . My books have become my companions. They are dearer to me than wife and children." His assistant (and posthumous biographer), Nanak Chand Rattu, noted that Ambedkar spent his last days "reading unto death."[10]

Siddhartha College, in Mumbai, holds a portion of this collection. V. Geetha, in a provocative essay, "unpacks" this collection to trace how Ambedkar's reading practices later manifest in his published work.[11] Her essay is compelling and imaginative in its scope, but we should be wary of too quickly replicating its methodology. An inventory of Ambedkar's books (and which passages he has underlined in them) is certainly interesting, but what it tells us is either redundant or empirically suspect. In the first instance, Ambedkar rarely hides his references, even if he does not always formally cite them. In the second instance, this methodology assumes that Ambedkar read every book in his library, and only read books he kept.

To be sure, Ambedkar was an avid scholar and reader. But a focus on his verifiable reading practices is undergirded by logics of autodidacticism organized around the telos of mastery and authority, concepts Ambedkar was fundamentally interested in dismantling. (This is a problem that haunts the study of other anticolonial thinkers, as we will see in our discussion of Bhagat Singh in Chapter 4.)

Ambedkar imagined reading is necessary. Ambedkar imagined reading to be central to his anticolonial critique. He was a theorist of reading, and especially reading in ways that *cannot* be catalogued. Under the signs of "reading" and "critique," Ambedkar imagined social and political practices that remained beyond recognition, or that would render recognition irrelevant.[12] As he writes in an early autobiographical note, being recognized, catalogued, and known are the conditions in which caste, and therefore caste oppression, is made possible.[13] My argument here is that Ambedkar theorizes a particular practice of reading that reclaims academic scholarship from its possible authoritarian uses (colonialism, casteism) by revealing the inherent inaptitude and irrelevance of authority within that textual or scholarly tradition. We will track Ambedkar's citations not simply to determine which books he read, but to show how Ambedkar thought those books might be read, or perhaps read *otherwise*.

The Crises of the European Sciences

Anupama Rao, in her particularly clear-sighted synthesis of Ambedkar's thought, shows four central aims of the thinker's life work: first, to dismantle the alleged transcendent authority of "Hindu law"; second, to reveal the incoherence and injustice at the core of "Hindu texts" and the practice of Hinduism; third, to reframe "Hindu laws" as mechanisms for securing Brahmanical power rather than asserting a code of conduct; and fourth, to extensively study Indian society by bringing together philology, Indology, and sociology/anthropology.[14] Ambedkar seems to have made few, if any, distinctions between his multiple projects. If "Dalits need theory as a social necessity," to borrow Gopal Guru's evocative demand,[15] Ambedkar offered theory for theory's sake, as a social necessity.

As Arun Mukherjee argues, reading Ambedkar "in isolation, without paying attention to ... an astounding number of other thinkers both contemporary and from the past, does justice neither to the richness and complexity of his thought."[16] We may borrow Edmund Husserl's description of this worldly conjuncture, wherein "the crisis of the European sciences" and "man" names not only a decisive shift in metaphysical thought but also debates what constitutes "science" and the "human" in academic institutions in the North Atlantic world. This chapter focuses on two of those sciences in the 1910s and 1920s: an emergent science, sociology; and a science in decline, philology.

Sociology's ascendance and philology's descent are not merely cotemporaneous. Their respective rise and fall center around a crisis about their methodological protocols: The social sciences were attempting to demarcate their disciplinary autonomy from the "natural sciences"; the "human sciences" were attempting to defend their relevance despite the institutionalization of national literatures, especially in the United States. Nevertheless, both "sciences" were still tethered to each other *and* the "natural sciences" in a way that this chapter will address. They were, moreover, attempting to distinguish themselves from each other.[17]

Ambedkar's work captures these fields at a curious interwar nexus.[18] "Ambedkar's failure was a failure of the state of anthropological and ethnographical knowledge of his times.... The failure is obvious in his recourse to anthropometry and ancient classical texts," Jaaware writes in a surprisingly shortsighted judgment.[19] On the contrary, Ambedkar's antiauthoritarian theory retains, amber-like, this moment of academic transition in the 1910s, to 1930–50s; it luxuriates in disciplinary fungibility and porousness; it forces the "human sciences" to fulfill their own political and aesthetic emancipatory promises.

We will take these disciplines in turn, testing out their critical force under Ambedkar: first, philology; second, sociology; and finally, their combination as an egalitarian political practice: sociophilia.

Minima Philologica

Philology had, by the 1910s, lost its exemplary status. To recall, the three interrelated missions of philology in the nineteenth century—the study of languages, historical linguistics, and comparativism—shared, despite their various projects, a methodological commitment to history as a particularly human practice (what Auerbach, Said, and others would later call "secular," or "this-worldly"). James Turner has traced philology's slow loss of its autonomy in the late nineteenth century, as "literature," "history," "anthropology," and "religious studies" became distinct disciplines.[20] Even if, as distinct "human sciences," they retained methodological commitments of philology, the object and unit of study became the defining feature of disciplinary order.[21]

Although it had been reduced to covert methodological commitment in the early twentieth century, nineteenth-century philology's contributions to the humanities had been safely secured. The Indo-European theory of language that eighteenth- and nineteenth-century philologists produced, as Said and others (including Ambedkar) have shown, promulgated a theory of race predicated on the notion of unique linguistic heritages.

Comparative philology, with its varied Herderian inheritance, largely took language as the expression of the "inner spirit" of the language's speakers, who formed an autonomous culture (and, consequently, an autonomous nation); language was therefore a reflection of a culture's creativity and freedom of thought. In her brilliant analysis of comparativism, Tomoko Masuzawa argues that the grammatical process of "inflection" became the primary feature of the difference between Indo-European/Aryan languages (Sanskrit, Persian, Greek, Latin, and modern European languages) and Semitic languages (Arabic and Hebrew). According to nineteenth-century philology, inflection, which Indo-European languages possessed, marked the ability for speakers to create new words and concepts; its lack, which forced languages to therefore rely on agglutination, meant that Semitic languages were fated to remain comprised, impure, and constrained.[22] (Other languages were haphazardly categorized.)

This philological-physiological-sociological card-trick was the alleged proof that Europeans were the descendants of a "Western tradition" ("the Romans" and "the Aryans," an ancestry that Europeans shared with South Asians) other than "the Semites" (Jews and Arabs). In the second instance, it justified European political and economic interest in South Asia. Philology named the linguistic proof (language) for a sociological theory (race); simultaneously, philology named the genealogical justification (shared ancestry) for political nonage (colonial exploitation). This philological endeavor served at least two purposes, which were "obviously not in harmony," Ambedkar writes succinctly: one, that "the Aryan race existed in a physiological sense with typical hereditary traits," and two, that "the Aryan race existed in a philological sense, as a people speaking a common language."[23] The conclusion that people who share a common ancient language must share a common ancestry and therefore must also share a common racial community is "an inference from an inference."[24]

For upper-caste anticolonial activists, however, nineteenth-century comparative philology offered the basis on which to assert equivalence and sovereignty. "Hinduism," and therefore "India," by way of Sanskrit, could assert its difference in the name of European universalism, rather than challenging it. As Masuzawa explains, Hindu universalism and Christian universalism could "negotiate the terms of their coexistence" through "mutual 'respect'—even 'sympathy'—that takes the form of complete and willful disregard for the other side's exclusivist claim for totality and universality."[25] The allegiance between philology, comparative religion, and political and social authority was secured, according to Masuzawa, by Max Müller's lectures on "The Science of Religion" in 1870, as well as by the publication of his multi-volume collection, *The Sacred Books of the East*, between 1879 and 1910.[26] This collection contained the text that would become the near sole focus of Ambedkar's philological critique, *The Laws of Manu* (or, alternatively, the *Manusmriti*).

The *Manusmriti* is an extensive list of protocols for proper Brahmanical behavior, concerning diet, dining habits, and sexual practices; "in sum, an encompassing representation of life in the world—how it is: and how it should be lived."[27] Numerous contradictory *Manusmriti* manuscripts circulated between this origin and William Jones's English translation in 1794 (an inaugural moment in Indology and Orientalist scholarship). Well before Jones, no matter Manu's original identity, "Manu" had already coagulated not simply into the figure of the "author," but the transcendent Hindu authority *par excellence*.[28] The long history of interpretation of *The Laws of Manu* is beyond the scope of this chapter, but by the nineteenth century, the *dharma-shastra* that make up Manu's "laws" had become the authoritative text for a variety of competing and interrelated interests: the British Raj, orientalist scholars, and Hindu reformers all drew on *The Laws of Manu* for their authority.[29]

For nineteenth-century European philologists, the *Manusmriti* was a document that demonstrated a calcified caste system, which was simultaneously the justification for Aryan supremacy and colonial intervention. Upper-caste anticolonial leaders, interested in demonstrating the equivalence between Vedic law and British law, also recuperated *The Laws of Manu*, which allowed them to reinforce caste difference and retain Brahmanical privilege. European philological scholarship agreed that the *Manusmriti* were "Vedic Laws" and helped render "Manu" a proper and authentic authoritative figure. The *Manusmriti* and its eponymous and anonymous author became the centerpiece in the canons of Sanskrit philology and Indological sociology.[30] This argument relies on strange reasoning: The *Manusmriti* was authoritatively "Hindu" because its interest in "Hinduism" was primarily a concern about authority.[31]

One particularly recalcitrant philologist relied heavily on the *Manusmriti*: Friedrich Nietzsche. Nietzsche saw clearly that Manu was the quintessential figure of dubiously calcified authority. In *Antichrist*, Nietzsche writes:

> to set up a law-book of the kind of Manu means to concede to a people the right henceforth to become masterly, to become perfect— to be ambitious for the highest art of living. *To that end, the law must be made unconscious:* this is the purpose of every holy lie.[32]

For Nietzsche, Manu represents the moment at which a culture ceases to interrogate its values and morals, and thus begins to enforce them as transcendent. Because the *Manusmriti* was the consolidation of traditional and textual authority, Nietzsche viewed it as the most important articulation of "Hindu law."[33] His praise for Manu's authority was enthusiastic, but he was hardly alone among nineteenth-century European philosophers, who believed Manu was the traditional and textual authority that Christianity (which was "weak") and Judaism (a tradition of "no discoveries") lacked.[34] In the absence of God, "tradition" would need to render itself transcendent, and the *Manusmriti* successfully achieved this.[35]

Despite his questionable interests, Nietzsche comprehended the "holy lie" at the heart of Manu's laws (or what they were by the 1860s): that any text could be used to justify "becoming masterly, becoming perfect" at the expense of others. Ambedkar saw Nietzsche's complicated analysis quite clearly: "Nietzsche was genuinely interested in creating a new race of men which will be a race of supermen as compared with the existing race of men. Manu, on the other hand, was interested in maintaining the privilege of a class who had come to arrogate to itself the claim of being supermen."[36]

Nietzsche consequently makes a fairly astute and foreboding prediction: "mastery over nature, the *idée fixe* of the twentieth century, is Brahmanism, Indo-German."[37] By the late 1930s, the sly transfiguration of philology to sociology was realized in its most horrific forms. It legitimized Nazism's monstrous "human sciences," which used philological difference to produce sociological/ethnic difference, for which a political "solution" was necessary. Simultaneously, it authorized extraordinary oppression and violence under the caste system, which used philological difference to assert the "equivalence" of "Hindu law" to "British law," thereby displacing caste, as sociological/religious difference, *outside* the reach of political concerns.

The slow textual accretion of Manu's *colonial* authority, over the eighteenth and nineteenth centuries, provided extensive documentation of the *Manusmriti's* internal divisions, splits, and contradictions. Ambedkar's citations here alert us to a particular philological practice that demonstrates the historical accretion of such authority, as well as its fundamental instability (and therefore, danger). In other words, Ambedkar uses a philological method to demonstrate philology's pernicious historical alliances.[38]

That Orientalist philology and European social sciences have been the justification for European colonialism as well as its beneficiaries should come as no surprise. That the same human sciences were also the basis for national (that is, nationalist) liberation movements in the twentieth century is, similarly, no new argument.[39] My argument here, however, has been to illuminate a very particular confluence of philology's assorted progeny that Ambedkar would mobilize for antiauthoritarian critique immune to the allure of identitarian expertise or autonomy (to which other nationalist thinkers would succumb). This critique relied on philological sources to reveal the anxiety, madness, arbitrariness, and therefore the total irrelevance, of authority located at the nexus of Brahmanical and British power.

The brilliance of Ambedkar's use of philological scholarship comes into clearer view. In order to attack the authority of caste, one had to begin with the production of authority: caste's canonicity in European philological and literary analyses. Ambedkar's anti-caste critique is, implicitly, as much a critique of colonial scholarly authority as it is Brahmanical authoritarianism. Both texts rely on other, arbitrary historical texts for authoritarian power in the present. Its critique works the other way, perhaps more damningly (especially for Gandhi and the Arya Samaj): It reveals these caste-Hindu thinkers' reliance on colonial institutions of authority for their own dominance an otherwise anticolonial discourse.[40] Ambedkar's Manu (like Gandhi's) spoke in English and German, not Sanskrit.[41]

Between Burning and Reading

In December 1927, Ambedkar burned a copy of the *Manusmriti* at a protest in Mahad, Maharashtra.[42] In his excellent account of the protest, Anand Teltumbde rightly identifies this as "the First Dalit Revolt."[43] In Ambedkar's words (published posthumously):

> The rock on which the Hindu Social Order has been built is the *Manu Smriti*. It is a part of the Hindu Scriptures and is therefore sacred to all Hindus. Being sacred it is infallible. Every Hindu believes in its sanctity and obeys its injunctions. Manu not only upholds caste and untouchability but gives them a legal sanction. The burning of the *Manu Smriti* was a deed of great daring. It was an attack on the very citadel of Hinduism. The *Manu Smriti* embodied the spirit of inequality which is at the base of Hindu life and thought just as the Bastille was the embodiment of the spirit of the *ancien regime* in France. The burning of the *Manu Smriti* by the Untouchables at Mahad in 1927 is an event which has the same significance and importance in the history of the emancipation of the Untouchables which the Fall of Bastille had in the liberation of the masses in France and Europe.[44]

We can see here the beginnings of Ambedkar's interest in revolutionary emancipation, with its antecedents in eighteenth-century France. Ambedkar would develop these revolutionary values, as we will see shortly, both in their liberal tradition as well as for an extra-liberal humanistic, impossible, political theory.

If burning the *Manusmriti* was a spectacular way to inaugurate an anticaste protest in 1927, it was also an augur, though not uncomplicatedly so, of Ambedkar's "scientific work" in the 1940s and 1950s. Prompted by his decision to move "outside the Hindu fold" in the mid-1930s, Ambedkar began a serious and sustained engagement with Manu and his laws. Ambedkar addressed Manu directly in his most famous publication *Annihilation of Caste* in 1936, but the majority of Ambedkar's writings on Manu were published posthumously, though Ambedkar circulated some versions among friends and colleagues: "India and the Prerequisites of Communism," "Riddles in Hinduism," "Revolution and Counter-Revolution," and "Buddha or Karl Marx."[45]

We might therefore describe Ambedkar's trajectory of anti-caste critique as the realization that burning the *Manusmriti* was insufficient for annihilating authority. Ambedkar's more radically antiauthoritarian critique theorizes a much more drastic measure: One must *read* the *Manusmriti*. By offering descriptions of his own reading practices and urging his colleagues (and adversaries) to read Manu *with* him, Ambedkar insists on the practice of social reading and interpretation of *The Laws of Manu* as a way of disavowing authoritarianism, rather than merely denying *an* authority. Put differently: Burning the *Manusmriti* is a rejection of Manu as Hindu authority; reading the *Manusmriti* is a rejection of authority and Hinduism entirely. Ambedkar's political vision, articulated by way of critique, relies not on dismantling the authorial presence of Manu as he lurks over both caste, colonial, and orientalist mastery, but rather of universalizing the stature of the "reader" as a critical and fundamental part of an egalitarian, anti-caste society.

Ambedkar does not deny Manu his authorship; he denounces transcendental authorship altogether as "madness." Ambedkar reveals the "madness" (if not the "holy lie") of the authorial position, which is "to become masterly, to become perfect." To refuse to become masterly, or to refuse perfection, is the precise refusal of authority heralded as an anticolonial reading practice.[46]

Between obeying Manu and burning Manu, we find the most radically egalitarian practice is reading Manu. Obeying Manu is a justification for continued authoritarian caste oppression. Burning Manu asserts authority over Manu, thereby gesturing toward, perhaps, caste *equality* (a value that is, as we have noted, necessary but insufficient). But when Ambedkar reads Manu closely—when Ambedkar *critiques* Manu—he reveals something more devastating to caste: Manu's authority, far from transcendent, is simply irrelevant. It is in this final move that Ambedkar offers the beginning of a model for the true *annihilation* of caste hierarchy.[47]

We have now arrived at a critique of authority produced by reading authoritative texts against their philological tradition. Ambedkar's readerly performance, with its near total destruction of authoritarian tradition, is impressive. We may stop here to admire the craft and deftness with which Ambedkar offers such critique, but let us not linger too long in mere destruction. Ambedkar's impossible political theory requires more than the annihilation of Brahmanism; it demands, instead, the annihilation of caste. The former might be satisfyingly destructive, but the latter is reconstructive and emancipatory. We should therefore press on, toward this creative annihilation.

Sociology Hesitant

Ambedkar was a sociologist when sociology was, to quote his contemporary colleague (and also underappreciated sociologist) W. E. B. Du Bois, "hesitant."[48] Crudely put, sociology had yet to fully develop its own social scientific protocols necessary for disciplinary autonomy, and therefore reveled in a moment of philosophical social science that unfortunately has since been lost (or, more optimistically, shifted to more historically sensitive forms of cultural studies). William James wrote that sociology, especially under John Dewey, "made biology and psychology continuous."[49] A heady blend of empiricism, psychology, anthropology, vitalism, political theory, pragmatism, and metaphysics was the foundation to this *fin-de-siècle* sociology.[50] When Du Bois and Ambedkar were sociologists, sociology was still pliable enough—"hesitant" enough—to be useful for a radical politics of anti-racism, anticolonialism, and anti-casteism. For example, during Ambedkar's time at Columbia University, leftist scholars debated the political use of rendering parallel the functions of "caste" in India and "race" in the United States—"color-caste," thusly named, is still considered one of the foundational moments in Afro-Asian solidarity, which emerged more fully, in the wake of Cold War decolonization and the Bandung Conference in 1955.[51]

"So deeply embedded is Dewey's thought in Ambedkar's consciousness that quite often his words flow through Ambedkar's discourse without quotation marks,"[52] notes Arun Mukherjee in her brilliant essay on the affiliations between Ambedkar and his mentor. "Unless we understand something of John Dewey," writes K. N. Kadam, an early biographer of Ambedkar, "it would be impossible to understand Dr. Ambedkar."[53] Ambedkar himself insisted on this relationship as well: "If Dewey died, I could reproduce every lecture verbatim," he allegedly told a student newspaper.[54]

Mukherjee notes that both thinkers share an interest in democracy, social change, communication, education, and individuals as always already social (and socialized) beings. Moreover, she writes, both thinkers share a wariness of teleological thinking, especially of crude versions of Marx and Hegel. At the same time, the stakes for Ambedkar are rendered much higher than those for Dewey. Unlike Dewey, whose personal views were likely more radical than the ones he published,[55] Ambedkar "drags Dewey . . . to the edge,"[56] and offers amore radical heterogeneous egalitarianism.

Rather than catalogue all citations of Dewey proffered by Ambedkar as a sign of his indebtedness to his advisor, we might instead understand Ambedkar as carefully curating a set of political terms to correspond more closely with an aesthetic/political vision of anti-caste critique.[57] Taken together, Ambedkar's selection pushes us closer to the curious sociological conglomeration of terms indebted to the study of crowd psychology at the turn of the century. "Communication," "social efficiency," and "consciousness of kind" might be closer aligned to a multitudinous politics of the crowd, wherein the central tenants of liberalism are called into question.

This brings to us the most curious of the terms in Ambedkar's sociological vocabulary, "endosmosis." The term was borrowed from biological sciences for use in philosophy, political theory, and psychology by a curious network of thinkers in the American and French academies. Approaching "endosmosis" by this route reveals the term's relationship to discourses of contagion and communion, rather than liberal democratic proceduralism. On the contrary, Ambedkar propels us toward a more radical form of democracy:

> In other words, there must be social endosmosis. This is fraternity, which is only another name for democracy. Democracy is not merely a form of government. It is primarily a mode of associated living, of conjoint communicated experience. It is essentially an attitude of respect.[58]

Rooted in an affective relationship with others ("an attitude of respect"), "associated living," held together by "organic filaments,"[59] is related more closely to a politics of heterogeneous collectivity than of liberal humanism. "There must be social endosmosis," in Ambedkar's analysis here, stands beyond the full reach of the recognizably political and yet not outside of its considerations.[60]

As Mukherjee has shown, Ambedkar's use of "endosmosis" appears as early as 1919, in his report before the Southborough Committee on Franchise: "Endosmosis among the groups makes possible a resocialization of once socialized attitudes . . . [which are] essential for a harmonious life, social or political and, as has just been shown, it depends upon the extent of communication, participation or endosmosis."[61] Again, even at this earlier point, Ambedkar's use of "endosmosis" occurs in the social realm but is not fully accountable to social-political democratic practice.

"Endosmosis" also shows up in Ambedkar's later work, especially in "What Congress and Gandhi Have Done for the Untouchables," in 1946, published shortly before independence, as well as "India and the Pre-

Prerequisites for Communism." In both cases, "endosmosis" refers to a practice of affiliation and disregard for difference:

> Gandhism insists upon class structure. . . . From the point of view of social consequences nothing can be more pernicious. Psychologically, class structure sets in motion influences which are harmful to both the classes. There is no common plane on which the privileged and the subject classes can meet. There is no endosmosis, no give and take of life's hopes and experiences. The social and moral evils of this separation to the subject class are of course real and obvious. It educates them into slaves and creates all the psychological complex which follows from a slave mentality.[62]

Mukherjee is correct to trace Ambedkar's use of "endosmosis" back to Dewey, especially in its longer form, "social endosmosis." Dewey uses the term most extensively in *Democracy and Education* (1916). Education, for Dewey, participates in the creation of a democracy-to-come insofar as it brings together people from multiple socio-economic backgrounds, and allows them to forge affiliations and associations across social differences. "A separation into a privileged and a subject-class prevents social endosmosis," he argues.[63] Dewey was productively unclear on whether democracy produces social endosmosis or vice versa; democracy, for Dewey, was not a teleological result but rather a process of perpetual practice. "'Social endosmosis,'" Dewey writes, "is blocked because society is divided into 'a privileged and a subject-class,'" which in turn "make[s] individuals impervious to the interests of others." Conversely, a pragmatic social endosmosis allows a properly democratic social imagination to emerge.[64]

In one of his most moving essays, "Creative Democracy: The Task Before Us" (1939), Dewey expands on the relationship between the duration of democracy and associated life, communication, and common life. The essay argues for the specificity of democracy as a social *and* political project as the cultivation of a "commonplace of living."[65] It seems likely that Dewey read *Annihilation of Caste*: "For everything which bars freedom and fullness of communication sets up barriers that divide human beings into sets and cliques, into antagonistic sects and factions, and thereby undermines the democratic way of life," Dewey notes.[66]

But it is worth noting that, in most cases beyond *Annihilation of Caste*, Ambedkar uses the term without Dewey's particular adjective. Stopping, as Mukherjee does, at Dewey only provides a partial account of Ambedkar's imagination—to say nothing of the imaginative reach of early sociology. To this end, we should move to sociology's now-repudiated ally, vitalism, in order to provide a richer account of "endosmosis" as the curious metaphor that unites early sociology and the literary imagination made available by the complete vibrancy of Ambedkar's anti-caste critique. Henri Bergson offers a definition:

> Thus, within our ego, there is succession without mutual externality; outside the ego, in pure space, mutual externality without succession: mutual externality, since the present oscillation is radically distinct from the previous oscillation, which no longer exists; but no succession, since succession exists solely for a conscious spectator who keeps the past in mind and sets the two oscillations on their symbols side by side in an auxiliary space. Now, between this succession without externality and this externality without succession, a kind of exchange takes place, very similar to what physicists call the phenomenon of endosmosis.[67]

In other words, Bergson's analysis of consciousness and duration relies on a biological/physics metaphor whereby cells freely interchange and are interdependent with one another. Similarly, the relationship between consciousnesses and the seemingly "external" world is one of interpenetration and oscillation.

Throughout his writings, Bergson clarifies the stakes of this metaphorical description. Endosmosis can explain how "perception and recollection always penetrate each other, are always exchanging something of their substance,"[68] and is "an intermingling of the purely intensive sensation of the mobility with the extensive representation of the space traversed."[69] The relationship between perception and recollection involves interpenetration and the exchange of substance.[70] Bergson solves, for James, "how a lot of separate consciousnesses can at the same time be one collective thing."[71] Endosmosis, for Bergson and James, thus describes a relationship of shared consciousness and perception, not only with people (that is to say, "social endosmosis") but also with objects, perceptions, and consciousnesses.

Equally true, however, for Bergson, is a practice that resembles what Dewey would later identify as "social endosmosis": "The members of a civic community hold together like the cells of an organism. Habit, served by intelligence and imagination, introduces among them a discipline resembling, in the interdependence it establishes between separate individuals, the unity of an organism of anastomotic cells," he writes in one of his few texts on social practice.[72] "Society, present within each of its members, has claims which, whether great or small, each express the sum-total of its vitality. But let us again repeat that this is only a comparison. A human community is a collectivity of free beings."[73]

Lawrence Westerby Howe, in his outstanding essay on Bergsonian endosmosis, asserts the importance of the Greek root *ōsm* ("push" or "impulse") in understanding Bergson's critique. In biology, endosmosis is "the process by which diffusion among substances occurs by a 'push' from the outside of a membrane to the inside of the membrane."[74] Bergson's understanding of endosmosis (like the biological process) insists on a type of *push* that thus allows liquid to move through a semipermeable membrane. For Bergson, this involved a physical correspondence between mind and world, but also a forceful exchange as a mixture of externality and succession. This mixture is promoted by habit, another trait of endosmosis, which accounts for the *semi*-permeability of the "membrane" of consciousness. Endosmosis thus refers to "a repetitious act of intelligence in which elements borrowed from the external world infiltrate interior states of mind [and] the interior states of mind are juxtaposed to one another and made to coincide with elements of the external world."[75]

Bergsonian endosmosis, containing both a concept of "habit" (duration) and the concept of interpenetration of membranes (space), metaphysically unites the seemingly perpendicular axes of human consciousness. In this sense, "time" is rendered in its spatial form as duration and habit interpenetrate human consciousness. Relatedly, a properly "social" endosmosis, with "contagion" and "association" as its references, imagines an egalitarianism beyond the confines of liberal humanism.[76]

These concerns become especially clear when this Franco-American philosophical triptych is contrapuntally refracted through the political critique of B. R. Ambedkar. Ambedkar's abandonment of the academic practice of sociology in the late 1910s in favor of legal activism meant that his sociological references, even in the late 1930s and 1940s (when sociology had emerged as a discrete field of social scientific inquiry, largely resembling the empirical science that we know now), were indebted to a much earlier, much messier, and much more humanistic moment of social scientific concern. If we are too quick to subsume Ambedkar's insistence on "social endosmosis" into an anti-caste project with liberal democratic practice as its sole end result, then we have, I think, fundamentally misunderstood Ambedkar's radical approach to political practice.

Contagious Fraternity

Ambedkar's *Annihilation of Caste*, self-published in 1936 as an "undelivered lecture," is a systematic deconstruction of the caste system and its justifications. It was meant to be a lecture for the Jat-Pat Todak Mandal, a faction of the Arya Samaj interested in dismantling the caste system as part of a broader project of Hindu reform movements. The lecture that became *Annihilation of Caste*, however, was deemed too radical for the collective, who insisted that the dismantling of caste come from within the privileged-castes, not from untouchables or Dalits.

The text moves forward by accomplishing a series of critical moves. It opens with a concern for contemporaneous social movements and an analysis of oppressive anti-Dalit events in Maharashtra and north India. Ambedkar then proceeds to offer a global analysis of demands for justice and national independence, with a particular focus on the ways in which "religious" and "social" movements have been put in opposition to the universality of "politics." On the contrary, as Ambedkar shows, these binaries elide many of the intersecting concerns of most revolutionary movements. Consequently, the status of the individual under an oppressive social or religious structure is no less "political" than that individual's claim to the right of democratic equality. Relatedly, caste—which, by justifying itself as a "religious" matter has been allowed to bypass "politics"—is, in fact, political, social, and economic. "The caste system is not merely a division of labor," writes Ambedkar. "*It is also a division of laborers.*"[77]

Section XIX of *Annihilation of Caste* returns, once more, to Manu. Ambedkar argues here that following the authority of Manu leaves no room for reason and individual thought:

> People are not wrong in observing caste. In my view, what is wrong is their religion, which has inculcated this notion of caste. If this is correct, then obviously the enemy you must grapple with is not the people who observe caste, but the *Shastras* which teach them this religion of caste. . . . Not to question the authority of the *Shastras* to permit the people to believe in their sanctity and their sanctions . . . is an incongruous way of carrying on social reform. . . . You must destroy the authority of the *Shastras* and the *Vedas*."[78]

For Ambedkar, Hinduism is a set of authorial regulations which must be totally destroyed in order to produce egalitarianism; Hinduism and egalitarianism are fundamentally incompatible. He was never unclear on this point.

The primary focus of *Annihilation of Caste* is on the idea that caste has prevented Indians from forming a "society," due to a lack of a shared consciousness.[79] Consequently, for Ambedkar, Hindu reliance on caste is anti-social in its essence. "Caste has killed public spirit," Ambedkar concludes. "Virtue has become caste-ridden, and morality has become caste-bound."[80] The last section describes the possibility for the annihilation of caste, which Ambedkar suggests is best accomplished through inter-caste marriage. Where the *Manusmriti* allows "no place for reason to play its part," caste Hindus "must give a new doctrinal basis to your religion—a basis that will be in consonance with liberty, equality, and fraternity; in short, with democracy."[81]

In Ambedkar's formulation, liberty and equality are subordinate to fraternity as the prerequisites of a proper democracy. Democracy, for Ambedkar, was more than a set of political institutions, but rather a mode of sociality and sociability. Ambedkar demanded "social democracy" throughout his career, but his most famous formulation is in *Annihilation of Caste*:

> In an ideal society there should be many interests consciously communicated and shared. There should be varied and free points of contact with other modes of association. In other words there must be social endosmosis. This is fraternity, which is only another name for democracy.[82]

We will recall this selection from our earlier analysis. In order to salvage this from interpretations overdetermined by Dewey's disciples, we may now focus on the full implications of "fraternity" in the context of caste. Ambedkar's definition of "democracy" here (and elsewhere) aligns closer to Bergson's definition in *Two Sources of Morality and Religion*: Democracy "proclaims liberty, demands equality, and reconciles these two hostile sisters by reminding them that they are sisters, by exalting above everything fraternity. . . . The essential thing is fraternity."[83] It is indeed about the vaguely republican ideal of "associated living," but it is, more radically, a claim to consanguinity.[84]

At first glimpse, we can trace Ambedkar's argument that "fraternity" asserts the fundamental sociability of humans after the annihilation of caste.[85] On additional inspection, however, "fraternity" *as* consanguinity reveals a different "madness" at the core of Manu and the caste system, which lays the seeds for its *own* annihilation.

Consanguinity was a fundamental "riddle of Hinduism" that Ambedkar would explicate in the 1950s. In Riddle 18, "Manu's madness or the Brahmanic explanation of the origin of the mixed castes," Ambedkar charts the caste system as described in the *Manusmriti*. The chart he produces reveals, indeed, a "madness" at the alleged authorization of the four-varna caste system. The chart, based on the particular combination of the person's (assumed biological) father and (known biological) mother, is comically extensive, as Ambedkar shows Manu's proliferation of mixed-caste identities. How can there be four discrete castes, Ambedkar asks, when Manu assumes everyone has already been contaminated with blood from other castes? If everyone is, by virtue of the *Manusmriti*, mixed-caste, how are we all not already linked fraternally?

Hereditariness, consanguinity, and kinship thus form the sociological-philological-biological roots of Ambedkar's *creative* critique (annihilation) of caste, which Ambedkar heralds under the seemingly French republican value of "fraternity" (though he does not, of course, misunderstand its French inheritance). Contagion, contamination, and contaminability: These are the grounds on which both sociological and philological analyses should align. In Ambedkar's critique, situated between John Dewey and William Jones, these two human sciences veer wildly away from the autonomous human subject, relinquishing its sovereign status to the much messier, porous, and fungible realm of cell biology. The mixing of blood (consanguinity), the interpenetration of cells (endosmosis), and the unknowability of hereditary belonging (fraternity) produce a much murkier, illiberal subject, whose sense of wild contagion and contaminability cannot possibly sustain the requirements of "caste."

This appears, first, as "kinship." For Ambedkar, "kinship" ends "social isolation" by forming "a physical unity." Ambedkar cites sociologist and Indologist Robertson Smith on this point, and by doing so, makes a decisive shift from "fraternity" as a social concern to "fraternity" as a biological concern:

> A kin is a group of persons whose lives were so bound up together, in what must be called a physical unity, that they could be treated as parts of one common life. The members of one kindred looked on themselves as one living whole, a single animated mass of blood, flesh and bones, of which no member could be touched without all the members suffering.[86]

Ambedkar's use of Smith's definition, which slides seamlessly between social description and biological metaphor, is particularly illustrative of Ambedkar's anti-caste critique. "Kinship" therefore becomes the combination of sociology and biology necessary to respond to Brahmanical philology.

Again, it is worth noting here that early sociology's interest in borrowing metaphors from biology is not merely an accident. Rather, it reveals how relatively unconvinced early sociology was of the autonomy or the exceptionality of the human being as a unit of study. Rather, in its moment of "hesitation," this early moment of sociology veered philosophical and biological, relinquishing even the seemingly exceptional figure of the human to the murkiness and interdependence of cell biology.[87] French criminologist and sociologist Gabriel Tarde, one of Ambedkar's key influences during his time at Columbia, proposed "contagion" as the key metaphor for social unity. For Tarde, biology and sociology were fundamentally inseparable.[88] Ambedkar's aesthetic and political critique, following this genealogy of hesitant thought, forced sociology and philology to make good on the promises of its imagined extra-liberalism egalitarianism.

Sociophilia

"That a man thinks is a biological fact what he thinks is a sociological fact," writes Ambedkar, citing psychologist Edward Thorndyke;[89] the study of which, we might add, is a philological fact. Under Ambedkar's promiscuous critique, philology, untethered from biology, becomes the grounds upon which it is possible to argue for a new sociology, retethered to biology, that renders caste unthinkable. If caste has prevented the formation of society, Ambedkar's sociology prevents the formation of caste.

By combining late nineteenth-century philology with early twentieth-century sociology, Ambedkar's critique invents a political subject on the basis of the chaos of cell biology: perpetually contagious, heterogeneous, and incapable of self-authorizing or claiming liberal sovereignty. This *sociophilic* subject would render caste unimaginable, and therefore be the basis for an endosmotic egalitarianism. Allow me to suggest, sociophilia, the love of society, as the proper name of this antiauthoritarian practice.

In *The Buddha and His Dhamma*, Ambedkar offers hints for a theory of sociophilic subjectivity, made possible by a particular scientific conjuncture:

> Nineteenth century scientists . . . conceived that the Universe was filled with indestructible atoms. Just as the nineteenth century was drawing to a close, Sir J. J. Thompson and his followers began to hammer the atoms. Surprisingly enough the atoms began to break up into fragments. These fragments came to be called electrons, all similar and charged with negative electricity. Atoms hailed by Maxwell as imperishable foundation-stones of the Universe or Reality broke down. They got broken into tiny particles, protons and electrons charged with positive and negative electricity respectively. The concept of a fixed unalterable mass abandoned Science for good. In this century the Universal belief is that matter is being annihilated at every instant. . . . Science has proved that the course of the Universe is a grouping and dissolution and regrouping.[90]

A sociophilic subject, having relinquished her sovereign ontological status to the murkiness of contagion and contamination, is perpetually dissolving and regrouping with others. In this re-imagining of a Buddhist convert, the renunciate is simultaneously more and less than an ascetic figure: She does not possess autonomy and sovereignty long enough to consider relinquishing it. In the same sense, no subject—following nineteenth-century cell biology and epidemiology—can claim to hold full authority over her "self," knowing its beginnings and its ends; in other words, no subject can claim to know its individual identification.

Even if "social isolation," in the form of the individual, provides the benefit of recognition to some in the short-term (though always at the expense of others), it is kinship that offers the *correct* "physical unity" of society. Society, rendered both literally and metaphorically biological, is the unit of political and aesthetic egalitarian critique.

We should be wary of reaching the conclusion that, through this philological-sociological-vitalist trajectory, Ambedkar attempts to universalize the *category* of "Dalit" (what Leela Gandhi briefly identifies as "*Dalit askesis*").[91] This is compelling but misses the radical antiauthoritarian claim at the core of Ambedkar's sociophilia. We should say, instead, that Ambedkar universalizes the *condition* of contamination. Recall that the Dalit body, by virtue of its alleged essential impurity, cannot be contaminated. It is the Brahmin body that is at perpetual risk of contamination from the varied impurities of its environment. The irony of caste, as Jaaware notes, is that vulnerability is the source of authority and power.[92] Instead of demanding that everyone be contaminated (a universalization of the Dalit), Ambedkar demands that everyone be contaminated and contaminatable (an egalitarianism of vulnerability).

This is not the same as demanding everyone become Brahmin, or that everyone attain the benefits that attend the Brahmin subject. The benefits of being Brahmin (of being touchable) today are undeniable and great, but we cannot predicate our utopian egalitarianism on that subject position for a few reasons. First, this political stance forgets that the Brahmin subject position is ineluctably produced by the domination of others. Second, it assumes that the Brahmin subject will always guarantee the greatest benefits (thereby ensuring that this status quo is, in fact, maintained). Finally, this requires that we assume in advance that autonomy and autochthony are utopian values. Instead, the demand here is for a society in which contaminability has rendered the Brahmin, as an autonomous subject position, fundamentally unthinkable.

By relinquishing the sovereign body to atoms that infinitely ungroup and regroup, *contaminability* becomes the foundational and irrevocable universal condition. To the extent that this is a renunciation—one must give up the autonomy of one's body—it is hardly one of loss, but one of rather infinite, multitudinous gain.[93] In Ambedkar's words:

> The first hindrance is the delusion of self.... Only when his eyes have been opened to the fact that he is but a tiny part of a measureless whole, only when he begins to realize how impermanent a thing is his temporary individuality can he even enter upon this narrow path.[94]

This is a particularly Buddhist iteration of Ambedkar's anti-caste critique, but it is not altogether different from his demand, in a more overtly secular vein, for endosmosis and fraternity. The problem of hierarchy and oppression is located in our commitment to the indivisible unit of the autonomous individual. Embracing its porousness, its fungibility, and its perpetual contagion (social and biological) allows us to loosen our grip, moving in both directions simultaneously: toward the cell, infinitely small and therefore possessing a shared contaminability; and toward the mass, infinitely large and therefore possessing a shared consciousness.

This is an illiberal political critique made possible by the aesthetic forms of European scientific crises. This is not an anti-humanist critique: Ambedkar retains a commitment to humanism, but one recreated otherwise. Let us "ungroup" our "selves" in order to be open for contamination so that, upon "regrouping," we find ourselves infinitely shared, multitudinous, tangled, and mutually constitutive. This is an impossible theory of egalitarian politics, and it is absolutely necessary to annihilate oppression. We must make it "impossible to touch a stranger," to borrow Jaaware's provocative phrase.[95] A properly contaminatable sociophilia would not prevent touching; it would prevent strangers.

Ambedkar is not alone in imagining cellular breakdown as the requirement for an emancipatory politics. Fanon, in his poetic introduction to *Black Skin, White Masks*, hints at a similar project: "How do we get out . . . ? I shall attempt a total lysis of this morbid body. I believe that the individual should tend to take on the universality inherent in the human condition."[96] Lysis is the disintegration of a cell by the rupture of its boundaries. We have tended to skip over this crucial turn in Fanon's opening provocation, even though it most closely aligns with his "concluding" demand: "I want the world to recognize, with me, the open door of every consciousness." It is therefore difficult to imagine that Fanon's final "prayer" ("O my body, make of me always a man who questions!")

is a request for a sovereign body that has the autonomy to ask questions. It is a prayer for a body that leaves the self-authorizing sovereign subject perpetually open for interrogation.[97]

Let us notice, finally, the method amenable to Fanon's last demand and prayer: "Why not the quite simple attempt to touch the other, to feel the other, to explain the other to myself?"[98] To touch and to feel, in order to be contaminatable: In direct opposition to untouchability, desiring contagion marks a sociophilic orientation to the world.

3 / M. K. Gandhi's Lost Debates

In 1943, one day before his twentieth birthday, John McAleer woke up early to write M. K. Gandhi a letter. "My own world being not so very great & yours having so thoroughly an intrinsic part in it," McAleer wrote, it was only appropriate that he begin his birthday celebrations with a letter of gratitude to his hero. McAleer, then an undergraduate at the University of North Carolina, claims to have read everything Gandhi had published and had, over the course of the previous year, fasted on Mondays to honor Gandhi's weekly vow of silence.[1]

What made McAleer—an otherwise proud Roman Catholic from Cambridge, Massachusetts—a devout Gandhian was his belief that only Gandhi had achieved a thing McAleer hoped to attain himself before his death: "congruity." McAleer saw in Gandhi a commitment to "unchanging" and "crucial fundamentals," but equally a desire to admit "that today you do not look upon everything you said a decade or two ago, in the same light, truth leading you on to truth."[2] This combination of relentless pertinacity ("consistency" and "orderliness") and perpetual self-correction ("inconsistency" and "humility") was, in McAleer's terms, the defining feature of the "congruity" that the twenty-year-old pledged to achieve in his lifetime.

McAleer's commitment to Gandhi's methods had "left [him] chagrined," as the "experiments in truth" McAleer had tried in the United States had been "completely ineffectual" and had "not borne the full fruit of effectiveness that I have so much desired of them."[3] Gandhi didn't quite make sense to the twenty-year-old, but McAleer, sadly unable to leave

Chapel Hill for Ahmedabad to help out in person, pledged "the succour of a spiritual nature" to Gandhi's anticolonial movement from abroad. Unlikely to demonstrate this to Gandhi in person, McAleer wrote, he hoped that Gandhi would be satisfied with his results when they could meet "in the next life . . . in the Elysian fields [that] await you."[4]

To my knowledge, there was no direct response from Gandhi to McAleer's letter. The undergraduate's insight in 1943, however, both participates in and bypasses a practice that has consumed the recuperation of Gandhi in academic inquiry: an anxiety that Gandhian anticolonialism could be "valuable" only insofar as it could possess the "consistency" of European political philosophy, which might make it recognizably equivalent to a proper canon of political theory or world literature. Gandhi's anticolonial career spanned at least forty years and his collected writings alone take up ninety-eight volumes. To my mind, no writing on Gandhi's thought has been as clear-sighted and concise as John McAleer's. Academics and activists, Gandhian and anti-Gandhian alike, have all tried their hand at what McAleer does in the course of a two-page note. It has taken a lot of verbiage (to which I now humbly add my own). McAleer's "congruity" identifies, with proper befuddlement, Gandhi's combination of consistent inconsistency and inconsistent consistency.[5] McAleer, although chagrined, acquiescently commits to Gandhi's "congruent" practice of not making any sense at all.

Waiting for the Mahatma

There is obvious appeal in claiming M. K. Gandhi as a political theorist equal to his European and North American contemporaries, but the task cannot be as straightforward as simply aligning him with Arendt and Adorno. Arendt was a political theorist and wrote as one; Adorno was a cultural critic and burrowed himself safely (if bitterly) within the academy. Gandhi was a politician, spiritual thinker, activist, and—quite often (knowingly or unknowingly)—an on-brand alibi for the unpleasant pragmatics of Indian state-building. Unburdened by the demands of the professional political theorist, Gandhi reveled in his ability to *not* make sense. Instead, one might locate Gandhi within the lineage he declared for himself: a proudly promiscuous assortment of late-Victorian liberalism, vitalism, and anti-modern utopianism, rather than the "sophisticated," "mature," and coherent inheritance of Kantian critique.[6]

Gandhi has been the central figure in the resuscitation of anticolonial thought as properly literary, properly political, properly ethical, or properly intellectual. This work has been outstanding. It has drawn necessary comparisons between M. K. Gandhi and nineteenth-century radical philosophers as well as interwar European pessimistic utopianists. In literary studies, it has attempted to correct what Pascale Casanova diagnoses (and occasionally herself performs) as the "hierarchies and various forms of violence" that "the world republic of letters" produces.[7] It has also allowed for a proper refutation of the allegation of aesthetic colonial belatedness by suggesting that the literary qualities of political texts reveal an aesthetic practice very much alive in the colonies and in the metropoles, concurrently. Because Gandhi has been at the center of this endeavor, he has taken on the same authorial transcendence that his moniker of "Mahatma" affords, even as scholars attempt to "secularize" him as a political theorist or literary author.[8]

Nevertheless, few thinkers openly renounced their authority and their coherence as often as Gandhi did. Fewer thinkers refused to think politics, ethics, religion, and aesthetics separately as obstinately as Gandhi did. Even fewer thinkers still *renounced their ability to renounce* their authority and coherence quite like Gandhi did. Our inattention to Gandhi's impossible demand for this doubled relinquishment has produced many outstandingly coherent, authoritative, and mature analyses of his thought.

Gandhi is not the Derrida of anticolonial theory (Derrida is the Derrida of anticolonial theory).[9] But more importantly, it seems likely that Gandhi would refuse to be even "*the* Gandhi" of anticolonial thought. In *Hind Swaraj*, the Editor warns the Reader against replicating "the tigers" of the British Raj. Lest we speculate about these "tigers," the Reader offers a short list: "Mill, Spencer, . . . and the English Parliament."[10] But more importantly for our concerns here, Gandhi's thought was messy, it was contradictory, it was impossible, it was experimental, and it requires substantially difficult analytical gymnastics (or at least a lot of caveats) to make him articulate *a* philosophy. Instead, allow me to humbly suggest that we relax and let Gandhi do what he claimed, repeatedly, to do best: fail. Gandhi failed spectacularly. We might say that Gandhi's failures, especially his failure to be consistent or to make sense, mark the "congruence" of his thought.

I suggest, then, that we begin our approach toward impossible Gandhian anticolonialism by way of his losses, failures, inconsistencies, and apologies. These are to be found most clearly in the debates Gandhi participated in—which is also to say, the debates that Gandhi lost. We will start first by examining Gandhi's three apologies for lost debates in his newspaper, *Harijan*, in the late 1930s. We will then consider two debates Gandhi held with Rabindranath Tagore and Margaret Sanger in 1934 and

1935; and one failed fast in 1933. Finally, we will return to Gandhi's most famous (but imagined) debate, *Hind Swaraj*, first published in 1909. This backwards trajectory will allow us to better approach Gandhian antiauthoritarianism across these thirty years of his career.

Giving Up Gandhi

It is true that Gandhian thought entices us to believe his aim was the uncomplicated attainment of mastery. But his writings tended to be grounded a bit more in the muck of practice and bad behavior, which was always at considerable distance to that imagined goal. What Gandhi documents, for the most part, are his repeated failures, or his courting of possible failure. More importantly, Gandhi documented his failures to articulate his own beliefs properly. In London, around his own twentieth birthday (in 1889), Gandhi clumsily began two of his fairly significant "experiments with truth": his interpretation of the *Bhagavad Gita*, and his abstinence from meat-eating.

What would become Gandhi's highly idiosyncratic explication of the *Gita* began with a chance encounter between the second-year undergraduate and two Theosophists, with whom Gandhi began reading Edwin Arnold's 1885 loose translation (from Sanskrit) of the *Gita*, *The Song Celestial*. Gandhi writes in his autobiography:

> I had read the divine poem neither in Sanskrit nor in Gujarati. I was constrained to tell them that I had not read the Gita, but that I would gladly read it with them, and that though my knowledge of Sanskrit was meagre, still I hoped to be able to understand the original.[11]

Gandhi's lectures on the *Gita*, which he delivered during the 1920s, relied almost entirely on Arnold's translation; in his *Autobiography*, Gandhi notes his failure to finish the text in Sanskrit and quotes Arnold's translations verbatim.[12] My intention here is not to chide Gandhi for relying on English sources.[13] The twenty-year-old (and the sixty-year-old) Gandhi considered himself a translator who, as Javed Majeed has shown, self-consciously trafficked in translations that were "always approximate and incomplete," thereby perpetually "revealing his ignorance" and his "ineptitude."[14]

Gandhi's interest in the *Gita* might have been the result of a chance encounter in London, but the text was an especially good choice for an aspirational incompetent translator: Nothing about the *Gita* could make sense until there was a "good translation," which Gandhi was unable to provide because he was never "able to understand the original."[15]

Later that same year, when forced to defend his vow of vegetarianism—a key tenet of self-purity in Gandhian thought—in a debate with his university roommate in London, Gandhi fails miserably. In his account:

> The friend once got disgusted with this state of things, and said . . . "You confess to having eaten and relished meat. You took it where it was absolutely unnecessary, and will not where it is quite essential. What a pity!" . . . One day the friend began to read to me Bentham's *Theory of Utility*. I was at my wits' end. The language was too difficult for me to understand. He began to expound it. I said: "Pray excuse me. These abstruse things are beyond me. I admit it is necessary to eat meat. But I cannot break my vow. I cannot argue about it. I am sure I cannot meet you in argument. But please give me up as foolish or obstinate."[16]

Ajay Skaria has argued for the importance of the "vow" in this passage, insofar as Gandhi insists on his own surrender to the power of absolute consistency.[17] I suggest we focus instead on Gandhi's final plea: "give me up as foolish." Where the vow assumes philosophical consistency, the relinquishment of "making sense" strikes me as the more radical stance, especially considering Gandhi's willingness to foreground the *inconsistency* of his vegetarianism, ventriloquized in the words of his friend.

As important as fulfilling a vow was, Gandhi acknowledged that even vows could be products of error and nonsense.[18] Gandhi reveled, moreover, in his inability to make an assured vow or a coherent argument. In an interview with *The Vegetarian* a few years after the debate, Gandhi recalled the friend's additional response:

> "Humph," said he, "childishness, rank superstition; but since, even after coming here, you are superstitious enough to believe in such nonsense, I cannot help you any more, I only wish you had not come to England."
>
> He never afterwards pressed the point seriously, except perhaps once, though ever since that he took me for little more than a fool.[19]

Immaturity, superstition, nonsense, incorrigibility, unseriousness, and foolishness: Might we identify these as the features of an impossible politics, rooted in perpetual relinquishment of mastery and its attendant values (maturity, reason, comprehensibility, seriousness)?[20]

Let us give Gandhi up as foolish: to renounce our own desire for him to "make sense," or even be an authority over something we might identify as "his own beliefs" or his interpretations. Instead, let us recuperate a Gandhi who reveled in illogic, un-mastery, and incertitude. We might therefore recover a form of Gandhian practice that resists colonialism by renouncing authority altogether, which would allow us to think Gandhian anticolonialism *as* antiauthoritarianism.

Gandhian Philology

If Gandhi admits to his Theosophist friends in London his knowledge of Sanskrit is scant, and he asks his friends to give him up as foolish, then our desire to take Gandhi and Gandhian mastery seriously stands at odds with his own philosophical demands. We might, instead, account for Gandhian antiauthoritarianism by refiguring the ground of Gandhian philology. Playfully indebted to Sanskrit, Gujarati, and English—and by no means masterfully so—Gandhi's vocabulary offers an impossible terminology for an impossible politics.

To rehearse, crudely, the most "congruent" of Gandhi's life-long arguments: In order to achieve "proper" independence from British rule, Indians should commit themselves to ethical and political self-cultivation rooted in non-violent resistance to colonial power. This self-cultivation, achieved on a large scale, would result in a radically different form of community than that of the European nation-state. Whereas violent resistance replicates the exact forms of dominance present in imperial rule, non-violent resistance reveals the inherent violence and hierarchy of the colonial project. Non-violence, concerned less with peace *per se* and more about the disavowal of violence, is a practice of risking death. In risking death, the non-violent activist makes herself radically open to the other, and therefore offers a model of ethical and political egalitarianism. Gandhi revisited these projects, in various spiritual, ethical, and political iterations, across a long public career. They appear, most notably, in *Hind Swaraj* (1909), *Satyagraha in South Africa* (1928), *An Autobiography* (1929), and lectures on the *Bhagavad Gita* (edited by Mahadev Desai as *The Gita According to Gandhi*, 1946).

Gandhian anticolonialism has its own vocabulary. *Satyagraha*, articulated by way of neologisms in Sanskrit (left "untranslated" in Gujarati and English), proceeds by way of a focus on *ahimsa*.[21] *Ahimsa* means "non-violence," but with an etymological emphasis on the prefix "non" (*a*); Gandhi's writings make it clear that, properly conceived as *ahimsa*, non-violence always retains its proximity to violence (*himsa*) rather than to peace (*shanti*). In other words, the practice of passivism or nonviolence was the renunciation of violence, not the assertion of peace. *Swaraj* literally means "self-rule," though on second glance, questions begin to proliferate: Who is this "self" (*swa*) that is yet to exist, and what is the "rule" (*raj*) that she is expected to enact or embody by way of renunciation? Gandhi translates *satyagraha* as "soul-force" or "passive resistance," though *satya* is "truth" and *graha* generally indicates overwhelming power, seizure, or total possession. Gandhi's curious slippage from "truth" to "soul" in his translations of the term provokes an ontological question, which is rendered in starker terms in *satyagrahi*, a person who attempts to cultivate (though likely fails to achieve) *satyagraha*.[22]

Satyagraha is achieved through its opposite, *aparigraha*, total renunciation (literally, non-possession); and it is "suffused with nothing."[23] Iterations of this practice are perpetually failed "experiments" (*duragraha*, seizure by falsehood): with truth, with self, with violence, and with obligations (or duties) toward others. These duties and obligations to others are most forcefully achieved by simultaneous surrender and restraint (*brahmacharya*). *Aparigraha* is, therefore, the total seizure of one's soul (*satya*).[24] It is for this reason that one practices *ahimsa* by embracing *himsa*; one achieves self-rule (*swaraj*) by relinquishing sovereignty (*swa-raj*); one restrains himself (*brahmacharya*) by losing control (*abrahmacharya*). Furthermore, the aspiring *satyagrahi* moves toward *satyagraha* by not simply abandoning (*tyaga*) the alleged benefits of *swaraj*, but by renouncing *swaraj* altogether (*samnyasa*). In other words, in order to achieve mastery over the self, one has to abandon both mastery and self.[25]

It seems, at first glance, that self-cultivation, self-mastery, and purity stand at the center of the Gandhian anticolonial project: the *satyagrahi*, as he writes in his *Autobiography*, attempts to "reduce [himself] to zero" in a process of "self-purification."[26] This process is not non-violent (especially toward one's own self), though its goal is *ahimsa*.[27]

Scholars eager to dismiss Gandhi align his desire for purity and mastery with fascism, Brahmanical Hinduism, and teleological thought. There are, of course, an equal number of cherry-picked quotations to support these claims as there are to refute them. Recent scholars, in various ways, have argued that Gandhian philosophy theorizes "mastery," "faith," "knowability," and "truth" in terms of purity, authenticity, sovereignty, and subjugation of others, but none of Gandhi's writings straightforwardly support these claims.[28] To be clear, Gandhi *was* a notably bad thinker on gender and caste due to his inability to theorize from a place of lived subordination (and, moreover, his inability to recognize the actual policy implications of his philosophical experiments). Gandhian resistance is the assertion of mastery *renounced* rather than authority sought.

Moreover, Gandhi's writings attest to his radical antiauthoritarianism, whereby mastery, knowability, and liberal selfhood, as the promises of modernity, are rendered unachievable (for we cannot know what achievement is) and undesirable (for we have relinquished the assurance of desire). Ajay Skaria provocatively identifies this as an "equality of deference."[29] If we trace the impossible and infinite deference in Gandhi's public career, we find ourselves propelled toward a project of radical obligationary (as distinct from, though not entirely opposed to, obligatory) egalitarianism. Obligationary egalitarianism is a politics of perpetually unfulfilled duties to others, circumscribed both by the insufficient finitude of the self and the infinite self-surrender of that limited self for others.[30] Such politics relies on many paradoxes: one must be a warrior in order to attain non-violence; one must abandon oneself in order to refuse abandoning others; one must relinquish oneself in order to grip oneself; one must relinquish truth to maintain obedience to "that still small voice"; and so on.

Gandhian philology perpetually guarantees its own impossibility: In order to fully achieve self-mastery (*swaraj*) one has to renounce herself (*aparigraha*) in order to be seized or possessed by truth (*satyagraha*). Waiting unknowingly to be possessed by truth that one cannot know is hardly the work of an authority or a master—indeed, it renounces even the possibility of a knowing, liberal subject (*swa*) completely. Faisal Devji's provocative claim that Gandhi was an "impossible Indian" is therefore particularly apt in three senses: Gandhi was impossible to deal with (a belief all of his opponents shared); Gandhi created for himself a project both necessary and impossible; and he demanded an impossible Indian as a necessary prerequisite for Indian self-rule. Gandhian philology is a literary project rooted in impossible translations from an impossible Sanskrit, impossible neologisms, and impossible reading.

Three Apologies

The winter of 1938–39 was a bad season for Gandhi: A fast in protest of failed negotiations around political reform in Rajkot had gone awry and a letter written to German Jews had received major backlash. Gandhi defended himself for a few issues of *Harijan*, his newspaper at the time. But starting in the May 1939 issue, his tone changed drastically. Regarding the misguided fast:

> I recognize my error. At the end of my fast, I had permitted myself to say that it had succeeded as no previous fast had done. I now see that it was tainted with Himsa [violence]. . . . This was not the way of Ahimsa [non-violence] or conversion. It was the way of Himsa or coercion. . . . I owe an apology to the Viceroy . . . I apologise to the

Chief Justice.... Above all, I apologise to the Thakore Saheb and Durbar Shri Virawala.... I must also own that, in common with my co-workers, I have harboured evil thoughts about him.... Suffice it to say that the way of Ahimsa was not and has not yet been applied to him.[31]

Regarding his essay, "The Jews" (and later, "The Jewish Question"), where he had argued that Jews fleeing Nazi Germany should instead practice non-violent resistance by remaining in the country:

In the face of foregoing weighty contradictions now enforced by the Editor of the *Jewish Tribune* and of the fact that I cannot lay my hands on anything on the strength of which I made the challenged observation, I must withdraw it without any reservation. I only hope that my observation has not harmed any single Jew.[32]

And finally, in September 1939, a summation:

My non-violence is made of stern stuff. It is firmer than the firmest metal known to the scientists. Yet, alas, I am painfully conscious of the fact that it has still not attained its native firmness. If it had, God would have shown me the way to deal with many local cases of violence that I helplessly witness daily.... And even at the risk of being misunderstood, I must act in obedience to the *still small voice*.[33]

These apologies are noteworthy not simply because Gandhi was perpetually reluctant to apologize for his actions on the basis that they were nevertheless rooted in *satyagraha* or *ahimsa*. Tagore, writing to Gandhi in 1934, praised his consistency while politely chastising Gandhi's obstinacy. Gandhi replied—and would consistently reply—by insisting on his perpetual *inconsistency*, repeatedly claiming that "as the great sage Emerson once said, 'consistency is the hobgoblin of small minds.'" Skaria has written that Gandhi had faith in "pure means" rather than "ends," which is how Gandhi easily justified his failures and contradictions. But the 1939 apologies are noteworthy because Gandhi admits the *fallibility* of the "pure means" of *satyagraha* itself: even in the moment of feeling seized by truth or God the *satyagrahi* could err; a *satyagrahi* could be possessed by a truth that might turn out to be wrong.

It would be easy to claim that this marks another way by which Gandhi attempted renunciation, and to claim that apologies and pleas to be "given up as foolish" are mere iterations of ascetic practice: the striving for complete relinquishment to the point of losing a debate about one's own ascetic practice. This would mean that Gandhian renunciation, in the form of loss or assertions of one's own illogic, circumscribes a set of enacted failures to stunt an otherwise teleological progression toward attainable *satyagraha*. This claim is compelling because it neatly and cleanly justifies Gandhi's mistakes, but this conclusion would be an apologia, not an apology. Gandhi was so adept at the former that we have tended to overlook the latter, and (to my mind) much more interesting, formulation. When Gandhi admits that he has *stumbled* on his way toward *satyagraha*, he nevertheless retains the authoritative claim that he knows the general contours of the "truth" that will eventually "seize" him. But when Gandhi admits that he doesn't even know where he is going, a more provocative claim emerges.

Allow me to describe two trajectories for this more radical claim, marked by the doubled meaning of *satyagraha* and Gandhi's citations. Gandhi relies on a produced slippage between "the truth" and "the self" in his formulation of *satyagraha*. First, the moments when Gandhi apologizes are moments where he confesses the more radical possibility of having been seized by the false truth in the first place, with little to no clue where the "correct" truth might be. We can find the articulation of this *aparigraha* in his September 1939 apology: "And even at the risk of being misunderstood, I must act in obedience to the *still small voice*."[34] Waiting blindly for a truth to arrive—and, additionally, being unsure of whether that truth is correct—is hardly a practice of mastery. This is to take more seriously the claim that Gandhi's *Autobiography* is an account of his *experiments* with (that is, *attempts* at) truth (*satyana prayogo*): an unsure stumbling toward *satya* ("truth"), which has yet to be known, or may never be known, or may be known falsely.

Second, the moments when Gandhi begs forgiveness or asks to be "given up as foolish" are moments when he abandons his *satya*, his "truth" *and* his "self." These are moments of *doubled* renunciation: Gandhi renunciates his own ability to renunciate, and therefore asks others to do it for him. Phrases like "please give me up as foolish," "allow me to lose this debate," and "allow me to be wrong" put Gandhi's self (*satya*) in the grip (*graha*) of others. Gandhi locates a position in which he asks the other to relinquish, on his behalf, himself. Put differently, this might look something like "please reduce me to zero": a claim that begs the other to renunciate the renunciant. In this process of renunciation, the other, too, is a renunciant. Losing the ability to lose yourself so that another person might lose you is a precarious and unsustainable politics of radical egalitarianism. To place this in the frame of Skaria's compelling equation, "surrender without subordination": This is an act of surrender because it gives up one's self; it is not an act of subordination because it demands, nevertheless, the production of two equal renunciants.

Mahadev Desai, Gandhi's editor, assistant, translator, and publicist, wrote an editorial in *Harijan* in 1940 defending Gandhi's apologies.[35] Repeating the line from Emerson, Desai theorized how "consistency might be inconsistency"—and therefore the perpetual misjudgment without apology—but that "inconsistency might reveal consistency," that is, that the celebration of apologies and misguided fasts, or the celebration of being seized by the wrong truth, might be the basis for a more radical approach towards *satyagraha*—a reduction of one's self to something that looks more like zero, nothing, or someone fumbling in the dark.

In the apologetic September 1939 issue of *Harijan*, Gandhi claims that, although it is a "crude" articulation of his beliefs, he would not change a word of *Hind Swaraj* upon its republication, and after thirty years of reflection.[36] On one hand, Gandhi admits his *satyagraha* has been, and could be again, essentially wrong (*duragraha*). On the other hand, Gandhi argues that his political philosophy is essentially correct, such that a single word needn't be changed. What do we make of these seemingly contradictory stances in the same September 1939 issue? Let us approach these claims by letting Gandhi fail spectacularly, tracing his failures backward from 1939 to 1909.

Two Lost Debates

A few years earlier, Gandhi participated in two bizarre debates: one with American reproductive rights activist Margaret Sanger about birth control in India in 1935; one with Rabindranath Tagore about the cause of earthquakes, in 1934. In advance, allow me to briefly give you Gandhi's *opening* gambit, which roughly proceeds as follows: What you say is correct and important. Others more knowledgeable than I have agreed with you. But I cannot agree with you. Please allow me to be wrong. Please allow me to lose this debate.

In late 1935, Margaret Sanger arrived in Bombay to tour India under the auspices of the All-India Women's Congress.[37] At their meeting in 1934, the All-India Women's Congress had passed a resolution in favor of birth control; Sanger was understandably thrilled to participate. She planned to meet with Gandhi in hopes that he would, like many of his colleagues (including Rabindranath Tagore), endorse women's use of contraceptives in India. She was sorely disappointed. When the two met, on December 3 and 4, Gandhi announced that he did not support the use of women's contraception, and, more devastatingly, its use was antithetical to the mission of the *satyagrahi*. For Sanger, sex was the manifestation of both love and lust (and was to be judged on the basis of quality); for Gandhi, lust was "animal passion" while love was self-regulating (and was to be judged on the basis of its intended result). Gandhi and Sanger carried on this debate for two days. Mahadev Desai and Sanger's assistant, Anna Jane Phillips, recorded the debate for publication in Gandhi's *Harijan* and the New York–based journal *The Illustrated Weekly of Asia*. The debate was so unflattering to both figures that it went largely unpublished.[38]

Here is Margaret Sanger's account:

> Mr. M. K. GANDHI says he knows women!
> When I talked with him at Wardha a few days after my arrival in India he said, "I have known tens of thousands of women in India. I know their experiences and their aspirations. I have discussed it (family relationships) with some of my educated sisters but I have questioned their authority to speak on behalf of their unsophisticated sisters because they have never mixed with them. The educated ones have never felt one with them. They have regarded me as half a woman because I have completely identified myself with them. . . . I feel I speak with some confidence because I have worked with and talked with and studied many women."
> This is an amazing boast to come from any man to claim that he knows women![39]

This quote from Gandhi appears verbatim in Desai's unpublished transcript of the meeting. It is a baffling argument at first glance, but even on its own it is not entirely out of line as a particularly Gandhian formulation. If we set aside its curious politics, however, it is hardly "an amazing boast," though it might certainly be a preposterous claim. The "some confidence" that Gandhi purports to possess is that of having dispossessed authority (which his "educated sisters" claim to possess). Authority is knowledge that is grasped from without (and above), whereas Gandhi has knowledge acquired by way of egalitarian "mixing." Because Gandhi has "completely identified" with "tens of thousands of women" who regard him as "half a woman," his claim is not so straightforwardly boastful as Sanger reports.

But Sanger's selection does a disservice to Gandhi's larger argument—though it is no less frustrating—from which this excerpt is a very small selection. Gandhi's heavily edited version, in *Harijan*, might therefore give us better insight into his argument. Here is the beginning of Gandhi's and Desai's rendition:

> Gandhiji poured his whole being into his conversation. He revealed himself inside out, giving Mrs. Sanger an intimate glimpse of his own private life. He also declared to her his own limitations, especially the stupendous limitation of his own philosophy of life—a philosophy that seeks self-realization through self-control, and said that from him there could be one solution and one alone:
> "I could not recommend the remedy of birth-control to a woman who wanted my approval. I should simply say to her: My remedy is of no use to you. You must go to others for advice."[40]

Gandhi's selection is even smaller than Sanger's—it is, in fact, an extremely condensed version of the transcript that Sanger and Desai agreed on—but it reveals more about Gandhi's debate style. Gandhi's line here is the composite of about three different responses to Sanger's plea for him to support birth control, all of which are from the final section of the two-day conversation. Gandhi does not hide his stance on birth control. But that is not his focus, although it would, at first glance, appear to be the primary concern of the article. The most significant aspect of the debate, in Gandhi's iteration, is that he was completely unqualified to address the issue in the first place. Gandhi, having given "his whole being," declares "his own limitations," and suggests that women "go to others for advice." This is hardly a "boast."

Gandhi not only finds himself ill-equipped to debate birth control. He asserts, in the first instance, "the stupendous limitation of his own philosophy of life": *satyagraha* and *brahmacharya*. In other words, Gandhi admits that his near sole ethical/political practice is grossly inadequate and insufficient. The practice of "self-control" has actively prevented Gandhi from being seized by the truth. This is a particularly messy formulation, worth elaboration: In order to be seized by a truth, you must attempt a lifelong practice of ensuring you will be ill-equipped to possess the truth that will also be your selfhood. Being seized by the truth, which you cannot know, is only possible (if even remotely so) if you attempt to renounce a self that you cannot possess. *Satyagraha* demands that you ask to be given up as foolish.

Gandhi's *Harijan* re-telling, though heavily edited, is closer to the chronology of the agreed upon transcript, which opens with Gandhi's unsettling response to Sanger's appeal for support:

> I suppose you know that all my life I have been dinning into the ears of women the fact that they are their own mistresses, not only in this but in all matters. I began my work with my own wife. While I have abused my wife in many respects, I have tried to be her teacher also.

> ... The animal passion in me was too strong and I could not become the ideal teacher. . . .[41]

Gandhi's opening response is horrifying: He admits to what would rightly be called rape before taking a vow of sexual abstinence (*brahmacharya*) in 1906.[42] Neither Sanger nor Gandhi address this directly, at least in the transcripts. For Sanger (though her views were surely more pointed than the ones she put into print), Gandhi's opening admission is proof for her argument that heterosexual marriage is a combination of "sex-lust" and "love-lust," thereby demonstrating the need for birth control.

For Gandhi, who published extended descriptions of his "brutality" in his *Harijan* account, this admission was proof of his "limitations," thereby demonstrating his inadequacy and inexpertise. It is a doubled admission of insufficiency: His life philosophy of "self-control" is inadequate for authority, and, furthermore, Gandhi is unable to adhere to his own life philosophy. The extreme brutality of the example Gandhi chooses to prove his "non-self-control" (*abrahmacharya*) is necessary to relinquish any possibility of eventual authority.

He reiterates this at the conclusion of his response, deferring to others' expertise and his inability to make sense:[43]

> I have been reading about this cause which you advocate so eloquently. I know some of the great people in the world agree with you. In India I would mention only two great representative names, Tagore and Mrs. Naidu. . . . Then too I gave long hours to Mrs. How-Martyn. She did not convince me but she prepared me for you. She said, "Ah, you are not convinced, but wait until Mrs. Sanger talks to you."[44]

In other words: "experts in the world agree with you; I am not one"; please let me lose this debate.

If she began by missing Gandhi's inexpert style, Sanger might have fully understood it by the end of her published account:

> I said to him, "But Mr. Gandhi, there are thousands, millions, who regard your word as that of a saint. How can you ask them who are not so strong nor wise as you, to follow such advice when you yourself acknowledge that it has taken you years to overcome and control the force that nature implanted in your being?"
> Mr. Gandhi merely smiled.

In the transcript, this interaction occurs halfway through the conversation as "G.—(Just smiled.)" But Sanger's description is far more accurate:

Gandhi "merely" answers with silence. Gandhi's mere-ness is an (infuriating) antiauthoritarian refusal to acknowledge one's own antiauthoritarianism. Gandhi relinquishes his ability to respond, and by doing so, demands that Sanger relinquish him.

In January 1934, a devastating earthquake occurred in Bihar, along the Bihar-Nepal border. Accounts estimated that up to 25,000 people died.[45] Gandhi, on a speaking tour across south India, announced that the earthquake was "a divine chastisement sent by God for our sins":

> For me there is a vital connection between the Bihar calamity and the untouchability campaign. The Bihar calamity is a sudden and accidental reminder of what we are and what God is; but untouchability is a calamity handed down to us from century to century. It is a curse brought upon ourselves by our own neglect of a portion of Hindu humanity. Whilst this calamity in Bihar damages the body, the calamity brought about by untouchability corrodes the very soul.[46]

Gandhi admits that this position might be naïve or overly superstitious, but cannot believe otherwise. In essays published in *The Hindu*, Gandhi acknowledges that "geologists and such other scientists will undoubtedly give us physical and material causes of such calamities," but that he wants his readers "to be 'superstitious' enough with me to believe that the earthquake is a divine chastisement for the great sin we have committed and are still committing against those whom we describe as untouchables."[47]

"Be superstitious enough with me": Let us give each other up as foolish. It is a renunciatory call for collective renunciation, and an obligatory egalitarian request, bolstered in the first instance by already having given oneself up for giving up. When asked why God delivered this message in the form of an earthquake and in the location of Bihar, Gandhi replied that he could not know, but that "guessing" must be the insufficient and necessary task of man.[48]

For Rabindranath Tagore, Gandhi's lifelong friend *and* often fervent adversary, this was beyond the pale. Gandhi invited Tagore to respond publicly in *Harijan*, which Tagore accepted. Although he agreed that untouchability needed to be addressed (but as a social/political issue, not a moral issue), Tagore lamented Gandhi's appeal to superstition to dismiss his critics. On February 16, Gandhi replied to Tagore:

> I admit my utter ignorance of the working of the laws of Nature. . . . I cannot help believing in God though I am unable to prove His existence to the sceptics. . . . Such a belief would be a degrading

superstition, if out of the depth of my ignorance I used it for castigating my opponents.⁴⁹

In February, Gandhi had begun to distance himself from his initial appeal to superstition (replacing it with "belief" and "faith"); by March, Gandhi had abandoned this approach entirely. Instead, Gandhi described the earthquake as a reminder that "we ought to be more humble, as death is inevitable," and that catastrophes reveal the fundamental equality of all humans.⁵⁰ We might identify Gandhi's rhetorical shift (from esoterically superstitious to acceptably platitudinous) as a nimble response to his critics, but this does not account for the specificity of Gandhi's moves (nor, for that matter, his recalcitrance to critics).⁵¹

Instead, we might track a move from invitation to plea, each of which raises the stakes of Gandhi's egalitarian relinquishment. "Be 'superstitious' enough with me" is a playful invitation to stop making sense, and therefore to consort in collective unknowing. "I admit my utter ignorance" is a demand to be given up as foolish, and therefore to participate in a renunciative equality. "Death is inevitable" is the urgent articulation of our shared condition, which should therefore humble us in preparation for unknowable community. In the face of inevitable death, we might finally relinquish ourselves to the egalitarianism of unknowability, unpredictability, and human insignificance.

A number of scholars have written about this debate, often to foreground Gandhi's irrationality and anti-modernism against Tagore's rational and scientific orientation. Sugata Bose offers an uninspired but representative conclusion: "Tagore was right, Gandhi was wrong."⁵² But what would it mean to claim that Gandhi *preferred* to be wrong, that he preferred to lose debates rather than win them?⁵³

One Fast

Dalit activist B. R. Ambedkar famously proposed that Gandhi's faith in his politico-spiritual methods had been irrevocably shaken by the specter of the 1932 Poona Pact, where Gandhi's fast had forced the Dalit leader into a compromise on untouchable rights that has had long-lasting effects in India.⁵⁴ D. R. Nagaraj has argued that debates they held about caste throughout the 1930s changed both men.⁵⁵

At the Third Roundtable Conference, in September 1932, British Prime Minister Ramsay McDonald granted separate electorates to religious minorities (including Muslims, Sikhs, Buddhists) and the "Depressed

Classes" (more or less, "Untouchables," represented at the Conference by Ambedkar). Gandhi opposed the resolution to grant Untouchables a separate electorate, and undertook a fast unto death on September 20. On September 25, facing the likelihood of Gandhi's death and its potential consequences, Ambedkar signed the Poona Pact, thereby giving up separate electorates for Untouchables. Gandhi ended his fast the next day. Gandhi took another one-day fast in December 1932, a twenty-one-day fast in May 1933, and a seven-day fast in August 1933, all against untouchability.

The reasons, implications, and consequences of these fasts are beyond the scope of this chapter.[56] Although he would continue to defend his actions, Gandhi wrote also of having been troubled by his own intentions. The May 1933 fast was intended, to some degree, to atone for the September 1932 fast (the two fasts are often, understandably, conflated). The September fast had a political goal (the alteration of a legal document); the May fast had a personal goal: the eradication of caste and untouchability from himself and his Hinduism. Or, to put it in Gandhi's words (with Skaria's help), the September fast was conditional because it was based on demands made externally. The May fast was "unconditional" because it intended to rid the world of untouchability, without the expectation that untouchability would be gotten rid of.[57]

Gandhi was to end his fast in May 1933 by eating an orange, given to him by a Dalit boy (a "Harijan boy" in Mahadev Desai's accounts). Gandhi, in order to demonstrate his commitment to Untouchables, had promised the Dalit boy financial support for education in exchange for his participation in the dramatic closing *mise-en-scène*. Famously, the Dalit boy did not show up. Mahadev Desai tracked him down and demanded his reasons; the boy first lied about having to go to work, and then later admitted that he felt too humbled to interact with Gandhi and that he feared envious retribution from his community (this is also why the Dalit boy never gave his name). A white British woman, Lady Thackersey, provided the orange instead.

The story, which Desai recounted in *Harijan* between June and July 1933, is one of fully acknowledged embarrassment and disaster. We might rightly conclude that the Dalit boy's response (even though his voice is absent in Desai's narration) illustrates the severe limitations of Gandhianism; namely, that it is available only to those with oranges enough to relinquish: upper-caste men and white women.[58] But Desai seems unable to see this critique, and brilliantly narrates instead a different failure of Gandhian thought. This failure, which actually stands at the center of Gandhian obligationary egalitarianism, is the belief that obligations can be made or fulfilled in advance of the egalitarianism which those obligations would ensure. Let us untangle this Gandhian knot in the context of the 1933 failed fast (and in advance of the 1939 failed fast).

First, Gandhi offers an obligation: specifically, that he *will not die* so that he can financially support the Dalit teenager's education. This obligation is sustained by another, equal, obligation: that the Dalit boy bring him an orange at noon on May 29. It is an "unconditional" obligation because, theoretically, Gandhi's life depends on the Dalit boy's orange. In Gandhi's words: "I assure you, I am not going to die. . . . [Because] on the noon of Monday 29th of May you come with an orange and I shall break my fast. . . ."[59] The order of mutual obligations (which would be infinite, presumably) is thus: 1) Gandhi will live; 2) the boy will bring an orange; 3) Gandhi will provide financial assistance; 4) the boy will be obligated, presumably, to go to school; and so on.

Second, mutual obligation between Gandhi and the Dalit boy produces an egalitarian relationship between the two. But herein lies the impossibility of this project: The Dalit boy cannot enter this obligatory relationship voluntarily. It is Gandhi who sets the conditions for this relationship, which can therefore not be egalitarian. Gandhian obligation requires the egalitarianism that it purports to create. Gandhi was not unaware of caste hierarchy and would have held no delusions that this obligatory relationship was forged under egalitarian conditions.

It is true that, as Nagaraj writes, "The Harjian boy who took a decision not to keep the appointment with Gandhiji was reborn as a Dalit youth."[60] But it is equally true that, by not showing up, he gave Gandhi up for foolish—even, perhaps, for dead. Without Lady Thackersey's assistance, Gandhi would have relinquished his ability to relinquish himself, thereby relinquishing his life. For Desai, that the teenager does not show is not proof of Untouchable unreliability;[61] rather, "it is we who are responsible for fostering this feeling of undue self-abasement."[62] In other words, Gandhi had failed to fulfill an even earlier obligation: the obligation to create the conditions for which others could be obliged.

The May 1933 fast was as much a spectacle as the September 1932 fast, but Ambedkar refused to recognize Gandhi's stance (he perpetually did, either strategically or tragically). Even if he ostensibly "won" the September fast and "lost" the May fast (and "lost" the 1939 Rajkot fast), to crudely summarize the events, these fasts marked Gandhi's desire to be "given up as foolish" in two senses: to "be given up" for death and to "be given up" for misrecognizing his alleged political allegiances.

Some Authorities

Let's return to the curious juxtaposition of Gandhi's two claims in the September 1939 issue of *Harijan*: on page 1, an apology for his misguided views; and on page 3, his more famous claim that he wouldn't change a word of *Hind Swaraj* upon its re-publication. Upon his suggestion, let us move to the allegedly unalterable text of 1909.

The story is fairly well-known: Aboard the *SS Kildonan Castle*, traveling between London and Cape Town in November 1909, Gandhi furiously wrote a dialogue on Indian self-rule entitled *Hind Swaraj*. It was first published in Gujarati in two installments in Gandhi's own South Africa–based *Indian Opinion*. It was banned by the British; Gandhi translated it into English in 1910.

Hind Swaraj is considered Gandhi's most authoritative text, and the central text in a corpus that draws together political theory with ethical experimentation, "continental" philosophy with Hindu textual practices, and philosophy with projects of ascetic self-cultivation. Antoinette Burton and Isabel Hofmeyr have rightly anointed it one of the "ten books that shaped the British Empire."[63]

Over the course of twenty short chapters, an Editor and a Reader debate the merits of Indian self-rule, which cannot be reducible to Indian political independence. Rather, over the course of the dialogue, the Editor carefully explains the necessary elements of a proper *Swaraj*: first, the development of a uniquely Indian version of government instead of replicating the British Raj; second, an Indian independence acquired only through passive resistance; third, a passive resistance acquired only through national self-reliance (*swadeshi*); fourth, a total and complete rejection of Western Civilization. The Reader questions each of the arguments in turn, and the Editor patiently replies. Consequently, it makes sense to assume that the "Editor" is Gandhi and the "Reader" is someone keen for Indian independence but in favor of a more expedient approach.

Gandhi proposed a series of reading and circulation strategies for his periodical, *Indian Opinion*, that reached from Durban to the world in ever-expanding concentric circles. "Slow reading" names, for Hofmeyr, the practice by which Gandhi reimagined the imagined community rooted both in the homogeneous experience of print-culture time but also in practices of memorization, recitation, orality, and collage that the *Indian Opinion* demanded. This produced an alternatively imagined community in its very condition of being time out of joint.

Reading (especially inexpert and non-literate reading) is a fundamental practice of Gandhi's anticolonialism. Gandhi theorized the social act of reading as crucial for the formation of an anticolonial subject, as well as the foundation for an anticolonial imagined community that stretched, even if asynchronistic, across the Indian Ocean. Unlike the western nation, Gandhi's imagined nation-to-come need not share a time, but merely a social act—and moreover one that leaves, at best, a minimal trace. Reading is non-productive and non-sovereign in this sense, and readers remain perpetually unknown to the historical record. Is the social act of reading the very method by which Gandhi urged his sympathizers to "reduce themselves to zero?"

Anthony Parel has written extensively about Gandhi's political vision for *Hind Swaraj*, the historical context of its emergence, and the concerns to which it seeks to respond. *Hind Swaraj* was shaped by Gandhi's encounter with Indian nationalists during his time in London. In this sense, it is easy to imagine (as is often the case) that the "Editor" is Gandhi and the "Reader" is likely an expatriate anticolonial revolutionary. Parel has expanded the role of "Reader" to include "the Extremists and Moderates of the Indian National Congress, the Indian nation, and 'the English.'"[64]

Similarly, Isabel Hofmeyr argues that it is difficult to imagine the Reader as a revolutionary figure, who would have not likely had the patience to interrogate the Editor in so patient a tone. In place of this "revolutionary," Hofmeyr argues that the Reader is the very model of the *satyagrahi* envisioned by Gandhi's Editor (and, by extension, Gandhi himself). What Hofmeyr calls "the Gandhian theory of reading" is a practice of self-rule and regulation, much like the practices Gandhi himself cultivated in South Africa while he was writing *Indian Opinion* from Durban. Because readers had to be self-ruling, Hofmeyr argues, Gandhi's instructions in *Indian Opinion* were strict and extensive: They involved not only reading, but also translating, reciting, cutting and pasting, and illicit circulation across Gujarati trading networks. In short, *Hind Swaraj* and *Indian Opinion*, when read together, reveal Gandhi's belief that reading and anticolonial practice were one and the same. The reader was the *satyagrahi*.

The debate of *Hind Swaraj* ends with the Editor's pragmatic four-item manifesto for true self-rule, ostensibly ending the conversation and the book. The Reader admits defeat. The Editor, having successfully won the debate by logical, patient, and generous argumentation appears to have the final word.

But in the English version there is a curious appendix, which Gandhi, in the introduction, has asked his audience to consult. The appendix is entitled, simply but provocatively, "Some Authorities." Under this title, Gandhi provides a brief list of some authorities—crucially, authorities who are not him:

The Kingdom of God Is within You—Tolstoy
What Is Art—Tolstoy
The Slavery of Our Times—Tolstoy
The First Step—Tolstoy
How Shall We Escape?—Tolstoy
Letter to a Hindoo—Tolstoy
The White Slaves of England—Sherard
Civilization, Its Cause and Cure—Carpenter
The Fallacy of Speed—Taylor
A New Crusade—Blount
On the Duty of Civil Disobedience—Thoreau
Life without Principle—Thoreau
Unto This Last—Ruskin
A Joy for Ever—Ruskin
Duties of Man—Mazzini
Defence and Death of Socrates—From Plato
Paradoxes of Civilization—Max Nordau
Poverty and Un-British Rule in India—Naoroji
Economic History of India—Dutt
Village Communities—Maine

The authors here could easily provide us with the general contours of Gandhi's philosophical lineage. Tolstoy's Russian mysticism and politics, Ruskin's aestheticism, Taylor's anti-technological modernism, Thoreau's transcendentalist anarchism, Carpenter's queer antimodernism, Mazzini's proto-fascism, and Dutt's Marxist analysis of British imperialism are all visible in *Hind Swaraj* in various forms. Leela Gandhi and Anthony Parel have traced some of these lineages, most notably through Carpenter and Thoreau. Other scholars have examined Gandhi's relationship with Tolstoy, and Shruti Kapila has traced "soul force"—*satyagraha*—from Herbert Spencer and Giuseppe Mazzini. Vinay Lal has illuminated the North American–South Asian–North American trajectory of transcendentalism and passive resistance from Thoreau to Gandhi to Martin Luther King Jr.[65]

Instead of tracing intellectual influence, we might argue that the textual foregrounding of one's own reading is a renunciation: It is an admission of not knowing, failing to know, and being unsure of, *satya*, the "truth" and the "self." In this context, Gandhi's reading list of "some authorities" gestures to a politics of non-authority, a project of reading as a political practice. By framing the question this way, we set aside the historical, empirical questions concerned with showing what Gandhi actually read or didn't read, which is a question fundamentally concerned with Gandhi's mastery. We also set aside the question of what practices Gandhi articulated as properly "theoretical," which accidentally reinforces his position as an expert of an anticolonial theoretical canon.

Instead, I suggest we endeavor to ask a slightly different question: What do the aesthetics of Gandhi's work implicitly demonstrate about Gandhi's antiauthoritarianism? This line of inquiry gets us closer to the anticolonial aesthetics of a postcolonial egalitarianism whereby anticolonial aesthetics are a textual practice rather than an explicit "theory." Viewed in this light, Gandhi's "Some Authorities" is much more revealing and interesting.

"Some Authorities" marks then, first and foremost, Gandhi's disavowal of his own authority in favor of "some" others'. The title of the appendix alone relocates the authority of *Hind Swaraj* somewhere else, and thus makes Gandhi the benefactor of others' ethical and political expertise. This makes more sense of the otherwise arbitrary list of twenty texts, which we shouldn't take as representative of the wide range of thinkers Gandhi drew on, even as early as 1909.[66]

One reason why Gandhi's list of "some authorities" is only twenty entries long is precisely that it is not exhaustive. The "some" of the title marks the partialness and incompleteness of Gandhi's bibliography. This is not to claim that Gandhi is withholding the full range of sources he drew on to write *Hind Swaraj*, but rather to demonstrate Gandhi's own rejection of a scholarly teleology. In other words, "Some Authorities" rejects not only the assertion of mastery and expertise in the present, but also any teleological realization of mastery at all: The list of "some authorities" will be *perpetually* incomplete. Instead, a properly Gandhian anticolonial practice revels in the endless deferral to an infinite number of others possessing authority, to others being correct. The proper genres for this, as we have been discussing, are the apology and the admission of defeat. One retains the muddy ontology of the in-expert and therefore participates in the quieter practice of criticism and readerly incertitude.[67] It is in this sense that Skaria has argued for "the conceptual necessity of the Reader," given the "equality of deference" often enacted between the Reader and the Editor.[68]

We might push a bit more, still, at the debate that *Hind Swaraj* stages: Why would Gandhi be the Editor if the Reader is the *satyagrahi*? In neither the English nor Gujarati edition does Gandhi claim a specific role. In his forward to the English edition (1910), Gandhi merely says that "the debate" (that is, as a whole) should be understood as his views on Indian self-rule. In the Gujarati edition (1909), he makes a more provocative claim:

> These views are mine, and yet not mine. They are mine because I hope to act according to them. They are almost a part of my being. But, yet, they are not mine, because I lay no claim to originality. They have been formed after reading several books.[69]

We should be hesitant to identify the referent of "these views" as specific to the Editor—and perhaps even more so because Gandhi admits to having arrived at them by being a reader.

Moreover, it is the Reader, not the Editor, who repeatedly admits defeat—and in ways that sound a lot like Gandhi. Here is a selection:

> I now begin to understand somewhat your meaning. I shall have to think the matter over, but what you say . . . is beyond my comprehension.[70]

> You are right. Now I think you will not have to argue much with me to drive your conclusions home. . . . I shall, therefore, endeavor to follow your thought, and to stop you when I am in doubt.[71]

> I cannot follow this.[72]

And finally:

> You have shattered my illusions. . . . You have left me with nothing.[73]

I offer this brief list of the Reader's confusion not simply to align it neatly with Gandhi's later admissions of illogic, defeat, and deference. It is because, in Gandhi's expansive oeuvre, only the Editor expresses the assuredness at having arrived at the truth. Even if Gandhi was the "Editor" in *Hind Swaraj*, it is a position he never holds again: Later he is but an *interpreter* of the *Gita*, an *experimenter* with truth, a *translator* of Ruskin, and, in his alleged final words, a *beggar* of god's acceptance.

Gandhi foregrounds his indebtedness (his obligations) and thus creates a network of texts and a network of readers (all of whom, by virtue of reading, are obligated to read it to others). He is, as Simona Sawhney has written, an "activist reader" whose reading renders the text open for endless interpretation.[74] The "Reader" in *Hind Swaraj* is someone in addition to the supposed audience of *Hind Swaraj*, though that person, too, is a "reader." The "Reader" is a person who reads, but she is also, in Hofmeyr's account, a *satyagrahi*; in this case, "Some Authorities" is an acknowledgement of an additional reader: Gandhi himself.

Gandhian renunciation in these particular aesthetic practices displaces authority to somewhere else and clings instead to the egalitarianism of fallibility, deference, and obligation. The reader is a person who reads, and thus participates in a collective fumbling for truth and self. ("Who am I when I read?" asks Michel de Certeau.) In this sense, the Reader, by virtue of reading, is a *satyagrahi*. It is, after all, the Reader who concedes to the Editor at the beginning, middle, and end of *Hind Swaraj*'s debate. Somewhere in between the Editor's successful argument and the appendix of "Some Authorities," there is a figure who begins to resemble Gandhi. Is it the Reader, whose confusion and hesitation ultimately lead him to admit that the Editor has "left me with nothing"? Could it be the Reader who seeks, like Gandhi, to be "reduced to zero"?

Rude Anticolonialism

John McAleer *did* meet Gandhi—on a visit to Pune in 1946. "Speak the rude truth in all ways," Gandhi allegedly told McAleer, quoting Emerson yet again. McAleer returned to the United States, where, having been "set on his lifelong path," he wrote a comprehensive biography of Emerson, *Days of Encounter*, in 1984.[75] McAleer dedicated the book to Gandhi.

Gandhi did speak a rude truth, not only in the sense that he was maddeningly recalcitrant, but also in the sense that he presented his thoughts before they were properly developed. Gandhi lost debates and apologized not to resolve disagreement or simply to be polite. Gandhi's lost debates are certainly not about retaining disagreement as some vague democratic political ideal. They are about foregrounding loss, defeat, and apology.

When the British Raj offered Indian sovereignty in exchange for proof of its political maturity, Gandhi responded with nonsensical philology, impossible egalitarianism, and immature critique. Childish refusal and petulant obligations of renunciation: These are the "mutually complementary gestures" necessary for a utopian politics in Leela Gandhi's manifesto.[76] But how do these gestures manifest when the utopia we want is utopian *because* of its impossibility, not in spite of it?

We might be immature by being impossible: This is why we might lose debates, apologize, and ask to be given up as foolish; in so doing, we can begin to imagine affinities with an impossible assortment of other losers, penitents, and fools. By doing this, Gandhi renders himself congruent with the collective ambiguous unknowingness that imperial power could not account for. By disavowing even *eventual* expertise and self-mastery, Gandhi asserted modes of perpetual refusal, irrelevance, inconsequence, in-expertise, and non-authority. In direct contrast to the values of British liberalism, these recalcitrant ideals were perfect for envisioning a radical egalitarianism rooted in a celebration of anticolonial unknowingness *ad infinitum*—a model by which a truly collective antiauthoritarian, anticolonial politics might be attained, even if in the compromised present.

Attended by infinite risks and no guarantees, an immature and impossible political theory imagines ephemeral egalitarianism in the present, for those who are unlikely to see its utopianism attained in their lives. Having relinquished (or at least not having been confined by) teleological thought—the demand to "mature," to make sense, to become an author— we can find ourselves seized by a nonsensical and messy, provisional and contingent, immature and rude, truth.

4 / Bhagat Singh's Jail Notebook

In June 1929, anticolonial agitator and leader of the Hindustan Socialist Republican Army (HSRA), Bhagat Singh, led his fellow prisoners in Lahore on a hunger strike for better jail conditions. His demands were as follows:

1. We, as political prisoners, should be given better diet and the standard of our diet should be at least the same as that of European prisoners. (It is not the sameness of diet that we demand, but the sameness of standard of diet.)
2. We shall not be forced to do any hard or undignified labour at all.
3. All books, other than those proscribed, along with writing materials, should be allowed to us without any restriction.
4. At least one standard daily paper should be supplied to every political prisoner.
5. Political prisoners should have a special ward of their own in every jail, provided with all necessities as those of Europeans. And all the political prisoners in one jail must be kept together in that ward.
6. Toilet necessities should be supplied.
7. Better clothing.[1]

Bhagat Singh's demands are provocative given his total willingness to die during the hunger strike. Of the seven demands, I find it particularly telling that two of them concern reading (3 and 4), which are signaled as being just as important as the demand for no hard labor (2) and better diet (1). What are Bhagat Singh's demands in the context of his awareness of his very likely death? Even if (or perhaps especially because) we understand that Bhagat Singh's revolutionary politics cannot be exhausted by the *telos* of his death, in the context of his apparent commitment to his own impending martyrdom, these demands appear rather inconsequential. Why demand to read in the face of death? Even if Bhagat Singh was demanding books *for others* (who might outlive him), the demand remains fairly inconsequential: Why books?

Although he is less well known outside of South Asia, Bhagat Singh remains one of the most celebrated anticolonial agitators and thinkers in India and Pakistan. Under the auspices of a revolutionary organization he helped found, the Hindustan Socialist Republican Army (HSRA), he assassinated British police officer J. P. Saunders in revenge for the beating of Punjabi activist Lala Lajpat Rai in 1928. A few months later, in 1929, he threw a smoke-bomb in the Delhi Legislative Assembly, proclaimed *inqilab zindabad* (long live revolution), and awaited his arrest. From jail, he debated M. K. Gandhi, wrote extensively, and staged hunger strikes with his fellow inmates. At the age of 23, Bhagat Singh was hanged by the British and became a martyr for the anticolonial cause—as well as a growing revolutionary movement that challenged the moderation of the Nehru-led Congress Party and the asceticism of Gandhian nonviolence. Especially in Punjab (both Pakistani Punjab as well as Indian Punjab), Bhagat Singh has sustained a vibrant afterlife, not least because of his iconographic studio portrait that he published in 1928. His image, as well as his revolutionary thought, continues to enjoy wide circulation today.[2] Academics have turned their attention to the previously overlooked activist, producing a significant amount of work under the rubrics of what Kama Maclean has called, provocatively, "the revolutionary turn."[3]

Scholars and hagiographers of Bhagat Singh point to these demands and other of his writings as a sign of Bhagat Singh's scholarship and wide-ranging reading practices, and flippantly conclude without further comment, "the revolutionaries were reading the revolutionaries."[4] This chapter takes that claim a bit more seriously. Revolutionaries reading revolutionaries not only suggests a global network of thinkers and agitators in communication with one another, though this is itself a significant revision of more provincial accounts of radical thought around the world. But moreover, revolutionaries reading revolutionaries should indicate the centrality of *reading* to the revolutionaries under our analysis. The revolutionary was always reading. Reading was revolutionary, I suggest, precisely because it was *not* in the service of scholarship, mastery, authority, or expertise. Reading, especially in the face of death, was revolutionary because it was inconsequential.

Postcolonial scholarship on anticolonial revolutionary writing has insisted, for politically pragmatic reasons, on the important consequences of anticolonial political agitation (namely, independence). "Revolution," in this sense, has tended to focus on the teleological assumption of mastery, authority, and power that have rendered some practices subordinate, unrecognizable, or irrelevant to the eventual success of a culminating event. In other words, our analytic commitment to a narrowly defined set of actions deemed, in retrospect, "properly" anticolonial, has only replicated the very language that structured colonial thought, including the forms of acceptable revolutionary behavior. We might therefore sympathetically ask: Of what postcolonial historiographical disorder is the desire for mastery a symptom? And, in response, how might we write postcolonial history and postcolonial theory without replicating the undergirding authorial logics of colonial rule?[5]

A focus on reading requires us to reconfigure our model of "revolution" itself, which has tended to privilege a singular, consequential event over and above the slow accretion of seemingly unimportant and irrelevant actions. A focus on reading brings to light a radical and egalitarian political theory implicit in actions previously relegated to the dustbin of inconsequence. Bhagat Singh's anticolonial reading offers us a model of revolution that depends on the perpetual displacement of, rather than the eventual assumption of, mastery.

To illustrate this point, this chapter takes the *inconsequence* of Bhagat Singh's list of demands as the basis for a revolutionary politics. Leela Gandhi has argued that a commitment to inconsequence reveals an attachment to minor forms of politics. It refuses the status quo of future realization by, instead, insisting on the present. Its insistence on the present is not an investment in the present, but a celebration of the present's "irrelevance"—its commonness, its inconsequentiality.

In order to approach a theory of revolutionary anticolonial inconsequentiality, we should begin by focusing on Bhagat Singh's jail notebook, a substantial if understudied piece of his corpus. It remains understudied primarily because, although it was written "by" Bhagat Singh, it offers no original contribution from the young anticolonialist. In my reading, Bhagat Singh's jail notebook reveals the young martyr's commitment to the inconsequential and, by extension, to the common and the revolutionary present.

Anticolonial Commonplace

The jail notebook is a 404-page notebook in which Bhagat Singh filled 75 pages, skipped 25 pages, and organized a separate section called "Sociology." Some pages feature one or two quotations, some have notes that would otherwise be marginalia, and others have extensive block quotations from major texts. Writers represented in the notebook include Karl Marx, Friedrich Engels, Bernard Russell, Patrick Henry, Thomas Paine, Horace Greeley, Maxim Gorky, Walt Whitman, J. S. Mill, Thomas Jefferson, Eugene Debs, Upton Sinclair and Leon Trotsky. In other words, the jail notebook is representative of European and American contemporaneous leftist thought in the late 1910s.[6]

"Sociology," the second portion of Bhagat Singh's jail notebook, begins on page 101 after 25 blank pages.[7] It opens with a quotation from the first few pages of Marx's *Capital*, and moves on to include a selection of writing from Victor Hugo, Fyodor Dostoevsky, Jean-Jacques Rousseau, Vladimir Lenin, Socrates, Plato, Aristotle, René Descartes, Thomas Aquinas, Niccolò Machiavelli, John Locke, John Milton, and many other European and American writers. It also includes a long section on Indian revolutionary history, including notes from the Ghadar Party, Rabindranath Tagore, Lala Lajpat Rai, and Bipin Chandra Pal, as well as long passages from Valentine Chirol's infamous *Indian Unrest*. "Sociology" also features more of Bhagat Singh's notes—large sections on Lenin are Bhagat Singh's own paraphrasing of Lenin's arguments rather than direct quotes (though direct quotes are interspersed throughout).

S. Irfan Habib claims to have extrapolated a "reading list of Bhagat Singh . . . from his unpublished diary" and published it as an appendix to his reflective manifesto *To Make the Deaf Hear*.[8] Habib's list includes twenty significant books mentioned in the jail notebook, ten additional books Bhagat Singh recommended to his friend Jaidev Gupta, and a list of poets. Habib's "unpublished diary" is the jail notebook, which has a much more confusing lineage than simply remaining "unpublished." Habib's "reading list" also might be overstating the *material* extent of Bhagat Singh's reading habits. Quotes from the poets and writers listed in Habib's appendix can be found in the jail notebook, alongside additional notes and questions; but most of the page numbers listed in Bhagat Singh's jail notebook correspond, instead, to Upton Sinclair's 1915 edition of *Cry for Justice*, a self-published compendium of radical Leftist thought. Sinclair's radical primer, at almost 900 pages, was published through a grant from John Hayes Holmes, himself a radical Unitarian preacher and anticolonial sympathizer,[9] and features an introduction by American novelist and progressive Jack London. For example, a quote from J. S. Mill, "Hitherto it is questionable if all the mechanical inventions yet made have lightened the day's toil of any human being," which appears on page 20 of the jail notebook, is cited as appearing on "page 199." The quote, in fact, appears on page 199 of *Cry for Justice*, in between passages by Antiparos and Edwin Markham.[10]

I suggest we briefly examine *Cry for Justice* as a compendium, and therefore a "commonplace," of contemporaneous radical Leftist thought. American revolutionary socialist Upton Sinclair was already famous when *The Cry for Justice* was published in 1915.[11] *The Jungle*, his most famous work, had been published to Leftist acclaim in 1906, and is generally acknowledged as one of the catalysts for the passing of the Pure Food and Drug Act in the same year. Like many of his contemporaries, his activism was multifaceted and wide-ranging: He was corresponding with socialists, anarchists, Indian anticolonialists, Irish revolutionaries, and trade union activists.[12] In the 1920s, however, Sinclair had not yet become an aspiring politician (1934) or Nobel Prize winner (1943). Drawing on his own resources and those of his friends, he published *Cry for Justice: An Anthology of the Literature of Social Protest* from his offices in Pasadena and New York. The cover promises "a gospel of new hope to the race"; it was "Illustrated with Reproductions of Social Protest in Art."

The book is divided into seventeen sections: "Toil," "The Chasm," "The Outcast," "Out of the Depths," "Revolt," "Martyrdom," "Jesus," "The Church," "The Voice of the Ages," "Mammon," "War," "Country," "Children," "Humor," "The Poem," "Socialism," and "The New Day." Jack London's introduction argues for the book's place next to "the Bible, the Koran, and the Talmud."[13] *Cry for Justice* features more than 450 entries "selected from twenty-five languages [and] covering a period of five thousand years."[14] At the same time, the radical primer is a selection very much of its time, and Sinclair predicts that the volume would have to be regularly updated to reflect the revolutionary vision for each age. This "whole movement,"[15] he notes, requires "a new Bible": "I believe that [this book] is, quite literally and simply, what the old Bible was—a selection by the living minds of a living time of the best and truest writings known to them. It is a Bible of the future, a Gospel of the new hope of the race."[16]

Consequently, *Cry for Justice* becomes a "humanist Bible" (in Jack London's phrase), devoted to the secular world. "We know how gods are made. Comes now the time to make the world," London proclaims at the end of his introduction.[17] Sinclair's insistence on this secular "Bible" takes on even greater weight in his particularly Protestant instructions:

> If the material in this volume means to you, the reader, what it has meant to me, you will live with it, love it, sometimes weep with it, many times pray with it, yearn and hunger with it, and, above all, many times pray with it. You will carry it with you about your daily

tasks, you will be utterly possessed by it; and again and again you will be led to dedicate yourself to the greatest hope, the most wondrous vision which has ever thrilled the soul of humanity.[18]

Sinclair prescribes a set of protocols for reading, encompassed in his expansive definition of "reading": loving, weeping, praying, hungering, and praying again. Similarly, Sinclair's call here associates "reading" with "revolution" and an egalitarian commitment to "humanity"—in other words, his call is for the development of a critical stance necessary for revolution.

The importance of this particular transnational circulation of texts and ideas cannot be understated. Due in large part to the Ghadr Party's San Francisco headquarters, and the circulation of texts between California and Punjab, I think it is necessary to consider Bhagat Singh a central figure in a network of interwar political and philosophical thought that is indebted to an extra-imperial circuit of influence. Bhagat Singh arrives at interwar European philosophy by way of California. Closer to Punjab, Bhagat Singh returns to theological Hindu, Sikh, and theosophical texts to render European and Anglo-American thought conducive to a radically inconclusive antiauthoritarianism. In other words, Bhagat Singh's atheism was as much a product of the particular forms of Russian anti-imperialism, leftist pulp publishing in the United States, and interwar European philosophy as it was a product of the practices of religious doubt within the British Empire.

Of course, Bhagat Singh's reading list was significantly broader than *Cry for Justice* alone. His definition of anarchism, taken verbatim from Emma Goldman, is not in *Cry for Justice*, but rather in Goldman's *Mother Earth* publications.[19] Bhagat Singh's notes include now-obscure poetry and socialist economic analysis. Interspersed with selections from *Cry for Justice* are Urdu poems, notes on economic practices in the United States, conversion rates between different world currencies, and selections from Rabindranath Tagore's lectures on Indian nationalism in Japan. Nevertheless, *Cry for Justice* is both the central component of Bhagat Singh's seventy-five pages of notes, as well as the primary reference for the jail notebook's structure.

According to Chaman Lal, the jail notebook was part of a set of writings that Bhagat Singh gave to Kumari Lajjawati, the secretary for the Bhagat Singh defense committee, to be passed on to Bejoy Kumar Sinha.[20] In any case, the notebook circulated privately within Bhagat Singh's family before being deposited in the Nehru Memorial Museum and Library Records in 1981.[21] Part of it first appeared publicly in L. V. Mitrokhin's 1981 book, *Lenin in India*. Bhupendra Hooja published the full notebook in 1994 as *A Martyr's Notebook*, and Chaman Lal edited the 2007 LeftWord edition.[22] The journal, originally written mostly in English, has been translated into Punjabi, Urdu, and Hindi.

The jail notebook is "by" Bhagat Singh in the fullest sense of the preposition: It is an agglomeration of texts that circulated *next to* or *alongside* him; but he "wrote" it only insofar as it is in his handwriting. As Isabel Hofmeyr explains in the case of M. K. Gandhi, books "by" anticolonial writers emerge to confirm an authoritative, "author" figure, often in retrospect. Anticolonial writing, in Hofmeyr's account, emerged under radically different, experimental "textual conditions," including practices that fundamentally trouble our notion of "author."[23] This sense of "by" is considerably more fungible than an indication of singular authorship, which is why it is curious that the jail notebook has become the corroboration of Bhagat Singh's authorial expertise.

I want to assert the importance of the jail notebook as a commonplace of anticolonial reading rather than anticolonial authority and authorship, not as a way of undermining Bhagat Singh's scholarly pursuits—I am not interested in charging him with having cribbed from a primer—but rather as a way of demonstrating his (and Upton Sinclair's) experimentation with textual production, including commonplace books and anthologies.[24] Commonplace books were collections of important quotations, notes, letters, poems, proverbs, and prayers. A commonplace book signaled a curatorial project, with each of these notes arranged according to the reader's interests. Readers used commonplace books to document their reading and as an aid for remembering especially important quotations.

A commonplace book was a way for the reader to practice self-cultivation without the demand to attain mastery. Unlike anthologies, commonplaces rarely feature an authorial editorial presence.[25] Indeed, both Bhagat Singh's jail notebook and Upton Sinclair's *Cry for Justice* insist on their creator's non-authority and non-authorial status. Bhagat Singh's and Sinclair's demands that other readers read *with* them signal a commitment to reading that is egalitarian in its orientation, actively disavowing mastery and expertise in favor of a commitment to reading in the present.[26]

As David Arnold has noted, jail writings often served as the documentation of a revolutionary identity, forged under conditions of incarceration as well as the injustice of colonial rule writ large.[27] Many scholars of Bhagat Singh point to the notebook as the sign of his developing scholarly authority and philosophical mastery; this is no doubt a politically sympathetic attempt to place Bhagat Singh in line with other radical writers, especially Antonio Gramsci.[28] Nevertheless, such an account of his impending "mastery" undermines, if not outright forecloses, the truly egalitarian vision that Bhagat Singh invokes in his published writings. It strikes me, therefore, that a greater focus on the *inconsequentiality* of Bhagat Singh's reading (and his documentation thereof) offers us a clearer vision of revolutionary egalitarianism.

Reading Revolutionaries

There exists a rich scholarly conversation about the literary strength and imagination of Bhagat Singh's *writing*, especially that written in jail. Simona Sawhney has traced the lineages of revolutionary martyrdom (*shaheedat, sarfaroshi*) and love (*ishq, prem*) through Bhagat Singh's writings and the *ghazals* of his co-conspirator, Ramprasad "Bismil."[29] Kama Maclean has written about his use of another sort of text—photography—to spread revolutionary sentiment.[30] Bhagat Singh's extensive body of writing is made even more enticing given that he wrote all of it before he was 23, to say nothing of the appeal of his scholarly approach to revolution, his attractive studio portrait, and his charismatic writing style.

Consequently, Bhagat Singh has been a vibrant figure for recent scholarly turns in South Asian history, especially those toward intellectual history, transnational studies, and radical and revolutionary histories. Historians of Bhagat Singh have long been eager to recuperate his extensive and expansive collection of writing—which reflects, as Bipan Chandra notes—a political philosophy "in motion."[31] Hagiography of Bhagat Singh appears to have started as soon as his death in 1931; collected writings and commentaries on his philosophy began to appear in the 1950s.[32] Scholars, wanting to claim Bhagat Singh as one of the "proper" leaders of Indian independence, point to the philosophical sophistication on display in his published essays, personal correspondence, and various other writings.

In the interests of making Bhagat Singh a "proper" authority of anticolonial revolutionary action, scholars and activists alike have been far too keen to sweep away his insistence on quieter forms of political agitation as being "improperly" ethical or personal.[33] Even accounts of anticolonial revolutionary thought that insist on agitators' reading practices have been ready to show that these reading practices were in the *service* of a greater, more authoritative practice (writing, bomb-throwing, publicity). This is no doubt related to the more nefarious version of an anticolonial hangover that is consumed with demonstrating masterful forms of anticolonial agitation and their political potency. Such accounts must, it seems, always be rendered "properly political" and "properly revolutionary."[34]

Bhagat Singh's *reading* practices, and revolutionary reading more generally, have likely been overlooked because reading is often relegated to the "inactive" and "passive," or to a instrumentalizable step in the process of "proper" revolution. Historians and politicians (across the political spectrum), wanting to resuscitate Bhagat Singh and his legacy, have tended to focus on those acts easily deemed "active" and "productive,"[35] and therefore properly revolutionary. To be sure, the publicity inaugurated by the Hindustan Socialist Republican Army contributed to this virile image. Nevertheless, Bhagat Singh's self-proclaimed interest in reading has been employed only to corroborate his more actively political pursuits and interests, as opposed to being taken seriously in its own right as articulating a theory of non-instrumentalizability and revolutionary action in the present. It is for this reason that Bhagat Singh is a particularly crucial figure in reconsidering the relationship between anticolonial reading and anticolonial revolution. A reconsideration of this relationship reveals that the formula of anticolonial "revolution" was a focus on method, process, and beginnings rather than ends, authority, and results.

That Bhagat Singh loved to read is no secret. Many of his colleagues recall his avid reading practices, and some of his correspondence from jail begs for specific books to be sent to him.[36] Jitendra Nath Sanyal, among others, recalls that one of Singh's favorite pieces was Leonid Andreyev's *The Seven That Were Hanged* (1908), about seven Russian peasants who were sentenced to hang; the short story traces how each of them dealt with their impending death.[37] Jaidev Gupta recalls that in his late teens, Bhagat Singh "was always seen with a book in English in his hands and a dictionary in his pocket."[38] Yashpal writes of seeing Bhagat Singh driving a camel-drawn cart for his father as "an interesting sight: the camel drove the cart and Bhagat Singh sat in the driver's seat, reading his book."[39] Durga Das Khanna remembers Bhagat Singh and Sukhdev praising his reading practices when he first met them.[40] Bhagat Singh allegedly read Charles Dickens and Oscar Wilde, and he spoke often of Kropotkin's and Bakunin's writings as having "transformed his life."[41] He also read Bankim Chandra Chattopadhyay's *Anandamath*.[42] Bhagwan Das Mahor recollects that Bhagat Singh had given him a copy of Marx's *Das Kapital* and thus "the seed that Bhagat Singh had planted into my heart . . . began to germinate and grow up. Thus, personally speaking, what I have upper most in my mind about Bhagat Singh is that he was my first teacher to turn me toward Socialism."[43]

Reading remains a crucial part of Bhagat Singh's afterlives, though often mentioned only in passing. Chaman Lal writes:

> When the time came to take him to the gallows on the last day of his life, he was reading Lenin. The revolutionary poet Avatar Singh Pash, slain by extremists many years later, paid tribute to Bhagat Singh by saying that the Indian youth needed to read the next page of the book that Bhagat Singh closed as he went to meet his death.[44]

Or consider journalist Kuldip Nayer's semifictional biography of Bhagat Singh:

> The warden had allowed Bhagat Singh to smuggle in all the books he wanted to read. It was all Marxist literature, strictly banned by the government. Still that was what he read or literally devoured. Hardly would a book on Marx, Lenin or Russia arrive when he would put in a demand for more. The secret supply by the local Dwarka Dass Library, founded by progressive nationalists, could not keep pace with his speed of reading. So keen was he about books that he once wrote to his schoolmate, Jaidev, to draw from the library, *Militarism*, by Karl Liebknecht, *Left-Wing Communism*, *Why Men Fight* by Bertrand Russell, *Land Revolution in Russia* and *Spy* by Upton Sinclair, and send them to him through Kulbir, his brother. . . . Indeed, Bhagat Singh's passion since his childhood was books.[45]

In both these examples, Bhagat Singh's passion for reading and his passion for books strike me as the overlooked aspects of the young martyr's constant interest in anticolonial self-cultivation and self-culture.

In his introduction to LeftWord's 2007 publication of Bhagat Singh's jail notebook, Chaman Lal argues that Bhagat Singh had three agendas in jail, one of which was to "develop himself ideologically and politically by undertaking a rigorous and serious programme of reading."[46] Lal goes on to describe what he thinks are the effects of this goal: the possibility of four unfinished manuscripts that Bhagat Singh might have written from jail.[47] S. Irfan Habib claims that Bhagat Singh wrote the four books, which were subsequently lost.[48] Lal is, of course, correct in identifying Bhagat Singh's interest in reading, but his efforts to portray Bhagat Singh as a fully developed political thinker elide other interpretations. Lal's (and others') dedication to the idea of a "developed" Bhagat Singh has enabled the conclusion that the jail notebook is a sign of the work that Bhagat Singh *could have written*—the elusive, incomplete four volumes—as opposed to considering the jail notebook itself as the key document in unpacking Bhagat Singh's fundamental approach to an antiauthoritarian politics.[49]

Indeed, the majority of the scholarship on Bhagat Singh has been invested in the futurity of his project: the *potentiality* of Bhagat Singh's political thought, illustrated by the existence of this jail notebook. As Chris Moffat has written:

> It can be difficult to untangle Bhagat Singh from his futures. The revolutionary's uncommon passion, taken alongside the event of a young death, seems to demand speculation—"what ifs" and "if onlys"—the now-familiar lament for potential unfulfilled, trajectories interrupted.[50]

Applied to our case, this requires us to disentangle the document we have—that is, the commonplace jail notebook—from the documents we could have had—allegedly, a book on socialism, a history of India, an autobiography, and a reflection on death[51]—"if only" Bhagat Singh had remained alive (or if they had not "been lost"). In other words, analyses of Bhagat Singh are so eager to endow him with the proper *authority* of an anticolonial leader that they point to his *potential* books as the sign of his status as an *author*.[52]

In the specific context of Bhagat Singh, this accounts for a myopic focus on the *possibility* of authoritative books rather than the actual notes and fragments. An insistence on authority, expertise, and productivity reproduces an authoritative vision of anticolonial activism focused exclusively on productivity, action, and expertise. It has, moreover, blinded us to a fundamental aspect of anticolonial thought and, consequently, anticolonial politics in the face of colonial rule. I think this excludes a more radically utopian strain of Bhagat Singh's anticolonial vision. In response, we need an account of Bhagat Singh's jail notebook that refers to it, not to its potential, as one crucial and overlooked strain of Bhagat Singh's anticolonial revolutionary vision. Our demand for Bhagat Singh to have authored a theory of revolution "in his own words" requires that we render him as the authorial figure that he himself was reluctant to become.

If we understand the jail notebook as a commonplace or an anthology, and we understand this document to contain no "original" material written by Bhagat Singh, we must abandon our fascination with the contents of the four allegedly written books in order to look at the theory implicit in the document we actually possess. In other words, Bhagat Singh's theory of anticolonial reading emerges at the exact moment when his jail notebook contains no traces of him as an author.

The jail notebook functions both as a private record of Bhagat Singh's own auto-didacticism, as well as a public document. In this sense, I think we can understand the jail notebook as a semi-public document. By semi-public document, I want to mark the ways in which the jail notebook was therefore neither fully "public" (it was not "published") nor fully "private" (even during his lifetime, his colleagues knew of the existence of the notebook and its contents). Bhagat Singh's reading was both an ethical practice (a "care of the self," frequently rendered "private" and therefore irrelevant to anticolonial activism) and a political vision (frequently rendered "public" and therefore celebrated as productive).[53] His practice of reading as a properly anticolonial practice confirms the centrality of reading as fundamental to anticolonial action. Bhagat Singh's insistence on his own readerly self-cultivation, without the goal of mastery (nor in order to become an author), is a politics that rests on non-instrumentalizable practices and inconsequential action. This is a far cry from the notions of revolution (or authority) that historians have tended to wrest from the scattered writings of Bhagat Singh.

Commonplace Anticolonialism

To diminish the importance of reading and critique is to fundamentally misinterpret the philosophical and political egalitarianism of radically antiauthoritarian anticolonial thought. It is *reading* as a non-instrumentalizable revolutionary practice, more than "active" revolt, which offers a fundamental piece of the unacknowledged inheritance of contemporary postcolonial theory.

With this in mind, I suggest we return to the list of demands at the beginning of this essay, which now comes into starker relief. If, from the moment of his arrest, Bhagat Singh knew he was going to die—indeed, he welcomed death—what does it mean to ask for more reading material?[54] Many scholars (to whom I am otherwise sympathetic) have been eager to suggest that this demand for books indicates, in conjunction with his jail notebook, that Bhagat Singh was working toward a scholarly mastery of Marxist and radical thought. This begs two questions: One, if Bhagat Singh knew he was going to die soon (even if he was able to slow the judicial process), why would he have had any desire to attain "mastery"? Two, if Bhagat Singh's politics were those of mastery and expertise, why would he have been willing to make his fairly inexpert jail notebook a semi-public document? In other words, Bhagat Singh's revolutionary thought was doubly "inconsequential" in the sense we have been discussing. Firstly, across his published writings, Bhagat Singh's preferred self-identification is marked by a willingness to die. Secondly, he consistently uses "master" and "expert" to describe others, especially regarding recommended reading.[55]

Not all reading is the same. I think it is more in line with the anticolonial martyr's own political vision to ask: What does it mean to read in the face of death?[56] What does it mean to read without seeking mastery or expertise? What does it mean, therefore, to read without consequence? What is inconsequential reading, and what might Bhagat Singh's inconsequential reading offer to a radical revolutionary politics and ethics?

For Leela Gandhi, consequence is the accrual of virtue on the basis of generativity, succession, and sequence. Consequentialism is thus marked by a filial logic, undergirded by the processes of procreation and futurity that mark both the units of the modern family and the modern nation. In response, inconsequence might "treat virtue as its own end, without care for rewards and commendations that might accrue [to] the bearer."[57] It originates from and signals a commitment to lives that have been deemed "inconsequential," "common," and therefore unrecognizable to the logics of state rule.

A focus on the revolutionary virtue to be accrued allows more critical historians of Bhagat Singh to conclude that the failure of the revolutionaries was "that of not linking their practice with their theory," wherein "theory" is assumed to be an *authoritative* philosophical vision and "practice" is defined as "individual action."[58] In addition to the "individual action" that Bipan Chandra envisions here (bomb-throwing, assassination, "terrorism"), Bhagat Singh's vision for "individual action" included, as we have been discussing, reading and the documentation of readerly self-cultivation rather than mastery. In other words, the practice *was* the theory.

Bhagat Singh envisioned that everyone read—or, in other words, he believed that reading should become common. In his introduction to Ram Saran Das's poetry collection, *Dreamland*, Bhagat Singh concludes:

> I strongly recommend this book to young men in particular, but with a warning. Please do not read it to follow blindly and take for granted what is written in it. Read it, criticise it, think over it, try to formulate your own ideas with its help.[59]

Bhagat Singh therefore openly advocated reading as an anticolonial practice. "Commonplace anticolonialism," in the first instance, refers to Bhagat Singh's practice of readerly collection and curatorial vision. "Commonplace anticolonialism," in the second instance, refers to the egalitarian politics inaugurated by the public documentation of one's own reading practices, and the demand to become a common reader.

Bhagat Singh's reading practices were not based in rote memorization and replication, but rather in practices of perpetual self-interrogation.

Michel de Certeau's seemingly sociological question, "*Who* reads?" becomes a political and philosophical conundrum.[60] Who does a person become when he or she reads and what political spaces are made possible from a textual interaction? Reading, in this sense, evokes a new evasively revolutionary subject, a virtue in the present, and a figure for whom mastery and authorship are beside the point. Bhagat Singh's quite successful praxis was the assertion of one's own radical inconsequentiality, commonness, and accessibility. This is seen most clearly in his practices of readerly reception and collection, and therefore his commitment to an egalitarian present rather than to future virtues earned through production and dissemination.

An ethics rooted in inconsequence refuses future possible outcomes in favor of an investment in the secular (that is, non-transcendent) present.[61] For Leela Gandhi, this is a political gesture: "we democratize our consciousness by sacrificing our *telos*," she notes.[62] If inconsequentialism names "a force of interruption in the worldly drama of repetition, reproduction, and duplication, so that newness might reenter the world,"[63] inconsequentialist reading is the practice of a revolutionary anti-authorial recalcitrance that both inaugurates and is made possible by a certain worldly commitment to the common, the impossible, and the ephemeral present.

Atheist, Secularist, Critic

Bhagat Singh explicates this relationship in his 1930 essay from jail, "Why I am an Atheist."[64] In this essay, it is studying without attaining mastery—"the cry that reverberated in the corridors of my mind"—that convinces him that "the moment the rope is fitted round my neck and rafters removed from under my feet, that will be the final moment.... Nothing further. A short life of struggle, with no such magnificent end, shall in itself be the reward."[65] A reward "in itself," without the promise of either future virtue or transcendental benefit, is the model of an inconsequential reading that Bhagat Singh offers in commonplace form. This impossible and inconsequential practice is especially necessary because it is rooted in an impatience with, and therefore a commitment to, the compromised present. Bhagat Singh understood that a relationship existed between unknowingness, reading, and public, which he dubbed "atheism."

It is unsurprising (given their insistence on his alleged or eventual mastery) that most scholars and hagiographers have taken Bhagat Singh's "atheism" to mean the confident refutation of the existence of God. Bhagat Singh's most ardent supporters therefore do him a grave disservice by rendering him the insipid anticolonial predecessor to Christopher Hitchens. Moreover, this interpretation relies rely on three fundamental misinterpretations of the essay: first, the equation of Sikh atheism with Christian atheism; second, the equation of "atheism" with religious non-belief; and third, the assumption that the title accurately describes the essay that follows it.

Instead, the essay inexpertly participates in the worldwide pessimistic utopianism in the aftermath of the Great War and the Bolshevik Revolution. Shell-shocked philosophers and intellectuals were forced to make sense of a world that appeared to lack transcendent reason. Gone, too, were grounds for philosophical universalism that had comforted European thought prior to the twentieth century. "Atheism" was the term most appropriate for imagining an unknowable world. In other words, "atheism" was the name given not to a confident knowingness of postwar philosophy, but rather to colonial doubt and anticolonial unknowingness—practices that resuscitated the secular human in the absence of metaphysical assuredness.[66] "Atheism" names not simply the absence of assurance in a "Supreme Being" but the absence of assurance in truth, one's own self, and the possibility of a future. In other words, the proper anticolonial agitator must relinquish theological transcendence, self-knowledge, and teleological certitude. In its place, the revolutionary subject must embrace unknowingness, self-critique, and contingency. For Bhagat Singh—like Emma Goldman, Leon Trotsky, Edmund Husserl, Randolph Bourne, among others—it was precisely the *lack* of metaphysical fixedness that made it possible to imagine new forms of worldly affiliation, including friendship (for E. M. Forster), love (in Ram Prasad Bismil's poetry), society (in John Dewey's radical pragmatism), and what William James called "muddy ontologies."[67] These forms of worldly affiliation, rooted in the *relinquishment* of metaphysical assurance, made the teleological acquisition of liberal value irrelevant.

In this sense, Bhagat Singh's "atheism" is more closely aligned with what we would identify as "secularism." Stathis Gourgouris, in his lectures on Edward Said's "secular criticism," clarifies this particularly well: Whereas "atheism" is the belief in the non-existence of God, "secularism" renders the question of God's existence irrelevant. Secularism, therefore, names an "all-out interrogation of transcendental authority [that] would hinge on how one can perform one's worldly existence without God," not out of conviction but rather by eschewing conviction altogether, which would in turn require a tentative and discontinuous (though perhaps constant) commitment to the ephemeral—the "utter singularity, untimely, ungrounded"—without a need for a transcendental guarantee.[68]

Bhagat Singh's atheistic criticism, properly aligned with Said's secular criticism, names a practice that not only assails obedience to mastery, but defies mastery altogether. This form of critique "does not seek to absolve the world of its unknowability, does not seek the incontestable, but submits its knowledge to the precariousness of living beings making history."[69] Bhagat Singh's commonplace anticolonialism asserts, to borrow Said's phrase, an "essential untidiness, [an] essential unmasterable presence."[70]

Said, we will recall, draws his inspiration from Erich Auerbach's "earthly" criticism, which took its fullest shape in what René Wellek once described as a "personal commonplace or rather an uncommonplace book": *Mimesis*.[71] Wellek's admittedly tepid praise is nevertheless illuminating. The allegedly monumental work of philological critique is a collection of fragments and synecdochal analyses, culled from makeshift libraries.[72] So, too, is Bhagat Singh's jail notebook.

Bhagat Singh's worldly ("atheist") anticolonial approach and Auerbach's worldly ("secular") philological approach share more than approximate contemporaneity: They are both attempts to rescue, by way of closely reading its most admirable fragments, the promises of European philosophy from Europe itself. Both are works produced in the absence of assured future (or the guarantee of no future), in the context of an entirely unknown audience, and under inexpert conditions. *Mimesis* famously offers neither theoretical method nor promise, despite the formalist New Critics who assured themselves its method was theirs.[73] Bhagat Singh's jail notebook, too, refuses to offer method or promise; nevertheless, as Chris Moffat has beautifully shown, his supposed benefactors have claimed a political inheritance from his corpse.[74] Most compellingly, both texts assert their likely inconsequence. Bhagat Singh reads unto death. Auerbach either writes for a reader he does not imagine he will find; or, alternatively, he finds himself reading for friends who are no longer alive.[75]

Philological and anticolonial critique, asserting their own status as "provisional and incomplete," are aesthetic and political projects without guarantees. Their radical investment in the present ("a particular time"[76]) is an assertion of aesthetic inexpertise for an unknown political collective. Anticolonial and philological critique asserts a world that *must* be otherwise, and so impossibly otherwise that we must commit to it without being its *figura*: We can neither prefigure nor preauthorize it. Instead, we might invest in the non-instrumentalizable virtues of reading, with and for others—whom we can neither know nor authorize admission into this amorphous "us." As Simona Sawhney writes, "love" in Bhagat Singh's writing is inherently secular, indebted to a politics of self-sacrifice.[77] By way of reading, perhaps "love" names the inconsequential political vision made possible by a refusal of mastery and authority, of an egalitarian relationship with others in the world.

The Terrorist and the Reader

In his fictional 1936 short story, "The Terrorist," Mulk Raj Anand describes two young revolutionaries, Bir Singh and Vasu Dev, in the minutes leading up to their throwing a bomb in the "Central Legislative Assembly." Bir Singh is able to enter the Legislative Assembly because of his "handsome, white-blonde face, with a forehead, shadowed by a khaki polo topee, inflamed by pink-white cheeks, which tapered from the edges of the sharp nose over a regular, expressive mouth down to the chin, whose determination was sadly flawed by the pit of a dimple."[78] Bir Singh is "histrionic," "wild and furtive," "full of molten lava," and filled with "youth's fire" and "the pure joy of violence, destruction, and annihilation."[79] He watches Congress Party members—whom he declares to be traitors, opportunists, and, worst of all, Swarajist traitors—enter the chamber as he prepares to explode the bomb. He remembers his past crimes—robbery, assassination—as he readies himself. As the story closes, he throws the bomb but it fails to go off; Congress Party officials flee only to return again to their seats. He is about to proclaim his mission: "'I sacrifice myself for . . .' he roared, but the roar ended in a hoarse whisper. . . . The word sounded hollow as it struck the dome of the Chamber."[80]

The short story is damning of these young revolutionaries, whose youthful rage blinds them against seeing the alleged wonders of the slow procedural lurch towards self-rule, and whose angry ignorance is ultimately impotent. Anand makes no attempt to hide the referents for his two revolutionary teenagers: Bir Singh and Vasu Dev are barely pseudonyms for Bhagat Singh and Sukhdev;[81] and Bhagat Singh's attractive pale skin and Trilby hat had famously allowed him to pass uncaught (as a British, or at least a cosmopolitan, figure) in the hagiographic iterations of his biography. Anand's almost mean-spirited dismissal of the HSRA revolutionaries is somewhat surprising. Anand, who had founded the Progressive Writers' Association (PWA) in the late 1930s with his fellow Leftist novelists, would have been a close colleague of at least two of Bhagat Singh's collaborators, Sachchidananda Vatsyayan (Agyeya) and Yashpal, both of whom spent time in jail following the collapse of the HSRA in 1930. Agyeya and Yashpal, who had each published accounts of their jail experiences, continued to defend the actions of the HSRA in fiction and memoir into the 1960s.[82]

On the other hand, it was no secret that Anand's sympathies aligned more closely with Gandhi's, at whose Sabarmati Ashram he had allegedly written *Untouchable* in 1935. Unlike Motilal and Jawaharlal Nehru, who expressed mild sympathy for the HSRA's actions,[83] Gandhi agreed fully with the British Raj that the revolutionaries were "terrorists" and members of "the cult of the bomb." Gandhi published an editorial in *Young India* in February 1930, in which he insisted that violence was a "cult" inconsistent with "the vast masses who have become conscious of the fact that they must have freedom . . . untouched by violence."[84] HSRA revolutionaries, by contrast, were "saturated with violence as to be beyond the pale of reason."[85] In this iteration of his quite complicated philosophy of non-violence,[86] Gandhi insists that violence only replicates the authority of British rule, whereas non-violence causes people to "bec[o]me conscious of their power. They ceas[e] to fear authority. . . . It [is] the true swaraj of the masses attained by the masses."[87]

In response, the HSRA released a statement, "The Philosophy of the Bomb," signed by 'Kartar Singh." The title refers to the subtitle of Har Dayal's 1912 pamphlet, "*Shabash!*," published from California by the Ghadr Party.[88] "Kartar Singh" refers to the nineteen-year-old Berkeley engineering student who was the first to be hanged in 1914 after the Ghadr Party's failed mutiny. These citations should alert us to a refusal of mastery and professed authority. A proper "philosophy of the bomb," as opposed to a "cult of the bomb"—in other words, a debate around the universalism or particularity of violent revolutionary agitation—argues that the violent revolutionary method "shatters the superiority of the ruling class," whereas Gandhi's methods are concerned with the reproduction of authority, except with Indian faces.[89] A significant part of the critique directed at "The Philosophy of the Bomb" is directed at Gandhi's insistence on his own authority: Instead of an egalitarian relationship with the masses, Gandhi provides *darshan* (ability to be devoted, to be beheld) and *updesh* (providing council, advice), two "services" that only replicate his own mastery and transcendent authority. By contrast, the HSRA "affirm that the masses of India are solidly with us because we know it from personal experience."[90] I have written elsewhere that this debate between Gandhi and the HSRA was about maintaining rhetorical command over the "masses" as the metonym for "humanity."[91] A different reading, however, reveals that the "masses" are also a thinly veiled metaphor for a commitment to egalitarianism, rooted fundamentally in a debate about authority. Both Gandhi and the HSRA attempted to publicly relinquish their own authorial and masterly presences as properly anticolonial political gestures. At the same time, both Gandhi and the HSRA attempted, in a seemingly counterintuitive move, to insist on the authority of the *other* and the other's methods. At the center of this debate, therefore, is an insistence on one's own anticolonial, anti-authoritative inconsequentiality.

In "Why I am an Atheist," Bhagat Singh presses this point further, connecting Gandhi's singular authority to theological assuredness:

> Because our forefathers had set up a faith in some Supreme Being, the Almighty God, therefore any man who dares to challenge the validity of that faith . . . shall have to be called an apostate. . . . Because Mahatmaji is great, therefore none should criticise him. Because he has risen above, therefore everything he says—maybe in the field of Politics or Religion, Economics or Ethics—is right.[92]

There is much to say about curious transition from "Almighty God" to M. K. Gandhi (sardonically anointed "Mahatmaji"). We should note firstly Bhagat Singh's consistent strategy of claiming Gandhi as having "risen above." As in HSRA's "The Philosophy of the Bomb," Gandhi is the *less* qualified anticolonial agitator because he is the *more* authoritative anticolonial leader. But Bhagat Singh presses the point further here. The argument here is not simply a renunciation of authority in deference to an other's, but rather the demand for the renunciation of authority altogether. Bhagat Singh's challenge to Gandhi's *satya* (his being "right") is not that "truth" does not exist, but that "truth" is unavailable.[93] In contrast, Bhagat Singh's anticolonial philosophy thus replaces the position of authority and expertise with the egalitarian social relationship founded on inexpert secular criticism *ad infinitum*. In other words, the grounds on which Bhagat Singh claims his "revolutionary" are not vanity and egoism, but rather total irrelevance and unknowingness. At the heart of the ongoing debate between Gandhi and the HSRA was a central concern about becoming common and inconsequential.[94]

Given both Gandhi's and Bhagat Singh's insistence on reading and reading practices as foundational to the cultivation of a properly anticolonial self, we should return to Mulk Raj Anand's short story to discover a central confusion around citation in the scene shortly before Bir Singh throws his bomb. The bomb—an actual bomb in the short story versus the smoke-bomb Bhagat Singh threw—is meant to explode at the same time as Bir Singh and Vasu Dev release hundreds of their manifestos into the crowd:

> 'The challenge! The challenge!' he said. 'The words which will spread throughout the length and breadth of India like wildfire, words as memorable as those of Proudhon and Mazzini: "I die for my mother-

land. I become a sacrifice for it. I have tried to avenge Bharat Mata against the devilry of the British!'" He exulted to think that tomorrow these words of his speech would form the headlines of all the newspapers in Hindustan. He had printed the words on leaflets, so that if all died in the Chamber, the printed matter would remain.[95]

Even if Anand's sympathies are more with Gandhi than Bhagat Singh, the flurry of quotation marks (and typographical errors) around Bir Singh's words reveal the confusion provoked by the referent revolutionary's citations. Even at the height of his revolutionary power, Bir Singh—much like Bhagat Singh—deflects and relinquishes his authorial status in favor of citing Proudhon and Mazzini. The obvious reference here is to Bhagat Singh's insistence that Auguste Valliant's words—"it takes a loud voice to make the deaf hear"—be the material of the smoke-bomb's "explosion" in 1929. At the precise moment when Bhagat Singh might have claimed true authority over the Legislative Assembly, the terrorist became a reader.

Epilogue: Stopping and Leaving

"Now comrades," Fanon begins his conclusion to *The Wretched of the Earth*, "let us leave this Europe which never stops talking of man yet massacres him at every one of its street corners, at every corner of the world. . . . Come, comrades, the European game is finally over, we must look for something else."[1]

We have been considering, in various iterations, practices of anticolonial antiauthoritarianism. I have suggested that the aesthetic form conducive for understanding these practices is "reading" and "critique" in their comparative philological tradition. Because radical anticolonial thought and comparative philology are invested in unknowability, unknowingness, and unknownness, they gesture toward an aesthetic and political criticism that envision a world that could be otherwise. That "world," despite its utopian spirit, remains purposefully uncharted and inaccessible. Either by relinquishing a telos for anticolonialism, or sacrificing the desire for scholarly totality, can we understand the importance of these shared critical projects.

Committed to retaining their proximity to the impure, the injured, the "ground-down," and the "wretched of the earth," anticolonial thinkers perpetually refused mastery and authority, two things that have been posthumously thrust upon them. I have tried to show, instead, that they were committed to practices of relinquishment, disavowal, and refusal necessary for anti-imperial survival in the compromised present. This type of anticolonialism thus operates at a seemingly paradoxical nexus: the incertitude of its fulfillment and the refusal to betray the mission of emancipatory politics.

What is to be done when we come to an end, when the "game is finally over?" Our final act of anticolonial refusal might be to quit: to stop, and then, to leave. It is an act for *an* end that is not *the* end. It is an anticolonial suggestion that appears last; sometimes it is a last resort, but sometimes it is simply the most impossible option of all the impossible options before it. It is also last because it is certainly never first; that is to say, a political collectivity does not *originate* by "stopping and leaving." An egalitarian collectivity should refuse any one "origin" or beginning. An egalitarian collectivity remains possible, or begins again, even if still tentatively and ephemerally, by stopping and leaving.[2]

Fanon died before Algerian independence, the absolute bare minimum for the world he demanded. His makeshift homeland gained independence in 1962. His birthplace, Martinique, is still under French rule. Har Dayal and Bhagat Singh died before independence. Gandhi lived to see Indian independence, but it was not the *swaraj* he had imagined. Ambedkar lived to see Indian national independence from the British Raj but had correctly predicted that colonial regimes would hardly atrophy in the shift from Viceroy Mountbatten to Prime Minister Nehru. In response, Ambedkar drafted one of the most radically democratic constitutions for the newly independent Indian republic but then watched as the Congress Party jettisoned its egalitarian assurances. Ambedkar died in 1956, "reading unto death," still "seeking Begumpura," Bhakti Sant Ravidas's imagined egalitarian utopia.[3]

The colonial world will outlive us, too. How do we retain a commitment to social, egalitarian, and emancipatory politics without deluding ourselves that those projects will be realized within our lives, or the lives of our friends? Despair and nihilism are insufficient for an anticolonial politics, but they guard against the equally unsatisfactory politics of optimism and hope. Rather than taking up an antisocial orientation, the anticolonial thinkers we have been following, I have demonstrated, suggest we turn instead to a radical politics of the present. Politics can only be "the art of the possible" for those whose lives are secured by the state, or, in other words, only for those who can confidently know that they will live to see the "possible" attained. Those whose lives are not guaranteed by the state, or those whose lives the state actively expects to end, cannot afford the luxury of such politics. The "wretched of the earth" require, instead, an impossible political theory, in the service of a contingent and unknowable present.

These anticolonial practices, which I have suggested are theorized under the rubrics of "reading" and "critique," are interested in envisioning a nonteleological egalitarianism. This egalitarianism might be tentatively staged in the present; it might occur in a future that will not be reached; it might occur fleetingly, ephemerally, unremarkably. To be unknown and unknowable, to abstain and be inconsequential, to relinquish and to disavow: Such readerly projects demand that we reconsider our impulse toward evaluation on the grounds of political "recognition," "success," "failure," "sustainability," and "productivity." These are precisely the imperious prescripts of liberal colonial rule, which promises national independence in return for the proof of liberal "maturity," properly demonstrated in the form of autonomous, self-knowing individuals. Rather than dismissing radical anticolonial projects as impossible or unattainable, it is instead precisely on the grounds of their impossibility that we find they are necessary to refute colonial logics of mastery and totality.

A politics and an aesthetics of impossibility exceed the confines of projects judged alternatively as "successes" or "failures" because the anticolonial and philological critic neither asserts judgmental authority nor appeals to external authorities for their ruling on the matter. To the British Raj, these minor anticolonial gestures were certainly "failures": Har Dayal's revolutionary reworking of nineteenth-century British liberalism did not cure liberalism of its ills, nor India of the British. Post-independence hagiographers of Indian anticolonialism (and anticolonialism more broadly) therefore argue that these insignificant acts were successes: Bhagat Singh's jail notebook is the corroboration for the martyr's role in Indian independence sixteen years after his death. Neither of these stances is satisfactory, but more troublingly, they share the same logic of teleological mastery—of the self and of the nation—which, *because* of its allure, we should relinquish.

Stopping and leaving gesture to the possibility of a collective not "bound by recognition," but rather committed to an unknowable heteronomy, heralded in the preceding example, as Fanon's "comrades."[4] I have written elsewhere that Bhagat Singh's interest in movie-going was a revolutionary practice formed on the basis of its ability to interrupt politics as such in favor of the collective experience of cinema.[5] Har Dayal asks that we stop existing in this world and depart, at least psychically, for that future "World-State," whose past will be our present exit. Anticolonialism is, in the final instance, a project of locating fleeting moments of egalitarian utopias in the relative opacity of an unguaranteed future.

We have reached (or will reach) our conclusion before colonialism will reach its. What antiauthoritarian, anticolonial projects are possible "in the final instance"? What shape does this recalcitrant anticolonialism look like "at the end of the day"? If the form of anticolonialism we are discussing refuses the secure telos of sovereignty or recognition, what are the forms it takes when it reaches an end? What does anticolonialism look like from a Bethesda hospital in 1961, or bedridden and nearly blind in Delhi in 1956? Allow me to suggest that *in the final instance*, anticolonial antiauthoritarian thought demands that we stop, and then, that we leave.

Let us return to two thinkers whom we have considered previously, B. R. Ambedkar and Frantz Fanon, who offer us conclusions that refuse to be ends. Ambedkar and Fanon, thought together, reveal a particular strain of utopian antiauthoritarian thought that was not and could not be exhausted by the telos of its alleged realization, heralded as either (individual) autonomy or (national) sovereignty.

Conscripted to participate in a world they had not chosen, Ambedkar and Fanon nevertheless endeavored to imagine that world otherwise. This vision of a postcolonial future, both alluring *and* grievous, stands at the center of most anticolonial thought. But it was a future that many anticolonial thinkers knew they would never inhabit. Anticolonial thought was written in exile, on deathbeds, in abjection, or in the face of "declined experience."[6] Anti-imperial thinkers sought vocabulary that could simultaneously capture both the grandiose utopianism and self-effacing acquiescence necessary to imagine a world that they would not live to see. They attempted to create a language sufficient to imagine political collectivities motivated by the very fact of their current impossibility. They invented aesthetic forms necessary to imagine a worldwide egalitarianism rooted in the implausibility of any future at all.

It is deeply compelling to align Fanon and Ambedkar to suggest they illustrate the "parallel logics" of race and caste, but this requires a willful and profound misreading of both writers. Put most simply, Fanon's primary concern was Blackness, not "race" (and was therefore psychological and phenomenological); Ambedkar's primary concern was caste, not "Dalit-ness" (and was therefore sociological and historical). More important, both thinkers insistently repudiated the simple parallelism on the grounds that it elided more than it revealed.[7]

Anupama Rao makes a compelling case for putting Ambedkar and Fanon in conversation around the issue of recognition,[8] but I think this runs the risk, similarly, of flattening out important distinctions between their two approaches. Ambedkar was concerned with political recognition in various forms—individual, collective, minoritarian, and national—and then, after resigning from the Constituent Assembly, with political action in the absence of recognition or recognition in excess of politics. Recognition, for Fanon, was phenomenological and existential, which would be, on one hand, to "be able to look the enemy in the eye without trembling,"[9] and, on the other, understanding the desire for various forms of recognition—Black people from white people, Black people as humans, Black people as autonomous but equivalent to white people—as a *mis*recognition (and therefore reification) of the full scale of colonialism and racism.[10] Both Fanon and Ambedkar do reveal, however, the essentially constitutive role that violence plays in the formation of their subjectivities, and the impossibly violent process required for the annihilation of those subjectivities.[11]

Let us instead align Ambedkar and Fanon on the basis of their shared commitment to rendering anticolonialism truly synonymous with antiauthoritarianism, as well as their shared acknowledgement that such political ideals were likely unattainable in their lives. We must, therefore, recognize in their anticolonial practices a particular antinihilist nonfuturity. They did not languish in the easy rejection of a postcolonial future, and they were not convinced that any predictable future was necessarily securable. It is possible to call this body of thought, in its most humble form, "a politics of the meantime," or a politics for those stuck in "the waiting room of history." What anticolonial practices could take care of people whose anonymous deaths would certainly precede utopia? But in grander terms, this is a radical politics of the present, or what Kama Maclean has called a "politics of impatience."[12] Unable to sit and wait for a formal revolution to occur, these thinkers imagined ways of enacting it in the present in minor, unintelligible, and illegible ways.

A Point of Departure

Fanon's conclusion to *The Wretched of the Earth* should draw our attention to a particular strain of "stopping and leaving" that refuses by abstaining, resisting, or walking away. Fanon's call to "leave [*quitter*] this Europe" is addressed to a heteronomous collectivity of "comrades" who are encouraged to stop trying to emulate Europe (for "they will do a better job than the best of us" at that murderous task). Instead, Fanon's comrades must "look for something else." Such a disruption makes it possible to "endeavor to create a new man." But despite its seemingly grandiose appeal, Fanon's call is mitigated by two curious rhetorical moments. First is his admission that there is nowhere to go: How does one leave "every corner of the world?" Second is his insistence that to "stop and leave" will only be in service of a mere attempt. "To endeavor to create" (*tenter de mettre sur pied*), a phrase he uses twice, is decidedly *not* synonymous with "to create," as most analyses have assumed. Stopping and leaving, in Fanon's formulation, is yet another experiment at the impossible. It is to leave without having anywhere to go. It is to stop a dominant continuity without guarantees, except one: that, by leaving, we will become an "us"; or, in other words, comrades.

We might be surprised by the addressee of Fanon's demand. After all, shouldn't it be Europe who stops and leaves? By 1961, Europe had, indeed, begun to leave: India, Pakistan, Ghana, Kenya, Vietnam, and Indonesia had achieved national independence from the English, French, and Dutch Empires. A year after Fanon's death, France would abruptly and disastrously abandon its North African colonial holdings. If you ask Europe to leave, it might eventually do so, but, as Fanon had diagnosed across his writings, there were plenty of people keen to take Europe's exact place.

Moreover, "the wretched of the earth" must stop and leave because, as Fanon had written in *El Moudjahid* in October 1958, colonialists (and colonial apologists) will perpetually insist that empire "stop leaving" (*halte à l'abandon*). To "stop leaving" is to insist on continuing and staying; to colonize is to insist on continuity.[13] Continuity, consequentiality, and progression toward maturity thus mark the logics of colonial rule. Colonial rule promises a future where we will come closer and closer to realizing ourselves as mature, self-knowing, productive, self-ruling subjects. To "stop leaving" this world is to reproduce it, to participate in engendering a future already mastered in advance.

To "stop and leave," on the other hand, is to refuse and therefore rupture this continuity. What happens if we stop "maturing," refuse the promises of liberal self-mastery that we might attain?

We, the Discontinuous

Fanon's more common phrase to describe the behavior of colonizers is that they "never stop" (*ne cesse*). Europeans "never stopped placing white culture in opposition to other noncultures," they "never stopped complaining that the 'native' was slow," and, in the conclusion: Europe "never stops talking of man yet massacres him at every one of its street corners."[14] National independence is no guarantee of colonialism "stopping"; Fanon is especially pessimistic on this point. Colonialism "never stops," even if it has changed faces, because new leaders have "slurped every lesson" from their European predecessors.[15]

Even if violence is necessary for national independence (a claim that Fanon makes ambivalently), it is also impossible, though perhaps in a different sense than the one we have been discussing. Violence will certainly rid a colony of its colonizers, but if it "never stops," then its end is "collective suicide."[16] "The apotheosis of independence becomes the curse of independence" because it is the end of *a* colonial rule but not of *colonialism*.[17] Declarations of national sovereignty, burdened with "narrow-minded nationalism" and "magnificently worded phrases straight out of Europe's treatises on ethics and political philosophy" are the proof that "colonialism has continued uninterrupted."[18] Or: that it has never stopped.

As David Marriott has written, Fanon should be read as "maintaining freedom as a difficult question that cannot be resolved," rather that committed to teleological freedom.[19] Instead, Fanon's anticolonial project is one of perpetual discontinuity, a "necessary interruption of all thought of purpose or final ends."[20]

Colonialism continues after colonial rule because, as Fanon repeatedly argues in *The Wretched of the Earth*, the post-independence subject insists on his individual sovereignty over and above relinquishing his power to the collectivity of the masses. The individual, with "his barely veiled wish to be assimilated to the colonizer's world," rejects spontaneity in favor of predictability, knowability, and colonial recognition.[21] The masses—anonymous, heteronomous, spontaneous—require the individual to "step aside" in favor of community.[22] The masses do not seek recognition; they seek "increased affinities" and act in ways that, to borrow Marriott's phrase, "cannot be entirely predicted or known in advance, and in whose future inheritance we necessarily remain bewildered and perplexed."[23]

Fanon's anticolonialism is a "strategy of immediacy" foregrounded on "the exemplary discontinuity of the revolutionary moment" and "the contingent, the singular, or the violent impropriety of his own thinking."[24] This politics requires imagining and foregrounding, in the face of imminent or certain death, projects not accountable to regimes of recognition but rather to the time being, the passing moment, and the final instance. We must stop; we must leave our own selves in favor of the collectivity of unknown comrades.

These unknowable masses are the "comrades" Fanon invites into being. Who are "we," these "comrades"? Sartre, in his introduction, makes a well-intentioned mistake of assuming it is *solely* Black men talking with one another.[25] But I think we cannot be so sure: This "we" is also an "invitation" or a "prompt to tune in" to an "unsettled collectivity."[26] It is a "we" that cannot be decided upon, decreed, or known in advance because it is also a "we" that will exist, at some point, without us.[27] To be sure, it is a "we" that can be ignored (or, alternatively, spied upon). Those who "never stop" (except to "stop leaving") are certainly set to receive significant benefits: recognition, sovereignty, and self-mastery. But this apotheosis is its curse because those individuals will have inherited a murderous antihumanism. The "us" that is formed by refusing to continue and refusing to stay is ephemeral, fleeting, and shifting; it is risky, unproductive, often unrecognizable. It is political and aesthetic; Jaaware calls "us" a "fiction of our togetherness" and "an impossible limitless ... that we need."[28] This "us" is both necessary and impossible. It is not created simply by stopping and leaving—we have relinquished the security of certitude. But if we stop and leave, and do so together, we can at least endeavor to create it.

Leaving the Fold

Ambedkar interrogated thoroughly the politics of stopping and leaving. Some of these experiments were to the chagrin of Dalit communities who sought his advice and support. In an address to Dalit sex-workers in Bombay in June 1936, Ambedkar says, "there are only two ways open to you. Either you remain where you are and continue to be despised and shunned or you give up your disgusting professions and come with us ... I insist you must give up this degrading life."[29] He is booed and chased out of the room by the women, who are shocked at his sudden resort to moralizing and respectability politics. Without denying the paternalism of Ambedkar's demand, I suggest we nevertheless note a fundamental distinction between Gandhi's and Ambedkar's projects: Where Gandhi might have said "stop" (a reasonable assumption based on his lectures to other sex-workers),[30] Ambedkar offers, additionally, "... and come with us." Stop, Ambedkar demands, and leave, *with us*—an "us" that now has expanded its reach and endeavored to create a new collectivity.

Ambedkar theorized "stopping and leaving" multiple times in his career in order to refuse colonial or Brahmanical authority. Allow me to describe two of them briefly so we can have time to linger on Ambedkar's final act of anticolonial refusal—a refusal he asserts "in the final instance."

One: At a protest in Mahad, Maharashtra in 1927, Ambedkar burns a copy of the *Manusmriti* and calls on the 3,000 Dalit protesters to stop scavenging, eating carrion, and begging.[31] In his address to women the following day, he demands they either stop having children or stop raising their children as "untouchable." An editorial written against the protest uses Ambedkar's own words to suggest that "untouchables have only themselves to blame for their untouchability." Ambedkar responds: for too long "untouchables" have enabled caste Hindus ("touchables") by remaining in their villages. Not simply is it necessary to stop, Ambedkar writes, but Dalits must "walk a new path ... It is difficult to walk a new path without one showing it. ... [I] hope that [Dalits] will take the lead in emancipating our own people."[32] In short: Stop, leave with us, endeavor to emancipate each other.

Two: Following the 1940 Lahore Resolution, in which the All-India Muslim League demands the creation of Pakistan as a separate nation-state, Ambedkar offers what seems like spiritless support. "If [Muslims] want to be a different nation, it is not because they have been, but because they want to be," he concludes.[33] Ambedkar, throughout his career, was deeply ambivalent about sovereignty, weighing the benefits of recognition (liberty) against the egalitarianism of an ever-shifting shared consciousness (fraternity).[34] A cohesively "shared sentiment" among Muslims, otherwise absent in Indian politics, produces an "us" that will stop negotiating with the Hindu majority and leave. But Ambedkar adds a significant warning: The Muslim League's demand for national sovereignty (as opposed to "community") will replicate the authoritarian logic of the British Raj *and* the Hindu-majority state. Because there are no minoritarian "organic filaments" that would have otherwise produced "occasional social cohesion," Pakistan will discover that it has not "stopped and left"; Pakistan will have inextricably tethered itself to the continuity of imperial dominance. Pakistan's Muslims will leave without stopping.

Ambedkar's protest at Mahad and his analysis of Pakistan represent two significant points in a career of theorizing minoritarian community, representation, authority, and sovereignty up to his work on the Indian Constitution. Moreover, these two moments portend Ambedkar's renunciation of politics altogether in 1951. Throughout the 1920s and 1930s, Ambedkar insistently argued that liberty and equality were necessary but insufficient conditions for a "society" that could guarantee egalitarianism; only fraternity could be the essential requirement for social, and therefore political, egalitarianism. The creation of Pakistan would ensure liberty, but its society would have been forged by the shared desire for recognition (perhaps equality), not a desire for egalitarianism (and therefore fraternity). In Ambedkar's estimation, this might be fine for Muslims. But for Dalits, *in the final instance*, Ambedkar chose fraternity.

In the final instance: Two months before his death, Ambedkar stopped and left. On October 14, 1956, alongside 500,000 Dalits, Ambedkar converted to Buddhism. The spectacle of his religious conversion has garnered much scholarly attention, which has tended to view Ambedkar's longstanding concern with Buddhism as proof that "conversion" as either a political stunt or a simple process of changing his mind.[35] Ambedkar's choice of Buddhism was measured, cautious, and studious, allowing him to, in Anupama Rao's phrasing, "underscore the impossible yet necessary task of annihilating caste."[36]

In the 1920s, Ambedkar had threatened to leave Hinduism, and had entertained the possibility of converting to Islam, Sikhism, and Christianity. He found none of these particularly appealing. Following his catastrophic loss to Gandhi in Poona in 1932, Ambedkar began to give lectures on "leaving the Hindu fold." In a speech to the Bombay Presidency Mahar Conference in Bombay in May 1936, Ambedkar offered Buddhism as the only possible way to eradicate caste. Shortly before his death he published *The Buddha and His Dhamma* and had just finished *Buddha or Karl Marx* when he died in December 1956. For twenty years, Ambedkar experimented hesitantly and unknowingly with religious conversion. Even though *Buddha or Karl Marx*, Ambedkar's posthumous essay, technically answers Ambedkar's two-decades-long question—which practice, Buddhism or Marxism, offers the greatest possibility of egalitarianism—the answer, Buddhism, hardly appears straightforward or assertive.[37]

But the October 1956 mass conversion was a fairly decisive moment, in both Ambedkar's life as well as in Dalit history. Rao has identified Ambedkarite religious and political experimentation as constituting (and perpetually re-constituting) a new collectivity. Ambedkar's decision to convert might be framed as follows: to stop being a Hindu (which is to say, an untouchable); to leave "the fold"; and to endeavor to create a new religious-social-political collectivity.

Buddhism was a purposeful and provocative choice. As Gail Omvedt has traced, moreover, Buddhism was an improbable, anachronistic, and irrelevant choice.[38] Dalits, as Hindu "untouchables," were (in theory) allowed "reservations," or guaranteed positions at universities, government positions, and jobs. By converting to Buddhism, Ambedkar not only stopped being "untouchable" but, more radically (especially for someone who had drafted its constitution), Ambedkar stopped seeking the security of the state. He left the privileges it might have offered on the conditions of obedience to its terms. Moreover, Buddhism's relationship with Hinduism asserts a minoritarian politics of entangled equivalence rather than difference (which is why Ambedkar, although he was attracted to Sikhism because of its historically anti-caste politics, found it nevertheless an unsatisfactory option).

Ambedkar's critics wondered what would be gained by conversion. He responded:

> The Untouchables it is true will not gain wealth by conversion. . . . Politically the Untouchables will lose the political rights that are given to the Untouchables. This is, however, no real loss. . . . Socially, the Un-

touchables will gain absolutely and immensely because by conversion the Untouchables will be members of a community whose religion has universalized and equalized all values of life. Such a blessing is unthinkable for them while they are in the Hindu fold.[39]

As Ajay Skaria has written, Ambedkarite Buddhism articulated an egalitarianism built on the grounds of Dalit universalism.[40] Christophe Jaffrelot writes that Ambedkar's conversion was "not an escape; nor was it purely an individual step. Collective conversion was the expression of a social revolt."[41] Conversion is social gain in two senses: first, in the sense of a value immediately granted; second, in the sense that the social itself gains and expands the conditions of its inclusion.

In *Buddha and His Dhamma*, his posthumously published guide to Dalit Buddhism—or Navayana (new-departure) Buddhism—Ambedkar argues for a collectively fraternal Buddhism that stops caste and walks away, but without leaving others to suffer. Ambedkar's particular form of Buddhist renunciation does not abandon others: Its perpetual and fungible fraternity renders the collective a site of asylum for others who have also stopped and left—as well as others who are not able to. In Leela Gandhi's formulation, Ambedkar's Buddhism is "an initiation into leaving," in order to "abandon abandonment and exit exclusion."[42] As Jaaware writes, "Running away, abandoning, is necessary for the annihilation of caste and the collective reconfiguration of the idea of equality and democracy."[43] To refuse to leave the stranger while simultaneously leaving the world in which that stranger might involuntarily remain is the core concern of Dalit Buddhism. In *Buddha and His Dhamma*, Ambedkar's formulation is somewhat more extensive, and we might track this by way of his reinvigoration of Pali vocabulary. The virtues are as follows:

First: *sila*, which is "to avoid to do evil."

Second: a combination of *nekkhama* and *dana*, which involve renunciation of the world, but tempered by *upekka*, which requires remaining in the world, an act that is a refusal to be detached from suffering.

Third: *virya*, which is "right endeavor. It is doing with all your might whatever you have undertaken to do"; to create anew. Coupled with *khanti* and *upekka* (doubled), this requires "forbearance" and "remaining unmoved by the result and yet engaged in the pursuit of it."

Fourth: *karuna* and *maitri*, the determination (*adhithana*) to extend "loving kindness," "fellow feeling," and universal fraternity to "all living beings."[44]

Ambedkar's new path of Dalit Buddhism might be tentatively phrased this way: We must stop and leave with others, but to leave our process of stopping if others are not able to stop and leave with us, and, in the meantime, to endeavor to create a world in which those others might, having attempted to leave, stop and find refuge. In so doing, one offers herself to a particular sociality of strangers who might not yet be known (or touched).

Ephemeral collective effervescence, marked by the elective (though constrained) affinities of mass conversion, is made possible by the fleeting politics of having stopped and left the fold, with thousands of anonymous others. Ambedkar's conversion to Buddhism is "leaving the Hindu fold," while relinquishing, simultaneously, the sovereignty of insuperable difference. Ambedkar's conversion thus foregrounds its own necessity and impossibility. This is a radical interruption to the procreative continuity of caste oppression. Ambedkarite Buddhism is an assertion that the world should be otherwise but that it won't be. It is on the *basis* of this tragic condition, not in spite of it, that we must endeavor to create a heteronomous egalitarian collectivity. That "us" will be ephemeral, incomplete, and imperfect, but that hotchpotch mélange "us" might "reconstruct the world."[45]

No Exit

Stopping, quitting, leaving, and exiting are by no means unique to anticolonial critique. Moses left Egypt (after he stopped being enslaved); Thoreau left Boston (after he stopped supporting slavery). Mark Satin refused to participate in the Vietnam War and left the United States for Canada. Richard Wright and James Baldwin left the United States for Paris, not despite their commitment to anti-racist activism, but in order to continue to disrupt racism's stronghold. Jennet Kirkpatrick has drawn on some of these thinkers to theorize "the virtues of exit" as a mode of political refusal and a demand for politics to be otherwise. The goal of exiting—of stopping and leaving—is "to disrupt, interrupt, or even unseat those in power." More important, exiting is never abandonment. Kirkpatrick emphasizes, correctly, the necessity of a *collective* exit as well as the necessity to conceive of the exit not as "a door" but as "an open threshold" so that even an exit remains, in her analysis, that which "invites returning and revisiting" because it remains "attached."[46] Kirkpatrick's exiles, émigrés, and fugitives are compelling figures because, as Alex Livingston has noted, she renders their exits spectacular, physical, and recognizable.[47] But Thoreau was hardly twenty miles from Boston;

Baldwin and Wright discovered in Paris and in Bandung that the grip of anti-Black racism knew few national boundaries.[48] Their exit was directed as a protest against the state: Thoreau and Wright, at least, recognized and demanded recognition from the state they claimed to have left.

M. K. Gandhi was a lifelong advocate of stopping *without* leaving. This manifested in especially pernicious demands on women, Dalits, and Jews, as we discussed in Chapter 3. His suggestion that "untouchables" (*harijan*) "stop" being impure did more to enforce the caste system than dismantle it. His demand that women "stop" being raped is appalling. His plea that Jews "stop" fleeing Nazi Germany was horrifically uninformed. None of these projects were outside of Gandhian logic that the practice of perpetual relinquishment would produce egalitarianism. The problem is that these communities had nothing left to relinquish. Gandhi was unable to theorize from a place of lived subjugation. Framed slightly differently, we might say that Gandhi's demand to stop was fundamentally misguided on two accounts. First, it offered only stopping—a rather blunt negation—without offering leaving. Second, and more important, Gandhi suggests stopping without offering a political and social collectivity that would make doing so possible in the first place.

The anticolonial practices we are tracing here are practices that seek to evade recognition while recognizing others. To recall, the goals of these collective practices are antiauthoritarian in the sense that they assert values of, variously: unrecognizability, indecipherability, unintelligibility, and untraceability in the face of, or perhaps under the nose of, authority. Juliet Hooker's brilliant elucidation of "Black fugitivity" offers another theory of stopping and leaving. "Black fugitivity is oriented . . . to sites of Black freedom that refuse . . . the logics of coloniality and the nation-state," she writes, drawing on Fredrick Douglass's writing.[49] But what does "stopping and leaving" look like when there is nowhere to go?

Ambedkar and his Dalit followers could not leave India: They were in an "impossible position . . . a minority with *nowhere else to go.*"[50] Fanon and his comrades could not leave "this world." The form of anticolonial refusal we have been discussing does not leave so straightforwardly as running and fleeing (though those are the conditions in which anticolonial writing is often produced). Stopping and leaving is a "declined experience" that reveals the egalitarianism of renounced expertise, unfulfilled mastery, and the disavowal of a self-knowing subject. It is the tentative assertion "that the *something* that [one is] should be openly expressed as provisional, revocable, insignificant, inessential, in a word: irrelevant."[51]

For Friends and Others

Readers will remember that points of departure (*Ausgangspunkte*) are also starting points (*Ansatzpunkte*). A philology conducive to *Weltliteratur* offers critique in which mastery is "virtually impossible" and which produces a "work of art" in which "unity is finally ungraspable."[52] It is a critical project whose only imperative is to depart in order to begin again. To enter into the "sudden fiction" of "us" with heteronomous unknown others in the world: such is the project of anticolonial and philological critique in the face of fascism (homogenization) and colonialism (conquest and mastery).[53] It forms what Didier Eribon calls a *morale minoritaire*:

> A set of guidelines of politics . . . an "us" that is at once impossible and inevitable, and which breaks up as it forms; . . . a life of "rupture" and "discontinuity" within a majoritarian world formed by the "continuous"; . . . a morality and a politics as aesthetic—that is to say, common self-creation and reorganization, always reformulating, for which it would be vain to want to eventually make whole, closed, or complete.[54]

Without any guarantees, such minor and inconsequential practices find points of departure for a world that must be otherwise, and, in the meantime, take them as starting points for an ephemeral egalitarianism.

Mimesis required a conclusion for a project that needed to end before an analysis of its inexhaustible subject could be finished because "it would be wholly impossible to give due recognition to everything instructive and interesting."[55] Most scholars think that Auerbach enters the book in his conclusion, where he becomes, perhaps, its protagonist. Auerbach willingly admits, in a later epilegomena, that "*Mimesis* is quite consciously a book that a particular person, in a particular situation, wrote at the beginning of the 1940s."[56] But to say Auerbach shows up as a diegetic character in the conclusion is not quite accurate: The character "Auerbach" has been our Dante (or perhaps our Beatrice) for the journey through "Western Literature," offering plenty of asides and personal commentary along the way.[57] Worse, this claim is often presented as a condemnation of Auerbach, symptomatic of the noxious though enduringly popular belief that humanist scholars should practice a sort of pious, ascetic, other-worldly objectivity (that is, authority) over the texts we study.[58]

Allegedly written without access to libraries and critical editions while in exile in Istanbul, Auerbach worries that his book is non-scholarly—though he is also keen to note that the book owes its existence to the lack of scholarly resources. Edward Said, in various iterations across his career, stretches the drama of Auerbach's claim to its limits—reading, as Aamir Mufti has suggested, Auerbach as text rather than *Mimesis*.[59]

It has now been exhaustively demonstrated that neither Istanbul lacked libraries nor Auerbach colleagues.[60] Istanbul, as Kader Konuk has written, was not uncomplicatedly "outside" of Western Europe in the 1940s (in many ways, it was quite central).[61] But we might place Auerbach's rhetorical excess less in the context of his forced exit from Marburg in 1935 and more in the context of his famous desire to exit the world, in 1952:

> *Paupertas* and *terra aliena*: or something to this effect, can be read in Bernard of Chartres, John of Salisbury, Jean de Meun and many others. *Magnum virtutis principium est*, Hugo of St. Victor writes (Didascali con III, 20), *ut discat paulatim exercitatus animus visi bilia haec et transitoria primum commutare, ut postmodum possit etiam derelinquere. Delicatus ille est adhuc cui patria dulcis est, fortis autem cui omne solum patria est, perfectus vero cui mundus totus exilium est.*
> ... Hugo intended these lines for one whose aim is to free himself from a love of the world. But it is a good way also for one who wishes to earn a proper love for the world.[62]

Said would repeatedly quote Auerbach quoting Hugo of St. Victor, but he rarely bothered with the preceding sentence. The longer selection veers toward a much more curious "sort of renunciation," and not one that can be straightforwardly aligned with asceticism or exile.[63] In his self-conscious reinterpretation of Hugo, Auerbach offers a different sort of politics for the critic. The renunciant who frees himself from a love of the world is a renunciant committed to purity and self-mastery. The critic is a figure, in contrast, who exits the world while knowing there is nowhere to go; she commits instead to the insufficient (*paupertas*) and the unknown (*terra aliena*). Her "philological home is the earth" not because she is an ethically righteous cosmopolitan, but because she has committed to an "earth" (*terra*) that is necessary and impossible to know in its fullness.[64] That is why we should insist that *Mimesis* is a text that is *necessarily* fragmentary, partial, incomplete, imperfect, and inexpert.

We might locate the beginnings of Auerbach's politics of incompletion and inexpertise in the fleeting moments of unknowability at the end of *Mimesis*.[65] The book's final chapter—on Virginia Woolf's *To the Lighthouse*—identifies the radical possibilities of the unaccounted moment, which in turn lays the groundwork for a "philology of world literature" a few years later. The passage that Auerbach chooses is of a particularly fleeting moment, which Woolf captures and extends through what Auerbach identifies as a failed attempt to grasp, from multiple perspectives, the "object truth" of Mrs. Ramsay. Woolf has not only abdicated her "position as the final and governing authority" over her text, but also relinquished her claim to possess a sovereign (if "extremely subjective" and "eccentrically aberrant") account of reality.[66] Woolf has abandoned the individual and "stepped aside in favor of community," to borrow Fanon's phrase.[67]

Seth Lerer argues compellingly that it is here that Auerbach, in Woolf's voice, reveals the underlying methodology of *Mimesis*: "Let's find another picture to cut out."[68] But we might go slightly further here by asking Auerbach's insistent question: "Who is speaking here?"[69] The answer in this case (unlike when Auerbach asks) is fortunately straightforward: It is Mrs. Ramsay, who had, a moment prior, briefly thought to herself: "books . . . grew of themselves. She never had time to read them. Alas! even the books that had been given her, and inscribed by the hand of the poet himself . . . disgraceful to say, she had never read them."[70]

Surrounded by books that she had never found time to read—and will likely never read—it is Mrs. Ramsay who invents a method from necessity. Auerbach, aware that he has not read all the books necessary for his impossible project, has had to rely instead on finding something else to excerpt, another picture to cut out. Unlike Woolf, who relishes in the insufficient sum of subjective accounts of reality, Auerbach—a particular person, in a particular place, in a particular time—offers a method closer to the form of incompletion marked by its extreme subjectivity and eccentric aberrance. Auerbach is the critic who realizes he will never finish reading—even "had we world enough and time."[71]

Lerer argues that Auerbach asserts his method by way of "the most allusive, fragmentary hints" (perhaps like Lala Har Dayal?), producing a "reality" that is, in James Porter's words, "constitutively and tragically incomplete," ineluctably contingent, and "fleeting and provisional."[72] In Auerbach's words, to read and to critique is to move "through the indeterminate and the contingent," to be "no one [who] is certain of anything," and to embrace "mere supposition."[73] Auerbach calls this *Wirklichkeitsauffassung* (literally, "reality-concept-ing" or "reality-conceptualization"): the fleeting experience of grasping the concept of a "reality" that "is diametrically opposed to locating, let alone supplying, definitive answers. Instead, it invites endless interpretation and speculation."[74]

Auerbach captures, in lieu of a total account, a fleeting moment. A fleeting moment in which multiple consciousnesses share an incomplete reality must be "stressed, not in the service of planned continuity, but for its own sake."[75] The moment, the random occurrence (*beliebege Vorgang*), seized from homogenizing continuity, is therefore that very moment when "we" emerge: It is here that we give our individually subjective selves over to the shared anonymity of unknown others' consciousnesses. These moments are "minor, unimpressive, random," and "insignificant."[76] For Auerbach, these are moments that the author has no access to, only the reader who will never have read enough: "For there is always going on within us a process of formulation and interpretation whose subject matter is our own self."[77] To read, to critique, is to relinquish one's self-mastery to the multitudinous collective "we," the discontinuously appearing formulation that is incapable of being absorbed into the authoritarian logics of homogeneity, continuity, and consequence.

Allow me to phrase this method slightly differently. Auerbach's philological critique is: first, to end a project in the face of its ineluctable incompletion and partiality; second, to abandon a world of homogenization in order to embrace a world of perpetual unknowability; and finally, to "surrender ourselves" in order to capture and emphasize that fleeting moment where we become a collective "subject of random moments."[78] Or, even more simply: to stop, to leave, and to endeavor to create a new world and a new human to inhabit it.

"Nothing now remains," *in the final instance*, "but to find him—the reader," Auerbach writes in his afterword to *Mimesis*.[79] At first glance, Auerbach's "reader" seems to stand in opposition to the reader that the thinkers we have been discussing attempted to theorize. That imagined reader, I have hoped to show, is *unfindable*—a figure who is unrecognizable to any authority, whose existence exists, fleetingly, in relative opacity.

Perhaps Auerbach has found himself.[80] Perhaps Auerbach finds himself in Woolf's Mrs. Ramsay, overwhelmed with books neither she nor he had read. But Auerbach presses on: "I hope that my study will reach its readers: both my friends of former years, if they are still alive; as well as everyone else for whom it is destined."[81] The readers—a collective of friends whom the book is "destined" to find—are unknown and unknowable.

What type of criticism is done for friends who might be dead? Auerbach is being literal here: he has read for friends who were unable to flee Nazi Germany, and who have therefore likely died (though he cannot know from Istanbul). Auerbach offers his "work of art" to the anonymous dead, and in the face of his lifelong exile.[82] The resigned, unsatisfied, and inexpert critic has ended an essentially incomplete task. He longs for friends: for friends who have not survived, but also for friends whom he will never know. His readers are inconsequential and anonymous friends, and reading with them will make a fleeting world. Anticolonial and philological thought offer us a model of critique in the service of a world we will not have lived to see. It is an impossible task for an impossible politics, and it is impossibly urgent.

Acknowledgments

Although I have written a book about "readers" who cannot be found and "reading" that leaves no traces, this book owes its existence to the readers I have had the immense fortune of knowing and whose fellow-reading has left its traces in a thousand configurations. While writing this book, my life has been immensely itinerant but rarely lonely. Strangers became friends, more often than not, by reading with me; they made unfamiliar places feel like homes by sharing their books. I am incalculably indebted to these gestures of hospitality and generosity.

Leela Gandhi, Dilip Gaonkar, and Janice Radway have indefatigably supported this project from the start. Their support came, in very different ways, as perpetual challenges to think the world otherwise. I cannot imagine better postdoctoral advisors than Caroline Levine and B. Venkat Mani, who treated me as a peer and colleague well in advance of my having earned that honor. I am grateful that these mentors have since become, additionally, friends. Their mentorship and their friendship are models not only for a professional life in academia, but for an intellectual life in addition to it.

I am grateful for the members of the "revolutionaries" writing groups, especially Kama Maclean and Chris Moffat, who are proof that humanistic inquiry is better when it is collaborative and social. Paul Fleming, Susan Stanford Friedman, and Mahesh Rangarajan are models for how one should endeavor to create intellectual community; they possess a rare combination of curiosity, commitment, and generosity that I can only hope to approximate.

John McGowan and Della Pollock taught me the benefits of asking questions rather than answering them. The following people asked the *exact* right question at the *exact* right time, whether they knew it or not: Nasia Anam, Prathama Banerjee, Laura Brueck, Andrew Campana, Giuliana Chamedes, Avigail Eisenberg, Evelyn Ender, Durba Ghosh, Isabel Hofmeyr, Isabel Huacuja Alonso, Yumi Lee, Alex Livingston, Ania Loomba, Joan Lubin, Deidre Lynch, Evan Mwangi, Arvind Narrain, Sarah Nuttall, Kwame E. Otu, Lucinda Ramberg, Anupama Rao, Simona Sawhney, Mitra Sharafi, Ajay Skaria, and Klaus Yamamoto-Hammering. I have wrestled with those questions in this book, though I doubt I have satisfactorily answered them.

Natalie Melas, Golnar Nikpour, Ragini Tharoor Srinivasan, Josh Tranen, and Parisa Vaziri and gave especially detailed comments on various manuscript verbiage, which made this book substantially better than it had been before them. Bart Scott's intellectual rigor, care, and companionship was a model for the ideal reader imagined in these pages. Three anonymous reviewers responded to this manuscript with so much acumen and care that it briefly felt like I had discovered for the first time my own insistence on the capacious sociability of unknown readers.

There were also afternoon walks in Jahanpanah; bicycle rides along Lake Michigan; midday breaks for swimming; secret dance parties and questionable karaoke; last-minute road-trips to rural towns; cheap frivolous vacations; circuitous conversations across multiple dinners; and that one reading group that will, one day, read all three volumes of Marx's *Capital*. For these necessary diversions, the following people are to blame: Begüm Adalet, Kaelin Alexander, Gregory Beck Rubin, Rehaan Engineer, Fai Jung Leun, Gauri Gill, Eric Green, Elliot Heilman, Michael Kushnir, Alysson Light, Anndrea Mathers, Mostafa Minawi, Seán McKeithan, Alex Mecattaf, Todd Michelson-Ambelang, Prithwindranath Mukherjee, Linde Murugan, Karuna Nundy, Jordan Osserman, Natasha Raheja, Danish Sheikh, Avery Slater, Justin Smith, and Leila Tayeb. My gratitude for these friendships is incalculable. These friends have made a peripatetic life possible by offering me a world full of homes.

My family, David, Mala, and Liz, have supported every one of my projects along the way. My parents have given me freedom and support in equal measure, and they have been role models for how to make a life in which there is always something new to discover. My sister has an unmatched sense of humor and creativity, and I am grateful that she is both a sibling and a friend.

Thomas Lay has been an outstanding editor. His responses to my work, from the beginning, have been incisive, supportive, and challenging. It has been a privilege to work with him and his colleagues at Fordham University Press. I am grateful to Padmaja Anant and her colleagues at Orient Blackswan, who have made it possible for this book to have a life in South Asia. Audiences at the Alternative Law Forum, Brigham Young University, Brown University, Cornell University, Lahore University of Management Sciences, Nehru National Museum and Library, Northwestern University, Queen Mary University London, the University of the Witwatersrand, and the University of Wisconsin–Madison endured lectures taken from earlier versions of this book, and asked difficult questions that made subsequent iterations better. Chapters 1 and 4 first appeared, in slightly different forms, in *Comparative Studies in South Asia, Africa, and the Middle East* and *South Asia: The Journal of South Asian Studies*. The Preface is a condensed version of an essay first published in *PMLA*.

I have relied on the expertise and work of many librarians, archivists, and staff members, especially those at the Bancroft Library (UC Berkeley), the British Library, the National Archives at San Francisco, the Maharashtra State Archives (Mumbai), the National Archives of India (Delhi), and the Nehru National Museum and Library (Delhi).

Two women taught me, in different ways, how to read and think. The first is my grandmother Dorothy Elam, who encouraged me very early on to remain a perpetual novice. Dot insisted on perpetual education in her life as well as mine. Before I was old enough for school, she passed along lessons from her classes in art history and botany; later, she demanded that I pass along lessons from my classes in geometry and minerology. Her book collection was seemingly infinite. The second is Lilian Furst, who, in the guise of an undergraduate independent study, taught me the full inheritance of Jewish philology and comparative literature. For Lilian, reading was the recuperation of a damaged life, even though it is attended by its own infinite risk. She refused to stop reading even after it had become impossible.

The full scope of these women's mentorship will take me more than a lifetime to grasp. To say that I am in perpetual debt to them would suggest that what they taught me could be tallied and enumerated. In the face of incalculability, I offer this book to them with my love and profound respect.

Notes

Preface

1. S. R Ranganathan, *The Five Laws of Library Science* (Madras: Madras Library Association, 1931), 121
2. Ranganathan, *The Five Laws of Library Science*, 126.
3. Ranganathan, *The Five Laws of Library Science*, 132.
4. Macaulay, "Minute on Indian Education," in Mia Carter and Barbara Harlow, eds., *Archives of Empire*, Volume 1 (Durham, N.C.: Duke University Press, 2003), 230.
5. Macaulay, "Minute on Indian Education," 237.
6. See Gauri Viswanathan, *Masks of Conquest: Literary Study and British Rule in India* (New York: Columbia University Press, 2015).
7. See Priya Joshi, *In Another Country: Colonialism, Culture, and the English Novel in India* (New York: Columbia University Press, 2002).
8. Here Ranganathan prefigures part of Bhabha's critique in *Location of Culture* (1994), as well as Viswanathan's in *Masks of Conquest*.
9. Ranganathan, *The Five Laws of Library Science*, 92.
10. Ranganathan, *The Five Laws of Library Science*, 323. Ranganathan's vision of Tompkins County is solely a product of his own imagination. Ranganathan likely chose Ithaca because, although the United States had established central public libraries in cities in the eighteenth century, the first nonurban association of networked libraries was established by Ezra Cornell in Tompkins County in 1864.
11. Ranganathan, *The Five Laws of Library Science*, 360.
12. Ranganathan, *The Five Laws of Library Science*, 360.
13. Ranganathan, *The Five Laws of Library Science*, 360.
14. M. K. Gandhi, *An Autobiography: Or, The Story of My Experiments with Truth* (Navajivan Publishing House, 1948), 268.
15. See B. Venkat Mani, *Recoding World Literature: Libraries, Print Culture, and Germany's Pact with Books* (New York: Fordham University Press, 2017).

Introduction: Impossible Subjects

1. For a thorough biography of Fanon, see David Macey, *Frantz Fanon* (London: Verso, 2000); Alice Cherki, *Frantz Fanon: portrait* (Paris: Seuil, 2000). See also Adam Shatz, "Where Life Is Seized," in *London Review of Books* (January 2017): 19–27.

2. Sartre says that the book stages a conversation occurring among Black men, but he nevertheless views that conversation as though it was staged for white witnesses.

3. Jean-Paul Sartre, "Preface," in Frantz Fanon, *The Wretched of the Earth* (New York: Grove Press, 2004), lxii. For an additional discussion of anticolonial/decolonial dialectics, see George Ciccariello-Maher, *Decolonizing Dialectics* (Durham, N.C.: Duke University Press, 2017).

4. Alice Cherki, "Preface," in Frantz Fanon, *Les damnés de la terre* (Découverte/Poche, 2002). Translation mine.

5. Sartre, "Preface," xlvii.

6. Hannah Arendt, "On Violence" in *Crises of the Republic* (New York: Harcourt Brace, 1972), 116n19, 122.

7. Paige Arthur has a compelling defense of Sartre as an anticolonial interlocutor; she argues that Sartre's *Critique of Dialectical Reason* is a more appropriate pairing with *The Wretched of the Earth* than his preface. See Paige Arthur, *Unfinished Projects: Decolonization and the Philosophy of Jean-Paul Sartre* (London: Verso, 2010). Robert J. C. Young has similarly argued for the importance of Sartre in the genealogy of postcolonial theory; see Robert Young, *White Mythologies: Writing History and the West* (London: Routledge, 2004).

8. I am not suggesting that I can see clearly what Sartre could not; indeed, my brief argument here is that Sartre's mistake was that he thought he could see clearly. Rather than replicate that error, what we might do instead is retain something of Fanon's opacity. This is in the spirit of David Marriott's beautiful work, which accounts for Fanon's "abysmal thought" against the masterly clarity that previous scholars had asserted on Fanon's behalf: "I have become more and more convinced that to have no certainty of judgment is the only certitude that Fanon's conclusion demands" (Marriott, *Whither Fanon?* Stanford, Calif.: Stanford University Press, 2018, ix). My goal here is to highlight the ways in anticolonial thought theorizes its own incertitude, its methods of unintelligibility, and its partial opacity. To render anticolonial thought "legible," in contrast, is the task for the police, not the critic.

9. Hannah Arendt, *Between Past and Future* (New York: Viking, 1961), 171.

10. Jonathan Lear makes a robust defense (and, to some extent, redefinition) of "hope" in his analysis of Plenty Coups. "Radical hope," in Lear's (and Plenty Coup's) sense, is not uncomplicatedly optimistic, but also ineluctably tragic. See Jonathan Lear, *Radical Hope: Ethics in the Face of Cultural Devastation* (Cambridge: Harvard University Press, 2009).

11. David Scott, *Conscripts of Modernity* (Durham, N.C.: Duke University Press, 2004); Talal Asad, "Conscripts of Western Modernity" in Christine Gailey, ed. *Dialectical Anthropology: Essays in Honor of Stanley Diamond: Civilization in Crisis* (Gainesville: University Press of Florida, 1992), 333–51.

12. Anne-Lise François, *Open Secrets* (Stanford, Calif.: Stanford University Press, 2008), xvi.

13. I want to foreground here that I am not arguing that there is "no future," in Lee Edelman's formulation. It is precisely against what has since been dubbed "antisocial

theory" that this project is set. Futures here are not absent—most of the time, they are actively imagined—but they are non-falsifiable futures: unguaranteed, unsecured, unpredictable. Related, readers will also note the absence of "failure" in my analysis. In this sense, my analysis finds Jack Halberstam's *The Queer Art of Failure* inappropriate for anticolonial politics. Although Halberstam's corrective of Edelman is among the most comprehensive and compelling, I find his identification with "failure" equally unsatisfactory. The anticolonial projects I am elucidating here did not have the privilege to "fail," even if some of their experiments never came to pass. Instead, I argue that anticolonialism foregrounds *impossibility* as the basis for political and aesthetical critique. Impossibility bypasses an unsatisfactory pass/fail assessment in favor of irrelevance. Whereas "failure" requires an appraiser, irrelevance seeks to evade such recognition altogether.

14. Henry James, *The Figure in the Carpet and Other Stories* (London: Penguin UK, 2007); William James, *Pragmatism* (Cambridge: Harvard University Press, 1975), 495.

15. Quoted in Sheldon Pollock, "Future Philology? The Fate of a Soft Science in a Hard World," *Critical Inquiry* 35, no. 4 (2009), 519; Edward Said, *Humanism and Democratic Critique* (New York: Columbia University Press, 2002), 58.

16. For an excellent history of philology, see James Turner, *Philology: The Forgotten Origins of the Modern Humanities* (Princeton, N.J.: Princeton University Press, 2014). See also Edward W. Said, *Humanism and Democratic Criticism* (New York: Columbia University Press, 2004); Edward W. Said, *Orientalism* (New York: Vintage Books, 2003).

17. I am indebted to Anna-Marie Jargose's *Inconsequence* (2002) for her conceptualization of this term, though my use here departs from hers in ways that will become obvious as the book moves forward. Leela Gandhi also uses it to reconsider Kant in *Common Cause* (2016). For me, it is additionally important as a rejection of "consequentialism" offered by utilitarian and liberal ethics, especially in Bentham and Mill.

18. I will not rehearse the debates about the uses and abuses of the prefix "post" in "postcolonial" here; it has been entirely unambiguous that most work produced under the name of "postcolonial theory" is built on the fundamental fact that we have yet to experience or reach a time "after" colonialism, though we now write in the wake of the formal colonial rule in most, though far from all, places. "Postcolonial," we should say instead, defines thought that imagines or envisions a world *beyond* colonialism, even if—or especially because—such a world does not and will not exist in the foreseeable present. Postcolonial thought, by this definition, occurred as much in the 1920s and 1930s as it did, as a more formal academic endeavor, in the 1980s and 1990s.

I have chosen to use the terms "anticolonial" and "postcolonial" rather than "decolonial" for a few reasons. "Anticolonial" and "postcolonial" have been the chosen names for scholarly and political traditions marked by impurity, contamination, imperfection, and limitless inclusion without guarantees. "Anticolonial" is *against* colonialism, and in the service of a world without colonialism, but it does not imagine a world uncontaminated by colonialism. Fanon is "anticolonial" in this sense because the "new man" he calls for will not "inherit the earth" but rather will remain *tethered to* the "wretched of the earth." I have not found these commitments and frameworks in the work of the most prominent proponents of "decoloniality" (though I do not presume to think that they are fully representative of the entire conversation). More importantly, I find that the most compelling decolonial theories (like those of Enrique

Dussel) are allies of postcolonial theories—and that the most compelling postcolonial theories are allies of decolonial theories—and so these terms might be more productive as roughly synonymous. Fanon, in French, uses "anticolonial" and "decolonial" interchangeably, though this is less apparent in most English translations of his work. See Walter D. Mignolo and Catherine E. Walsh, *On Decoloniality: Concepts, Analytics, Praxis* (Durham, N.C.: Duke University Press, 2018), especially pages 3–11. For a robust critique of Mignolo, see Timothy Brennan, "Joining the Party," *Postcolonial Studies* 16, no. 1 (2013): 68–78. For a compelling and alternative view, see Enrique Dussel, *Philosophy of Liberation* (Eugene, Ore.: Wipf and Stock Publishers, 2003).

19. Dipesh Chakrabarty, *Provincializing Europe: Postcolonial Thought and Historical Difference* (Princeton, N.J.: Princeton University Press, 2008), 7.

20. Kama Maclean, *A Revolutionary History of Interwar India* (New York: Oxford University Press, 2015).

21. Stefanos Geroulanos, *An Atheism That Is Not Humanist Emerges in French Thought* (Stanford, Calif.: Stanford University Press, 2010); Edmund Husserl, *The Crisis of the European Sciences and Transcendental Philosophy* (Evanston, Ill.: Northwestern University Press, 1970).

22. See Leela Gandhi, "Postcolonial Theory and the Crisis of European Man," *Postcolonial Studies* 10, no. 1 (March 2007): 93–110.

23. Most notably, Ania Loomba's recent work, *Revolutionary Desires* (2018), provides a necessary and long overdue corrective to work in South Asian anticolonial history, which has nearly ignored women activists altogether.

24. In this sense, I hope that this book is in conversation with recent work, especially: Saidiya V. Hartman, *Wayward Lives, Beautiful Experiments: Intimate Histories of Social Upheaval* (New York: Norton, 2019); Avery Gordon, *The Hawthorn Archive: Letters from the Utopian Margins* (New York: Fordham University Press, 2018); and Adam Zachary Newton, *To Make the Hands Impure: Art, Ethical Adventure, the Difficult and the Holy* (New York: Fordham University Press, 2016). See also Ernst Bloch, *The Spirit of Utopia* (Stanford, Calif.: Stanford University Press, 2000); Homi Bhabha, "Introduction to the 1986 Edition," in Frantz Fanon, *Black Skin, White Masks*, trans. Charles Lam Markmann, (London: Pluto Press, 2017).

25. Marriott, *Whither Fanon?*, 236.

26. Bloch, *The Spirit of Utopia*, 229.

27. Leela Gandhi, "The Pauper's Gift: Postcolonial Theory and the New Democratic Dispensation," *Public Culture* 23, no. 1 (January 2011): 27–38.

28. Leela Gandhi, *The Common Cause: Postcolonial Ethics and the Practice of Democracy, 1900–1955* (Chicago: University of Chicago Press, 2014).

29. Gandhi, "Pauper's Gift."

30. Faisal Devji, *The Impossible Indian: Gandhi and the Temptation of Violence* (Cambridge: Harvard University Press, 2012); Julietta Singh, *Unthinking Mastery: Dehumanism and Decolonial Entanglements* (Durham, N.C.: Duke University Press, 2018); Ajay Skaria, *Unconditional Equality: Gandhi's Religion of Resistance* (Minneapolis: University of Minnesota Press, 2016); Joseph S. Alter, *Gandhi's Body: Sex, Diet, and the Politics of Nationalism* (Philadelphia: University of Pennsylvania Press, 2000); Nico Slate, *Colored Cosmopolitanism: The Shared Struggle for Freedom in the United States and India* (Cambridge: Harvard University Press, 2017); Partha Chatterjee, *Nation and Its Fragments Colonial and Postcolonial Histories* (London: Oxford University Press,

1997); Shruti Kapila, "Self, Spencer and Swaraj: Nationalist Thought and Critiques of Liberalism, 1890–1920," *Modern Intellectual History* 4 (2007): 109–27; Maia Ramnath, *Haj to Utopia: How the Ghadar Movement Charted Global Radicalism and Attempted to Overthrow the British Empire* (Berkeley: University of California Press, 2011); Gandhi, *The Common Cause*.

31. Leela Gandhi, *Affective Communities: Anticolonial Thought, Fin-De-Siècle Radicalism, and the Politics of Friendship* (Durham, N.C.: Duke University Press, 2006), 176.

32. One of the most vibrant and overt anticolonial aesthetic critiques is *negritude*, which is unfortunately beyond the scope of this book, though its thinkers' concerns have certainly framed the project. See Gary Wilder, *Freedom Time: Negritude, Decolonization, and the Future of the World* (Durham, N.C.: Duke University Press, 2015).

33. Kandice Chuh, *The Difference Aesthetics Makes: On the Humanities "after Man"* (Durham, N.C.: Duke University Press, 2019), 5. In this book, I follow Chuh's use of "illiberalism." This use is not synonymous with its more common usage, which is meant to describe despotic political practices across the world that are anti-democratic. (This usage is itself imprecise because contemporary anti-democratic practices appear to thrive in "liberal" or "neoliberal" contexts.) The way I am using it—and the way I understand Chuh to use it—renders "illiberalism" as roughly synonymous with "non-liberal" or "extra-liberal." The reason I have chosen to use "illiberal" instead is that it captures, simultaneously, politics that both exceed the boundaries of liberalism ("extra-liberalism") as well as politics that fall radically below its purview ("non-liberal").

34. For a detailed account of these jumps and shifts, see Peter Uwe Hohendahl, *The Institution of Criticism* (Ithaca, N.Y.: Cornell University Press, 1982).

35. Benjamin, *Illuminations*, 254, 263, 255.

36. Philip Weinstein, *Unknowing* (Ithaca, N.Y.: Cornell University Press, 2005), 254. See also Jürgen Habermas, "Walter Benjamin: Consciousness-Raising or Rescuing Critique" in Gary Smith, *On Walter Benjamin: Critical Essays and Recollections* (London, 1991), 90–128.

37. See "The Theory of Criticism" in Walter Benjamin, *Walter Benjamin: Selected Writings*, Howard Eiland and Gary Smith, eds. (Cambridge: Harvard University Press, 1996).

38. "Walter Benjamin Responds to Theodor Adorno," in Theodor Adorno and Fredric Jameson, *Aesthetics and Politics* (London: Verso, 2007).

39. Walter Benjamin, "On *Elective Affinities*" in Benjamin, Eiland, and Smith, *Walter Benjamin*, 334. The possibility of knowing this "truth," however, should remain perpetually foreclosed.

40. Benjamin, "On Elective Affinities," 351.

41. Frantz Fanon, *A Dying Colonialism* (New York: Grove/Atlantic, Inc., 1994).

42. Edward Said, "Introduction," in Erich Auerbach, *Mimesis: The Representation of Reality in Western Literature* (Princeton, N.J.: Princeton University Press, 2013), xix.

43. Virginia Woolf, "How Should a Person Read?" in Virginia Woolf, *The Second Common Reader* (New York: Houghton Mifflin Harcourt, 1986).

44. Marcel Proust, "Days of Reading," in Marcel Proust, *Against Sainte-Beuve and Other Essays* (New York: Penguin, 1994).

45. Walter Benjamin, *Berliner Kindheit um neunzehnhundert: Fassung letzter Hand* (Berlin: Suhrkamp Verlag, 2013).

46. Michel de Certeau, *The Practice of Everyday Life* (Berkeley: University of California Press, 1988); Roland Barthes, *The Pleasure of the Text* (New York: Hill and Wang, 1975).

47. Pascale Casanova, *The World Republic of Letters* (Cambridge: Harvard University Press, 2004), 2–3.

48. Newton, *To Make the Hands Impure*. Rimbaud, quoted in Newton, 31.

49. See D. A. Miller, *The Novel and The Police* (Berkeley: University of California Press, 1988); Eve Kosofsky Sedgwick, *Epistemology of the Closet* (Berkeley: University of California Press, 2008); Anne-Lise François, *Open Secrets: The Literature of Uncounted Experience* (Stanford, Calif.: Stanford University Press, 2008).

50. Dohra Amhad, in a different vein, has argued that anticolonial projects are "incomplete utopias that invite and even demand reader participation." See Dohra Ahmad, *Landscapes of Hope: Anti-Colonial Utopianism in America* (Oxford: Oxford University Press, 2009).

51. Bruno Latour, "Why Has Critique Run Out of Steam? From Matters of Fact to Matters of Concern," *Critical Inquiry* 30, no. 2 (2004): 225–48. "Critique" here aligns with ideology critique and its progeny. See also Rita Felski, *The Limits of Critique* (Chicago: University of Chicago Press, 2015); Elizabeth S. Anker and Rita Felski, eds., *Critique and Postcritique* (Durham, N.C.: Duke University Press, 2017).

52. We should not understate the historical fact that comparativism (in many of its disciplinary formations: including philology, literary studies, history, religion, and anthropology) has colluded with European imperial domination. Nor can we ignore the ways in which imperialist comparativism—marked by belatedness, radical otherness, developmental slowness, and apathetic relativism—continues to structure academic practices today.

53. Édouard Glissant, quoted in Natalie Melas, *All the Difference in the World: Postcoloniality and the Ends of Comparison* (Stanford, Calif.: Stanford University Press, 2007), 37. Glissant's concept of *tout-monde* (roughly, "the world in its totality") is particularly helpful for thinking totalities are not totalizing (not unifying), made possible by infinite and errant relation. See Édouard Glissant, *Traité du tout-monde* (Paris: Gallimard, 1997).

54. Melas, *All the Difference in the World*, 43.

55. Melas, *All the Difference in the World*.

56. Edward Said, "Secular Criticism," in *The World, the Text, and the Critic* (Cambridge: Harvard University Press, 1983).

57. I offer a brief catalogue for the interested reader: In a review of René Wellek's work, Erich Auerbach asks if his *own* life's work could ever form a "unified subject" (quoted in Levin, 50). George Watson concluded that literary criticism is "a record of chaos marked by sudden revolution" (quoted in Wellek, 33). Henry Levin celebrates philological critique as "an endless approximation" (56). In order to resist the temptation to become authoritative, René Etiemble once suggested that comparativists address one another by transliterating their own European languages into Chinese characters. Auerbach famously apologizes at the end of *Mimesis* for an insufficient book. Charles Bernheimer concludes that "comparison is indeed the ... what is it?—activity, function, practice? all of these?—that assures that our field will always be unstable, shifting, insecure, and self-critical" (quoted in Melas, 2).

58. Marcel Detienne, *Comparing the Incomparable* (Stanford, Calif.: Stanford University Press, 2008).

59. Detienne, *Comparing the Incomparable*, 98–99.
60. See Auerbach, *Mimesis*, 557.
61. Timothy Brennan has written extensively on this underappreciated (though by no means hidden) strain in Said's work, especially Said's indebtedness to scholars who were equally committed to a secular world (most notably, Vico and Lukacs). See essays in Adel Iskandar and Hakem Rustom, eds. *Edward Said: A Legacy of Emancipation and Representation* (Berkeley: University of California Press, 2010); Michael Sprinker, ed. *Edward Said: A Critical Reader* (London: Blackwell, 1992). Additionally, Aamir Mufti and Timothy Brennan have addressed these issues in some detail, in different ways. See Aamir Mufti, *Forget English!: Orientalisms and World Literatures* (Cambridge: Harvard University Press, 2016); Aamir R. Mufti, "Global Comparativism," *Critical Inquiry* 31, no. 2 (2005): 472–89; Timothy Brennan, "Edward Said as a Lukácsian Critic: Modernism and Empire," *College Literature* 40, no. 4 (2013); Timothy Brennan, "Fanon for the Present," *College Literature* 45, no. 1 (2018); Timothy Brennan, "Vico and Modern Scientism," *Italian Culture* 35, no. 2 (September 2017): 129–49; Timothy Brennan, *Borrowed Light* (Stanford, Calif.: Stanford University Press, 2014). Edward Said addresses this most directly in *Humanism and Democratic Criticism*, though his interest in Vico and Auerbach appear as early as *Beginnings* and essays in *The World, the Text, and the Critic*.
62. Said, *Humanism and Democratic Criticism*, 59, 73, 61. An analysis that takes texts as existing in history is the foundation for what Said considers "secular criticism" and "worldliness." For Said's original cultivation of these terms, see his essay "Secular Criticism."
63. Said, *Humanism and Democratic Criticism*, 82–83.
64. Sheldon Pollock, "Future Philology," 935. Pollock's notes on Said's "return to philology" here are very interesting but are ultimately ungenerous.
65. This is one of many guiding concerns of Werner Hamacher's curious and provocative *Minima Philologica*. Werner Hamacher, *Minima Philologica* (New York: Fordham University Press, 2015).
66. See Said, *Humanism and Democratic Criticism*; and Édouard Glissant, *Poetics of Relation* (Ann Arbor: University of Michigan Press, 1997); Édouard Glissant, *Caribbean Discourse: Selected Essays* (Charlottesville: University Press of Virginia, 1989); Glissant, *Traité du tout-monde*.
67. John Stuart Mill, *"On Liberty" and Other Writings* (London: Cambridge University Press, 1989).
68. Liberalism names the perpetually amorphous configuration of values, pedagogical projects, practices, and justifications of the British Empire—as well as the alibi for its despotic practices and the supposed conditions for its disingenuously promised departure. For brilliant (though very different) analyses of the interconnections between liberalism and colonialism, the following books are highly recommended: Lisa Lowe, *The Intimacies of Four Continents* (Durham, N.C.: Duke University Press, 2015); J. Barton Scott, *Spiritual Despots: Modern Hinduism and the Genealogies of Self-Rule* (Chicago: University of Chicago Press, 2016); Uday Singh Mehta, *Liberalism and Empire: A Study in Nineteenth-Century British Liberal Thought* (Chicago: University of Chicago Press, 1999); Karuna Mantena, *Alibis of Empire: Henry Maine and the Ends of Liberal Imperialism* (Princeton, N.J.: Princeton University Press, 2010).
69. For histories and analyses of "actual" reading practices, as well as the historicity of reading, in South Asia, see Priya Joshi, *In Another Country: Colonialism, Culture,*

and the English Novel in India (New York: Columbia University Press, 2002); Francesca Orsini, *Print and Pleasure: Popular Literature and Entertaining Fictions in Colonial North India* (Delhi: Permanent Black, 2017); Sanjay Seth, *Subject Lessons: The Western Education of Colonial India* (Durham, N.C.: Duke University Press, 2007); Swapan Chakravorty and Abhijit Gupta, *Print Areas: Book History in India* (Calcutta: Orient Blackswan, 2004); Robert Darnton, "Literary Surveillance in the British Raj: The Contradictions of Liberal Imperialism," *Book History* 4, no. 1 (2001): 133–76. For discussions of English as a South Asian language, see Ragini Tharoor Srinivasan, "South Asia from Postcolonial to World Anglophone," *Interventions* 20, no.3 (April 2018): 309–16; Akshya Saxena, "A Worldly Anglophony: Empire and Englishes," *Interventions* 20, no. 3 (April 2018): 317–24; Rashmi Sadana, *English Heart, Hindi Heartland: The Political Life of Literature in India* (Berkeley: University of California Press, 2012). See also Gauri Viswanathan, *Masks of Conquest: Literary Study and British Rule in India* (New York: Columbia University Press, 2015).

70. De Certeau, *The Practice of Everyday Life*, 170.

71. The thinkers here participated in—or have been conscripted to participate in—genealogies of nationalist anticolonialism. To be sure, their political experimentations were rooted in the demand for Indian independence. But their vision for anticolonialism exceeded national boundaries or nationalist sentiment. Indeed, these activists' anticolonial philosophies were often in direct opposition to nationalism. Bruce Robbins has offered an excellent analysis of the relationship between nationalism and postcolonial theory. See Bruce Robbins, "Secularism, Elitism, Progress, and Other Transgressions: On Edward Said's 'Voyage in,'" *Social Text*, no. 40 (Autumn 1994), 25–37.

72. Gloria Fisk's work on "the good of world literature" offers a particularly lucid account of "good" politics in current defenses of the humanities. See Gloria Fisk, *Orhan Pamuk and the Good of World Literature* (New York: Columbia University Press, 2018).

73. Gandhi, *Common Cause*, 153.

74. Simona Sawhney discusses this in greater detail. See Simona Sawhney, "Death in Three Scenes of Recitation," *Postcolonial Studies* 16, no. 2 (2013); J. Daniel Elam, "The 'arch Priestess of Anarchy' Visits Lahore: Violence, Love, and the Worldliness of Revolutionary Texts," *Postcolonial Studies* 16, no. 2 (2013): 140–54.

75. For a discussion of these circuitously sympathetic anticolonial politics, see Gandhi, *Affective Communities*.

76. Walter Benjamin, "On the Concept of History," in *Illuminations*.

77. Erich Auerbach, "Philology and Weltliteratur," *Centennial Review* 13 (1969); Erich Auerbach "Philology der Weltliteratur," in Walter Muschg, ed., *Weltliteratur; Festgabe für Fritz Strich zum 70. Geburtstag* (Bern: Francke, 1952), 39–50. Edward Said and Marie Said produced the first English translation of this essay (1969), but it is not a particularly good translation. The English translation to consult is in James I. Porter and Jane O. Newman, eds., *Time, History, and Literature: Selected Essays of Erich Auerbach* (Princeton, N.J.: Princeton University Press, 2014).

78. Barbara Johnson, "Philology: What Is at Stake?" in Jan Ziolkowski, ed. *On Philology* (University Park: Pennsylvania State University Press, 1990), 26–29, 29.

79. Hamacher, *Minima Philologica*, 110–11. Hamacher identifies philology as a sort of immaturity (*Unmündigkeit*).

80. Glissant, *Poetics of Relation*, 21.

81. Chuh, *The Difference Aesthetics Makes*, 125.

82. Jaaware, *Practicing Caste* (New York: Fordham University Press, 2019), 195.

83. B. Venkat Mani, *Recoding World Literature: Libraries, Print Culture, and Germany's Pact with Books* (New York: Fordham University Press, 2017), 13.

84. Jaaware, *Practicing Caste*, 10.

85. Departing radically from the inherited tradition of comparativist unknowing and anti-mastery I have traced here, recent scholars have insisted on "world literature" regimes of mastery and knowability, or, in lieu of that, containment and recognizability. To proffer a few examples from the first regime, of mastery and knowability: The world is a "the sum of all forms of literary expression in all the world's languages" (Apter), "one and unequal" (Cheah), a "unity and permanence" (Mufti), a "regime of . . . finite set of entities and relations" (Ganguly), an "ecology" (Beecroft), a "self-organizing, self-enclosed, and self-referential totality" (Hayot), a "universal spirit" (Tagore). Concerningly, most of these conceptions of "the world" are mobilized with reference to Heidegger, whose worlding (*welten*) forces are (at least) sympathetic to world domination. "World literature" under these rubrics is a project that shares the logics of colonial exploration and exploitation.

Relatedly, the second regime, of containment and recognizability, can be largely summarized by reference to the ongoing debates concerning canonicity in the wake of "new critical humanities" and literary interventions in the 1980s and 1990s. Accumulation and expansion of world literary knowledge are necessary endeavors, to be sure, but not without a pernicious logic. This logic envisions a "world" made possible by what Pascale Casanova calls *littérisation*, the process by which texts become literature; or, framed in this book's vocabulary, the granting of literary recognition to texts. Practically speaking, this has tended to involve academics asking recognition for writers from the formerly colonized world on the grounds that they are, in fact, the "Zulu Tolstoy" of Saul Bellow's xenophobic diatribe.

Gloria Fisk, Michael Allan, and Andrew Rubin have interrogated "world literature" as a *practice*. In this sense, they have revealed how "world literature" operates at the nexus of imperial expansion, economic globalization, and local debates about cultural authority.

86. Auerbach, "Philology of *Weltliteratur*," in Porter and Newman, *Time, History, and Literature*, 254.

87. Auerbach is invested, as James Porter has argued, in incompletion, unfulfillment, ungraspability, and contingency. See Auerbach, "Philology of *Weltliteratur*." See also James I. Porter, "Disfigurations: Erich Auerbach's Theory of Figura," *Critical Inquiry* 44, no. 1 (September 2017): 80–113; James Porter, "Old Testament Realism in the Writings of Erich Auerbach," in Shai Ginsburg and Jonathan Boyarin, eds., *Jews and the Ends of Theory* (New York: Fordham University Press, 2019), 187–224. In a different vein, Seth Lerer provocatively argues that philological scholarship *begins* in error, and proceeds with an awareness of its own errantry. See Seth Lerer, *Error and the Academic Self: The Scholarly Imagination, Medieval to Modern* (New York: Columbia University Press, 2002).

88. For a different formulation of this thought, see Jaaware, *Practicing Caste*, 117–18.

89. Didier Eribon, *Une morale du minoritaire: variations sur un thème de Jean Genet* (Paris: Fayard, 2001), 319; translation mine.

90. Didier Eribon, *Une moral du minoritaire*, 294; translation mine.

91. François, *Open Secrets*, xvi.

92. Auerbach, *Mimesis*, 10.

93. Auerbach, *Mimesis*, 552; translation modified.

1. Lala Har Dayal's Imagination

1. Har Dayal, *baraabari de arth*, University of California, Berkeley Bancroft Library, South Asians in North America Collection, no. 342. Hereafter referred to as SANA.

2. Most of the members of the Hindustan Republican Army were jailed or killed in 1925. Chandrashekar Azad, one of the few members to evade capture, reformed the group with others (including Bhagat Singh) and added "Socialist."

3. See Kama Maclean and J. Daniel Elam, "Who Is a Revolutionary?" *Postcolonial Studies* 16, no. 2 (2013): 113–23.

4. That Har Dayal would have known about Bhagat Singh is not surprising. There are many connections between the two writers, including textual citations and familial friendships. Ajit Singh, Har Dayal's colleague in San Francisco, was Bhagat Singh's uncle. Bhagat Singh quoted from Har Dayal's pamphlets in his own publications. See also Kama Maclean, "The Portrait's Journey: The Image, Social Communication, and Martyr-Making in Colonial India," *The Journal of Asian Studies* 70, no. 4 (November 2011): 1051.

5. Har Dayal, "The Social Conquest of the Hindu Race and [the] Meaning of Equality," SANA no. 347; Har Dayal, "The Social Conquest of the Hindu Race," *Modern Review* VI, no. 3 (September 1909): 239–48.

6. Isabel Hofmeyr, *Gandhi's Printing Press* (Cambridge: Harvard University Press, 2013); and Benedict Anderson, *Imagined Communities* (New York: Verso, 1983).

7. HW Hale, *Political Trouble in India 1917-1937* (Allahabad: Chugh Publications, 1973), 64; William C. Hopkinson, CID Reports, National Archives of India—New Delhi, Home Department, Political B, June 1913, no. 5–17.

8. Bhagat Singh's specter, too, haunts our present. See Simona Sawhney, "Death in Three Scenes of Recitation," *Postcolonial Studies* 16, no. 1 (2013), 202–15.

9. For a discussion of "affiliation," see Edward Said, *The World, The Text, The Critic* (Cambridge: Harvard University Press, 1983); and, in the context of anticolonial thought, J. Daniel Elam, "The 'Arch Priestess of Anarchy' Visits Lahore: Violence, Love, and the Worldliness of Revolutionary Texts," *Postcolonial Studies* 16, no. 1 (2013), 140–54.

10. In a conversation with early biographer Dharmavira in 1933, Har Dayal mentions that the book is for the "Hindu youths" obsessed with communalism and "pseudo-nationalism." Emily Brown, *Har Dayal* (Tucson: University of Arizona Press, 1975).

11. Har Dayal, *Hints for Self Culture* (London: Watts & Co., 1934), vii–viii.

12. National Archives of India, New Delhi (hereafter referred to as NAI); Home Political 1934 (35/10/34).

13. Robert Darnton, "Literary Surveillance in the British Raj: The Contradictions of Liberal Imperialism," *Book History* 4 (2001), 133–76.

14. As an example, in 1907, the Director General of the Post Office complained that it should not be his duty to determine sedition by textual analysis (in this case, opening and reading private correspondence) alone. He argued that his office could halt shipment of pre-determined seditious texts, but could not make the decision based on text alone. See NAI Home Political A August 1907 (243–50).

15. NAI Home Political 1934 (35/10/34).

16. Leela Gandhi, "The Pauper's Gift: Postcolonial Theory and the New Democratic Dispensation," *Public Culture* 23, no. 1 (2011), 27–38.

17. Michael Hardt and Antonio Negri, quoted in Leela Gandhi, "The Pauper's Gift," 31.

18. SANA 314.

19. Har Dayal, "Two Things Are Necessary," *Ghadr*, August 11, 1914. National Archives at San Bruno, California, 118. Records of the Office of the U.S. Attorney, Northern District of California. Neutrality Case Files, 1913–1920 (hereafter referred to as NCF); Accession Number 118-72-001, 188-73-001, box 1, folder 2.

20. Maia Ramnath, *Haj to Utopia* (Berkeley: University of California Press, 2011). For Ramnath, this often means "anarchist" in a contemporary (and thus anachronistic) sense. Consequently, many of the most revolutionary religious writings are blanched to an innocuous secularism.

21. The Ghadr Party was not the only organization to rewrite the Indian Mutiny. Marx and Engels had published a series of essays on the Revolt in 1857–1858. Nor was the Ghadr Party's version the first to render the Mutiny into an event for reenacting; V. D. Savarkar's infamous *The History of the First Indian War of Independence* was published five years earlier from London.

22. Har Dayal, "Shabash," South Asians in North America Collection, Bancroft Library, University of California, Berkeley.

23. British Library, Asia/Africa Collection EPP 1/53.

24. The quotation in the heading is from Har Dayal to S. R. Rana, July 29, 1934, in Dharmavira, ed. *Letters*, 131.

25. See the NCF case files at San Bruno.

26. Seema Sohi, "Sites of 'Sedition,' Sites of Liberation: Gurudwaras, the Ghadr Party, and Anticolonial Mobilization," *Sikh Formations* 10, no. 1, 5–22; Har Dayal, *Hints for Self-Culture* (Delhi: Rajkamal Publications, 1948).

27. Dharmavira, "Lala Har Dayal: An Appreciation," in Har Dayal, *Thoughts on Education: Reprint of Articles Originally Published in 1908* (New Delhi: Vivek Swadhyaya Mandal, 1969), 76.

28. Dharmavira, "Lala Har Dayal (A Sketch)," in Har Dayal, *The Letters of Har Dayal*, ed. Dharmavira (Ambala: Indian Book Agency, 1970), 11.

29. See the Har Dayal (Dharmavira) Collection at Nehru Memorial Museum and Library, Manuscript Room, in Delhi, India. Hereafter referred to as NMML.

30. Har Dayal to Madame Rana, May 21, 1910 (NMML).

31. *Collected Works of B. R. Ambedkar*, vol. 5, 136–37. Hereafter referred to as CWBRA.

32. Har Dayal, "Our Educational Problem: Ideals of Education," *Thoughts on Education* (New Delhi: Rajdhani Granthagar, 1969), 1. For more on "association," see Ambedkar's sociological analyses in Chapter 2.

33. Har Dayal, *Hints*, viii.

34. Har Dayal to Raghubar Dayal, July 8, 1925, in Dharmavira, ed *Letters*, 116–18.

35. Har Dayal, *Hints*, 102.

36. Har Dayal, *Forty-Four Months in Germany and Turkey* (London: P.S. King & Son, 1920); Dharmavira, *Lala Har Dayal and Revolutionary Movements of His Time* (Delhi: India Book Company, 1970); and E. Jaiwant Paul, *Lala Har Dayal* (Delhi: Roli Books, 2008).

37. Leela Gandhi, "Postcolonial Theory and the Crisis of the European Man," *Postcolonial Studies* 10, no. 1 (2007): 93–110; and David Omissi, ed., *Indian Voices of the Great War: Soldiers' Letters, 1914–1918* (London: Palgrave Macmillan, 1999).

38. Har Dayal, *Hints*, 360–62.

39. Har Dayal, *Hints*, viii.

40. See Timothy Brennan, *Borrowed Light* (Stanford, Calif.: Stanford University Press, 2018).

41. Har Dayal, *Hints*, 302.

42. Bipin Chandra, quoted in Simona Sawhney, "Bhagat Singh: A Politics of Death and Hope," in Anshu Malhotra and Farina Mir, eds., *Punjab Reconsidered* (Delhi: Oxford University Press, 2012), 377–408; Leela Gandhi, *Affective Communities* (Durham, N.C.: Duke University Press, 2006).

43. In Anupama Rao's words, *Hints for Self Culture* was "secretive and sought possibilities for self-making beneath the state's radar: ethical possibility was cultivated as a response to political foreclosure and [Har Dayal's] own betrayal." See Anupama Rao, "Introduction: Insurgent Thought," *Comparative Studies in South Asia, Africa, and the Middle East* 34, no. 1 (Spring 2014): 6.

44. Har Dayal, *Hints*, viii.

45. At more than fifty pages, "History" was the longest section in "Intellectual Culture." Har Dayal had begun work on a companion volume, "History of Civilization." (Har Dayal to Van Wyck Brooks, August 12, 1934, Special Collections, University of Pennsylvania.)

46. Har Dayal, *Hints*, 71.

47. It should be noted that this section is the only time Har Dayal disagrees with Herbert Spencer.

48. Har Dayal, *Hints*, 83.

49. Har Dayal, *Hints*, 37.

50. Herbert Spencer, *Social Statics* (London: John Chapman, 1851).

51. Christopher Herbert, *Victorian Relativity: Radical Thought and Scientific Discovery* (Chicago: University of Chicago Press, 2001).

52. Shruti Kapila, "Self, Spencer, and *Swaraj*: Nationalist Thought and Critiques of Liberalism, 1890–1920," *Modern Intellectual History* 4, no. 1 (2007), 109–27. Harald Fischer-Tiné, *Shyamji Krishnavarma* (Delhi: Routledge, 2014).

53. See Har Dayal, *Our Educational Problem* (Lahore: Tagore & Co., 1922).

54. SANA 347.

55. Emily Brown considered Har Dayal a "cultural nativist," a simultaneously understandable and also troubling claim given texts like "The Meaning of Equality." The essay opens with the contributions of Buddhism and the Vedas to notions of "equality" but flatly rejects "all the silly talk about reincarnation and realization" when shifting to the bulk of his proposal.

56. That Har Dayal's 1909 "Meaning of Equality," written against the imperial state, returned in 1938 as a defense of Bhagat Singh's anti-state actions, even as Har Dayal himself was crafting *Hints for Self Culture*, seems just. Bhagat Singh's own afterlives are equally unconstrained. Such is the problem of afterlives. See Simona Sawhney, "Death in Three Scenes of Recitation"; Chris Moffat, *India's Revolutionary Inheritance* (Cambridge: Cambridge University Press, 2019).

57. Har Dayal, *Hints*, 4.

58. Har Dayal, *Hints*, 193.

59. Har Dayal, *Hints*, 198–99.

60. Leela Gandhi, *Affective Communities* (Durham, N.C.: Duke University Press, 2006), 19.

61. Har Dayal, *Hints*, 362.
62. Har Dayal, *Hints*, 305.
63. And perhaps, in a particularly Derridean vein, a World-State to-come.
64. See, among others, David Long and Peter Wilson, eds., *Thinkers of the Twenty Years' Crisis* (London: Oxford University Press, 1996); Aldous Huxley, *Brave New World* (1932); H. G. Wells, *The Shape of Things to Come* (1933); George Orwell, "Wells, Hitler, and World State," *Horizon* (London), August 1941.
65. Har Dayal, *Hints*, 362.
66. Har Dayal, *Hints*, 362.
67. Har Dayal, "Shabash," 1912, SANA.
68. Har Dayal, *Hints*, 363.
69. The epigraphs are presented without formal citation. First, from William Morris's "All for the Cause":

There amidst the world new-builded shall our earthly deeds abide,
Though our names be all forgotten, and the tale of how we died.

And Arthur Hugh Clough's "Where lies the land to which the ship would go":

Where lies the land to which the ship would go?
Far, far ahead, is all her seamen know.
And where the land she travels from? Away,
Far, far behind, is all that they can say.

70. *Hints for Self-Culture* is dedicated to "Young-Rationalists," and Har Dayal warns that "if all the children obey and imitate their parents, Mankind is lost.... Old men and women are, as a rule, mere bundles of antiquated prejudices and reaction-patterns, living fossils fit only for a museum of Sociology" (276–77).
71. "Manifesto of the Hindustan Socialist Republican Army," 1929. For a long discussion of "youth" and Bhagat Singh, see Chris Moffat, "Experiments with Political Truth," *Postcolonial Studies* 16, no. 2 (2013).
72. Jack London, *The Little Lady of the Big House* (New York: Macmillan, 1916).
73. See Said, *Beginnings* (New York: Basic Books, 1975).
74. Quentin Skinner, *Visions of Politics* (London: Cambridge University Press, 2002), 86.
75. Brennan, *Borrowed Light*, 64.
76. Har Dayal, *Hints*, 45.
77. Anecdotally, Har Dayal's *Hints for Self-Culture* remained in wide-circulation, especially in Delhi, through the 1970s, where it was often available from street-side kitab-wallas. Even more speculatively, the article I wrote for Nehru Memorial Museum and Library receives at least one hit a day, and often with the search terms "Har Dayal Self Culture." Digital humanities' blind fetishization of data aside, we might at least suggest that this reveals a continued interest in the thinker well beyond any interest in mutiny.
78. Har Dayal to Van Wyck Brooks, April 8, 1934, Van Wyck Papers, University of Pennsylvania Special Collections.

2. B. R. Ambedkar's Sciences

1. James Shotwell, *The Faith of an Historian and Other Essays* (New York: Walker and Company, 1964), 230.

2. The exact topic of the course is unknown, but Boas and Dewey exchanged notes about a collaborative project on comparative ethics. See Gabriel Alejandro Torres-Colona and Charles A. Hobbs, "The Intertwining of Culture and Nature: Franz Boas, John Dewey, and Deweyan Strands of American Anthropology," *Journal of the History of Ideas* 76, no. 1 (2015): 139–62.

3. Beard resigned from Columbia in 1917 and Robinson resigned in 1919; they became two of the founders of the New School for Social Research.

4. Ambedkar's transcript can be found at Francis Pritchett's online collection of documents relating to Ambedkar and his time at Columbia: http://www.columbia.edu/itc/mealac/pritchett/00ambedkar/timeline/graphics/courses.html.

5. Jesús Francisco Chaírez-Garza, "B. R. Ambedkar, Franz Boas and the Rejection of Racial Theories of Untouchability," *South Asia: Journal of South Asian Studies* 41, no. 2, (2018): 281–96.

6. For excellent work about Dalit activism beyond Ambedkar, see Anand Teltumbde, *Dalits: Past and Future* (Delhi: Routledge, 2017); Eleanor Zelliot, *Dr. Babasaheb Ambedkar and the Untouchable Movement* (New Delhi: Blumoon Books, 2004); Eleanor Zelliot, *From Untouchable to Dalit: Essays on the Ambedkar Movement* (New Delhi: Manohar Publications, 1992); Gail Omvedt, *Seeking Begumpura: The Social Vision of Anticaste Intellectuals* (New Delhi: Navayana, 2008); Gail Omvedt, *Understanding Caste: From Buddha to Ambedkar and Beyond* (New Delhi: Orient Blackswan, 2011).

7. B. R. Ambedkar, *Collected Works of B. R. Ambedkar*, vol. 17, p. 53. Hereafter referred to as CWBRA.

8. Aniket Jaaware, *Practicing Caste* (New York: Fordham, 2018).

9. Jorge Luis Borges, "The Library of Babel," in *Collected Fictions* (New York: Penguin Books, 1999).

10. These are all quotations from Nanak Chand Rattu, *Reminiscences and Rememberances [sic] of Dr. B. R. Ambedkar* (New Delhi: Falcon Books, 1995).

11. V. Geetha, "Unpacking a Library: Babasaheb Ambedkar and His World of Books," October 29, 2017, https://thewire.in/caste/unpacking-library-babasaheb-ambedkar-world-books.

12. See Jaaware, *Practicing Caste*, 193–96.

13. See B. R Ambedkar, *Ambedkar: Autobiographical Notes* (Pondicherry: Navayana, 2003).

14. See Anupama Rao, *The Caste Question* (Berkeley: University of California Press, 2009) 149–50.

15. Gopal Guru and Sundar Sarukkai, *The Cracked Mirror* (Delhi: Oxford University Press, 2012), 24.

16. Arun Mukherjee, "B. R. Ambedkar, John Dewey, and the Meaning of Democracy," *New Literary History* 40, no. 2 (2009): 345–70, 368.

17. See James Turner, *Philology: The Forgotten Origins of the Modern Humanities* (Princeton, N.J.: Princeton University Press, 2014).

18. This is the list of sources (collected to the best of my ability) in *Annihilation of Caste* and *Who Were the Shrudras?*, to give a glimpse of the expansive assemblage of Ambedkar's thought, which is not reducible to any individual discipline. Philologists, Indologists, and classicists: E. W. Hopkins, Ferdinand Lassale, M. A. Sherring, George Bühler, George Grote, George Smith, James Bryce, James Burgess, Jean-Antoine

Dubois, John Muir, Julius Jolly, Max Müller, P. V. Kane, R H. Barrow, and William Jones. Sociologists, Social Theorists, Legal Theorists, and Economists: A.E. Crawley, Charles Ellwood, Edward L. Thorndyke, Gabriel Tarde, William Ripley, William Graham Sumner, Emile Durkheim, Franklin Henry Giddings, Henry Mayhew, Stanley Rice, John Dewey, Leslie Stephen, Robertson Smith, William Bateson, and William McDougall. Philosophers and Political Theorists: Albert Venn Dicey, Henri Bergson, J.S. Mill, Karl Marx, Matthew Arnold, Thomas Carlyle, Thomas Strange, and William Morris.

19. Jaaware, *Practicing Caste*, 137.

20. James Turner, *Philology: The Forgotten Origins of the Modern Humanities* (Princeton, N.J.: Princeton University Press, 2014).See also Natalie Melas, *All the Difference in the World: Postcoloniality and the Ends of Comparison* (Stanford, Calif.: Stanford University Press, 2007). See Michel Foucault, *The Order of Things; an Archaeology of the Human Sciences*. (New York: Vintage Books, 1973); Edward W. Said, *Orientalism* (New York: Vintage Books, 2003).

22. Tomoko Masuzawa, *The Invention of World Religions, or, How European Universalism Was Preserved in the Language of Pluralism* (Chicago: University of Chicago Press, 2005). As we will see shortly, that these supposed philological (scientific) "facts" aligned easily with increased anti-Semitism and Islamophobia became increasingly convenient.

23. CWBRA, vol. 7, p. 70. Ambedkar cites Max Müller for proof of this philological argument.

24. CWBRA, vol. 7, p. 78.

25. Masuzawa, *The Invention of World Religions*, 288.

26. Masuzawa, *The Invention of World Religions*, 263.

27. Wendy Doniger and Brian K. Smith, Introduction, in Wendy Doniger, ed. *The Laws of Manu* (New York: Penguin, 1991), page xvii.

28. Patrick Olivelle has most recently argued that "Manu" was a single person, but someone who relied on a team of researchers to collect, distill, and comment on previous assortments of customs and laws. *Manu* means "the wise one" and also serves as the root for the word for "mankind"; in general, laws of these kind were organized around a particular figure whose laws they became. Olivelle notes that *smrti* also means "maxims" (in the sense of platitudes), which would suggest that the book has a considerably less direct relationship to "laws" than it receives credit for. Siraj Ahmed lays the blame squarely on William Jones, which strikes me as an outdated and/or unnuanced claim. See Manu, Patrick Olivelle, and Suman Olivelle, *Manu's code of law: a critical edition and translation of the Manava-Dharmasastra* (New York: Oxford University Press, 2005); Siraj Ahmed, *Archaeology of Babel: The Colonial Foundation of the Humanities* (Stanford, Calif.: Stanford University Press, 2018).

29. For the purposes of this discussion: Most recent scholarship has generally agreed that the *Manusmriti* should be viewed as a *record* of local customs (not law) in the second century BCE. Later commentary and *puranas* (around the eighth century) declare Manu "the authority" (see Olivelle, 69). Warren Hastings proposed British East India Company law based on *Manusmriti* in 1772; William Jones's English translation followed in 1794. Ambedkar works from both Jones's translations as well as later iterations, especially Max Müller's. Ambedkar addresses the use of *Manusmriti* for Hindu

reform movements, especially the Arya Samaj, in *Who Were the Shudras?* For a more comprehensive historical account, see Olivelle's introduction. Doniger and Smith offer a very good history in their introduction (1991).

30. Dorothy Matilda Figueira, *Aryans, Jews, Brahmins: Theorizing Authority through Myths of Identity* (Albany: SUNY Press, 2002), 67.

31. Figueira notes the irony of Manu's authority on the basis of its imaginary author. Figueira, 88.

32. Friedrich Nietzsche, *The Anti-Christ, Ecce Homo, Twilight of the Idols: And Other Writings*, ed. Aaron Ridley (New York: Cambridge University Press, 2005), 177.

33. Nietzsche's footnotes indicate his primary source was Louis Jacolliot's *Les législateurs religieux: Manou-Moïse-Mahomet* (1876). Figueira has shown how most of what Nietzsche claims to find in the *Manusmriti* is actually culled from other sources, and that Nietzsche's "Manu" bears only a philosophical relationship to the versions of Manu that were available to the philologist. A Manu hobbled together from European sources, to recall Said, is not particularly outstanding in nineteenth-century philological philosophizing!

34. Nietzsche outlines these thoughts in, respectively, *Twilight of the Idols* and *Will to Power*.

35. It is curious that Ahmed does not discuss Nietzsche's writings on the *Manusmriti* even though he praises Nietzschean genealogy as the way to resist the alleged authorizing logics of philology. Nietzsche's various considerations of the *Manusmriti* show clearly how philology has always foregrounded, rather than ignored, how its sources become authoritative at the expense of other practices.

36. CWBRA, vol. 3, p. 123.

37. Nietzsche, *Untimely Fragments* (quoted in Figueira, 50).

38. This might be called, in Ahmed's and Porter's use, a "counter-philology."

39. The implications of this second argument, however, should concern us: Claims of cultural authority and expertise, from political representation to debates about world literature, reveal that the strength of nineteenth-century racist human sciences is no less institutionally powerful in the twenty-first century. In Figueira's words, the "brahmanization of theory is complete" (164).

40. See Figueira, 152–53.

41. Ambedkar was upfront about this. See his preface to *Who Were the Shudras*, CWBRA, vol. 7, p. 11.

42. I discuss Mahad in greater detail in the Conclusion. I am using the word "protest" here based on Ambedkar's revisiting of the event in his writings from the 1940s. At the time, Ambedkar called the protest a *satyagraha*, taking the word from Gandhi's lexicon. Ambedkar's declared that his protest was "an insistence on truth" while Gandhi's reliance on Hindu scripture appeared more "as *duragraha* (insistence on untruth)." Ambedkar's discussion of this is reproduced in full in Teltumbde, *Mahad*, 301–3. I discuss *satyagraha* in Gandhi's writings in Chapter 3.

43. Anand Teltumbde, *Mahad: The Making of the First Dalit Revolt* (Delhi: Aakar, 2016).

44. CWBRA, vol. 5, p. 255.

45. See the Editors' Note at the beginning of CWBRA, volume 5.

46. Ambedkar cites, as a model, Lala Har Dayal's early essays on reading. CWBRA, vol. 5, pp. 136–37.

47. My interpretation of Ambedkar differs significantly here from Aishwary Kumar's (whose focus on equality, sovereignty, and autonomy produce a very liberal Ambedkar), though I certainly agree with his claim that "there was no annihilation without faithful, close, and intimate reading" (281).

48. W. E. B. Du Bois, "Sociology Hesitant," *boundary 2* 27, no. 3 (2000): 37–44.

49. William James, *Pluralistic Universe* (Cambridge: Harvard University Press, 1977).

50. See Amanda Anderson and Joseph Valente, eds. *Disciplinarity at the Fin de Siècle* (Princeton, N.J.: Princeton University Press, 2002); Manu Goswami, "'Provincializing' Sociology: The Case of a Premature Postcolonial Sociologist," in *Political Power and Social Theory 24* (Bingley, UK: Emerald Group, 2013); George Steinmetz, ed. *Sociology and Empire* (Durham, N.C.: Duke University Press, 2013).

51. Beginning a history of Afro-Asian solidarity with "color-caste," however, can only really offer a precious and blanched history of solidarity below the color line. The term was offered mostly by well-meaning white sociologists and anthropologists; Du Bois and Ambedkar, among others, were never fully convinced that the term was either useful or accurate. On the contrary, Du Bois and Ambedkar demanded a considerably more difficult (and pessimistic) vision for Afro-Asian solidarity than the trajectory that "color-caste" inaugurates. For a celebratory but comprehensive history of the "color-caste" trajectory, see Nico Slate, *Colored Cosmopolitanism* (Cambridge: Harvard University Press, 2013).

52. Mukherjee, "B. R. Ambedkar, John Dewey, and the Meaning of Democracy," 247.

53. K. N. Kadam, *The Meaning of Ambedkarite Conversation to Buddhism and Other Essays* (Mumbai: Popular Prakashan, 1997).

54. Quoted in Mukherjee, "B. R. Ambedkar, John Dewey, and the Meaning of Democracy," 347.

55. Quoted in Mukherjee, "B. R. Ambedkar, John Dewey, and the Meaning of Democracy," 347.

56. Mukherjee, "B. R. Ambedkar, John Dewey, and the Meaning of Democracy," 349.

57. It should be made clear that Ambedkar was not merely a dutiful advisee who uncritically attempted to implement his advisor's political theory. Scott Stroud has documented nearly every time Ambedkar quoted Dewey, with the implication that Ambedkar could possess no thought that did not first appear in *Democracy and Education* (1916). See, as a representative essay, S. R. Stroud, "The Rhetoric of Conversion as Emancipatory Strategy in India: Bhimrao Ambedkar, Pragmatism, and the Turn to Buddhism," *Rhetorica* 35, no. 3 (2017): 314–45.

58. *Annihilation of Caste*, CWBRA, vol. 1, p. 57. Dewey's words, without quotation marks here, are from *Democracy and Education*, 97–98, 101–2.

59. This term is found elsewhere in *Annihilation of Caste* and is Thomas Carlyle's; its biological references will come into use in Ambedkar's "sociophilic" anti-caste critique, which we will discuss at the end of this chapter.

60. It is important to note here that I am not attempting to reinstate a tired binary of "religious/social" and "political" wherein caste is rendered apolitical through a dehistoricization of its relationship with Hinduism. In this sense, I am following scholars such as Anupama Rao, Eleanor Zelliot, and Anand Teltumbde. At the same time, Ambedkar offers us, in the guise of an anti-caste critique, a model of democracy that exceeds the boundaries of mere politics.

61. Ambedkar, "Evidence Before the Southborough Committee on Franchise," CWBRA, vol. 1, p. 258.
62. "What Gandhi and Congress have Done for the Untouchables," CWBRA, vol. 9, p. 285.
63. Dewey, *Democracy and Education*, 84.
64. Dewey, *Democracy and Education*, 141.
65. John Dewey, "Creative Democracy," in *The Later Works: 1925–1953* (Carbondale: Southern Illinois University Press, 1988).
66. Dewey, *The Later Works: 1925–1953*. Scott Stroud speculates that Dewey's "Creative Democracy" influenced Ambedkar's writings on Buddhism in the 1950s. My claim here, that Ambedkar influenced Dewey, is much easier to textually defend, though it does require that we consider Ambedkar a critic with his own expansive imagination, rather than Dewey's lackey and mimic. See Scott Stroud, "Creative Democracy, Communication, and the Uncharted Sources of Bhimrao Ambedkar's Deweyan Pragmatism," *Education and Culture* 34, no. 1 (2018): 61–80.
67. Henri Bergson, *Key Writings*, ed. Keith Ansell (London: Bloomsbury, 2002), 63.
68. Bergson, *Key Writings*, 117.
69. Bergson, *Key Writings*, 112.
70. Bergson, *Key Writings*, 72.
71. James, *Pluralistic Universe*, 752.
72. Bergson, *Key Writings*, 298.
73. Bergson, *Key Writings*, 296.
74. Lawrence Westerby Howe, "The Process of Endosmosis in the Bergsonian Critique," *The Modern Schoolman* LXV, November 1987, 29–45.
75. Howe, "The Process of Endosmosis in the Bergsonian Critique," 35.
76. For a rich and provocative discussion of this, see Alexandre Lefebvre, *Human Rights as a Way of Life* (Stanford, Calif.: Stanford University Press, 2013).
77. Ambedkar, *Annihilation of Caste*, CWBRA, vol. 1, p. 56.
78. *Annihilation of Caste*, CWBRA, vol. 1, p. 69.
79. Jaaware redefines "society" in favor of "sociability" in his brilliant analysis of touch and caste.
80. *Annihilation of Caste*, CWBRA, vol. 1, p. 56.
81. *Annihilation of Caste*, CWBRA, vol. 1, pp. 72, 77.
82. *Annihilation*, CWBRA, vol. 1, p. 57.
83. Henri Bergson, *The Two Sources of Morality and Religion* (New York: Henry Holt, 1935), 282.
84. In his writings on Buddhism, Ambedkar translates "fraternity" as *maitri*, or "sympathy." On "fraternity" against "isolation" in Ambedkar's writings, see Anjani Kapoor and Manu Bhagavan, "Beyond the Nation: Ambedkar and the Anti-Isolation of Fellowship," in Suraj Yengde and Anand Teltumbde, *The Radical in Ambedkar: Critical Reflections* (Delhi: Penguin Random House, 2018).
85. This is also a critique of caste-Hindu anticolonial activists who claimed "India" as a coherent unit worthy of national sovereignty; the persistence of caste reveals that there is insufficient "shared consciousness" to claim unity.
86. CWBRA, vol. 5, p. 413.
87. Henry Harris, *The Birth of the Cell* (New Haven: Yale University Press, 1999). See also Alexandre Lefebvre and Melanie White, eds. *Bergson, Politics, and Religion* (Durham, N.C.: Duke University Press, 2012).

88. See Gabriel Tarde, *Gabriel Tarde on Communication and Social Influence: Selected Papers* (Chicago: University of Chicago Press, 2011); Tarde Gabriel, *Les lois sociales* (Paris: Les empêcheurs de penser en rond, 1999). John Dewey, in *Democracy and Education*, makes a similar claim: "Society exists through a process of transmission quite as much as biological life" (6).
89. *Who Were the Shudras*, CWBRA, vol. 7, p. 16.
90. *Buddha and His Dhamma*, CWBRA, vol. 11, pp. 596–97.
91. Leela Gandhi, *Common Cause* (Chicago: University of Chicago Press, 2014), 26.
92. Jaaware, *Practicing Caste*, 99.
93. In the same idiom, Jaaware theorizes that one can maintain the individual body, reconceptualized properly as "a macrolevel collection, probabilistically held together" (*Practicing Caste*, 4).
94. *Buddha or Karl Marx*, in CWBRA, vol. 3, p. 448.
95. Jaaware, *Practicing Caste*, 181.
96. Fanon, *Black Skin White Masks*, 4, translation modified; note the doubled meaning of *univers* here, both "universe" and the narcissistic "body," which is its own universe: "Comment s'en sortir . . . ? Nous travaillons à une lyse totale de cet univers morbide. Nous estimons qu'un individu doit tendre à assumer l'universalisme inhérent à la condition humaine." (See Fanon, Frantz. *Peau noire, masques blancs*. Paris: Éditions du Seuil, 1952.)
97. Fanon, *Black Skin White Masks*, 181. This formulation is clearer in the French: "O mon corps, fais de moi toujours un homme qui interrogee!" The demand is not straightforwardly "concluding" in that Fanon describes this final chapter as a "guise of a conclusion." To be clear, this is neither straightforwardly emancipatory nor optimistic. See D. S. Marriott, *Whither Fanon?: Studies in the Blackness of Being* (Stanford, Calif.: Stanford University Press, 2018).
98. Fanon, *Black Skin White Masks*, 181.

3. M. K. Gandhi's Lost Debates

1. Nehru Memorial Museum Library, special collections file (hereafter referred to as NMML): Pyarelal Misc. 21. Published writing by Gandhi is published in the multivolume set, *The Collected Works of Mahatma Gandhi* (New Delhi: Publications Division, Government of India, 1955–1984); hereafter referred to as CWMG. It seems likely that McAleer read *Hind Swaraj* published in its U.S. iteration, *Sermon on the Sea*; regarding the fast, McAleer is referring to an article in *Young India*, July 28, 1920 (CWMG, vol. 21, p. 94). See Gandhi and Haridas Thakordas Muzumdar, *Sermon on the Sea* (Chicago: Universal Publishing, 1924).
2. Pyarelal Files, Misc. 21, NMML.
3. Pyarelal Files, Misc. 21, NMML.
4. Pyarelal Files, Misc. 21, NMML.
5. To my knowledge, Gandhi never uses the word "congruity" or "congruent," though, as we will see shortly, "inconsistency" and "consistency" are, in Gandhi's usage, often interchangeable terms.
6. See Leela Gandhi, *Affective Communities: Anticolonial Thought, Fin-De-Siècle Radicalism, and the Politics of Friendship* (Durham, N.C.: Duke University Press, 2006); Ritu Birla and Faisal Devji, "Guest Editors' Letter: Itineraries of Self-Rule,"

Public Culture 23, no. 2 (May 1, 2011): 265–68; Anthony Parel, *Gandhi's Philosophy and the Quest for Harmony* (Cambridge: Cambridge University Press, 2006).

7. Pascale Casanova, *The World Republic of Letters* (Cambridge: Harvard University Press, 2004).

8. "Secular," in this case, meaning "non-religious." For a clear-sighted focus on Gandhi's commitment to religion, see Ajay Skaria, *Unconditional Equality: Gandhi's Religion of Resistance* (Minneapolis: University of Minnesota Press, 2016).

9. See Aijaz Ahmad, "'Show Me the Zulu Proust': Some Thoughts on World Literature," *Revista Brasileira de Literatura Comparada* 17 (2017): 11–45.

10. Gandhi, *Hind Swaraj and Other Writings*, ed. Anthony Parel, (Cambridge: Cambridge University Press, 2009), 28. See also Gandhi's conclusion to his *Ruskin: Unto His Last; a Paraphrase* (Ahmedabad: Navajivan, 1951), 61–62.

11. M. K. Gandhi, *An Autobiography: Or, The Story of My Experiments with Truth* (Navajivan Publishing House, 1948), chapter 20.

12. See Chapter 52 in Gandhi's *Autobiography*. That Gandhi's *Gita* is largely Anglophone (with its sources going back to William Jones) is more proof that philology's affiliations are neither straightforwardly "colonial" nor "nationalist" but rather multitudinous and unpredictable.

13. Just as Derrida is the Derrida of postcolonial thought, a tangential conclusion to Said's *Orientalism* might argue that English, German, and French are the languages of oriental scholarship. Chapter 2, on Ambedkar's philology, covers this in greater depth.

14. Javed Majeed, *Autobiography, Travel and Postnational Identity: Gandhi, Nehru and Iqbal* (Basingstoke: Palgrave Macmillan, 2007), 289, 239, 241.

15. Majeed, *Autobiography, Travel and Postnational Identity*, 241.

16. Gandhi, *Autobiography*.

17. Skaria, *Unconditional Equality*, 226.

18. Gandhi explains this in a letter to Mirabehn, February 28, 1927: "A vow should be taken, but it may be wrong; not taking a vow is to trust in yourself, but a vow requires that you trust you have heard God correctly—in short, vows themselves are perpetually risking nonsense and falsehood." CWMG, vol. 38, p. 171.

19. *The Vegetarian*, June 20, 1891 (in CWMG, vol. 1, p. 48).

20. These are the values that Nehru complains, in his own *Autobiography*, that Gandhi lacked.

21. Faisal Devji, in a personal conversation (April 12, 2018), provocatively suggested that some of Gandhi's words appear to have been translated *into* Gujarati *from* English (and then back again).

22. Shruti Kapila's work on this is especially compelling. See Shruti Kapila, "Gandhi before Mahatma: The Foundations of Political Truth," *Public Culture* 23, no. 2 (May 1, 2011): 431–48; Shruti Kapila, "Self, Spencer and Swaraj: Nationalist Thought and Critiques of Liberalism, 1890–1920," *Modern Intellectual History* 4 (2007): 109–27.

23. Skaria, *Unconditional Equality*, 291.

24. Gandhi, *An Autobiography*, Chapter 28.

25. For a dense but rewarding discussion of this, see Sibaji Bandyopadhyay, *Three Essays on the Mahabharata: Exercises in Literary Hermeneutics* (New Delhi: Orient BlackSwan, 2016), 129–30.

26. Gandhi uses this term repeatedly in his *Autobiography*.

27. Devji's *Impossible Indian* makes this claim more thoroughly, and in the context of the 1857 Mutiny.

28. See Julietta Singh, *Unthinking Mastery: Dehumanism and Decolonial Entanglements* (Durham, N.C.: Duke University Press, 2018). Suresh Sharma and Tridip Suhrud, "Editors' Introduction," in Tridip Suhrud et al., *An Autobiography, or, The Story of My Experiments with Truth: A Table of Concordance* (New Delhi; London: Routledge, 2010); Tridip Suhrud, "Translating Sovereignty," in Antoinette M. Burton and Isabel Hofmeyr, *Ten Books That Shaped the British Empire: Creating an Imperial Commons* (Durham, N.C.: Duke University Press, 2014), 153–67; Aishwary Kumar, *Radical Equality: Ambedkar, Gandhi, and the Risk of Democracy* (Stanford, Calif.: Stanford University Press, 2015). Gandhi repeatedly explains that he is uninterested in "completion" or "complete renunciation." See, for example, his notes on this in CWMG vol. 78, pp. 368–69.

29. Ajay Skaria, "Relinquishing Republican Democracy: Gandhi's Ramarajya," *Postcolonial Studies* 14, no. 2 (2011): 221.

30. This is part of a larger argument that Gandhi makes; Gandhian thought prefers "duties" (to others) over (and against) "rights." See Faisal Devji, *The Impossible Indian: Gandhi and the Temptation of Violence* (Cambridge: Harvard University Press, 2012).

31. *Harijan* (Ahmedabad), May 20, 1939.

32. *Harijan*, May 27, 1939. See Matthew Baxter's outstanding essay on Martin Buber's response to Gandhi: Matthew H. Baxter, "The Jewish Gandhi Question, or, Ich and Swa: Martin Buber and the Five Minute Mahatma," in Daniel Kapust and Helen Kinsella, eds. *Comparative Political Theory in Time and Place: Theory's Landscapes* (London: Palgrave, 2016). See also *Harijan*, September 30, 1939.

34. The italics in this printed apology stand in place of the quotation marks Gandhi did not use. The most obvious source for this phrase is the Bible (1 Kings 19:12; "And after the earthquake a fire; but the LORD was not in the fire: and after the fire a still small voice."), when God speaks to Elijah. To recall, Elijah wanted to prove God's existence by demonstrating the uselessness of sacrificing an animal to false idols. God's lesson for Elijah is that a prophet looks for truth not in the powerful but in the powerless. Elijah refuted idolatry on the basis of power, whereas God speaks not in fires and earthquakes but in a "still small voice." But it seems more likely to have reached Gandhi by a much more circuitous path, not least because Gandhi's "still small voice" almost always comes from "within," which aligns Gandhi's use of the phrase with Quaker abolitionists' use of the phrase in the nineteenth century. Gandhi claims to have learned the phrase from a monk in a Trappist monastery in South Africa (CWMG, vol. 32, p. 197). This was most likely Franz Pfanner, the founder and abbot of the Mariannhill Monastery from 1882 to 1909.

35. *Harijan*, August 18, 1940.

36. See CWMG, vol. 69, p. 197.

37. Margaret Sanger was an early advocate for women's birth control; she was the founder of Planned Parenthood. She was also actively interested in eugenics and was influenced by Katherine Mayo's racist 1927 book, *Mother India*, which argues that Indians are simultaneously too sexually profligate and too sexually emaciated, and therefore in need of foreign intervention. See Mrinalini Sinha, *Specters of Mother India: The Global Restructuring of an Empire* (Durham, N.C.: Duke University Press, 2006); Kumari Jayawardena, *The White Woman's Other Burden: Western Women and South Asia during British Colonial Rule* (New York: Routledge, 1995).

38. The transcript is available in Pyarelal's files at NMML. It was partially published in *Asia* and *The Illustrated Weekly of India* as "Does Mr. Gandhi Know Women?

What He Told Me At Wardha," January 19, 1936. In India, it was published in *Harijan* as "Interview to Margaret Sanger" and "Mrs. Sanger and Birthcontrol" (in CWMG, vol. 68, pp. 190–94). See also Thomas Weber, *Going Native: Gandhi's Relationship with Western Women* (New Delhi: Lotus Collection, 2011).

39. Margaret Sanger, "Does Mr. Gandhi Know Women? What He Told Me At Wardha," *The Illustrated Weekly of India*, January 19, 1936.

40. "Interview to [*sic*] Margaret Sanger," CWMG vol. 68, pp. 190–94.

41. Pyarelal Files, Correspondence (1935–1936), NMML.

42. Gandhi elaborates on this in other parts of the conversation, in passages that need not be reproduced here. The curious reader may find them in Gandhi's *Harijan* account of the interview.

43. Gandhi makes this suggestion a few times throughout the conversation, most notably: "[C.F.] Andrews opposes me tooth and nail. We laugh at each other," and, "Romain Rolland laughs at me."

44. Pyarelal Files, Correspondence (1935–1936), NMML.

45. Gandhi's count fluctuates between 15,000 and 25,000 over the course of his writings and speeches in 1934, likely depending on news reports. British reports suggested fewer deaths.

46. *Harijan*, February 2, 1934 (in CWMG, vol. 63, pp. 38–39).

47. *The Hindu*, January 29, 1934 (in CWMG, vol. 63, p. 50); *The Hindu*, January 26, 1934 (in CWMG, vol. 63, p. 40).

48. CWMG, vol. 63, p. 82.

49. *Harijan,* February 16, 1934 (in CWMG, vol. 63, pp. 165–66).

50. *The Indian Nation*, March 28, 1934 (in CWMG, vol. 63, p. 312).

51. Gandhi might be accused of relinquishing authority in an ironic manner—that is, performing non-authority in order to assert authority or "win" an argument. My argument here, as I have noted throughout this chapter, is to take Gandhi at his word, rather than read him suspiciously. If this a naïve interpretation, please give me up for fooled.

52. Quoted in Paranjape. For a summary and further analyses, see Makarand R. Paranjape, "'Natural Supernaturalism?' The Tagore–Gandhi Debate on the Bihar Earthquake," *The Journal of Hindu Studies* 4, no. 2 (July 2011): 176–204. Ananta Kumar Giri, "Gandhi, Tagore, and a New Ethics of Argumentation," *Journal of Human Values* 7, no. 1 (2001): 43–63. Vinay Lal, "The Gandhi Everyone Loves to Hate," *Economic and Political Weekly.* 43, no. 40 (October 4–10, 2008): 55–64. For a collection of Tagore and Gandhi's correspondence, see Gandhi, Rabindranath Tagore, and Sabyasachi Bhattacharya, *The Mahatma and the Poet: Letters and Debates between Gandhi and Tagore, 1915–1941* (New Delhi: National Book Trust, India, 1997).

53. The next chapter discusses Gandhi's debate with revolutionary activist Bhagat Singh, the only adversary who seemed to have figured out Gandhi's desire for irrelevance. In 1929, the two publicly debated who was *less* in control of the masses, and who was therefore *most* prepared to lead them in political action.

54. B. R. Ambedkar, *Collected Works of B. R. Ambedkar*, vol. 5, p. 387; hereafter referred to as CWBRA.

55. Nagaraj makes the convincing case that, despite their differences, Gandhi finally accepted Ambedkar's argument that caste was social and economic (hence his *khadi* scheme), and Ambedkar finally accepted Gandhi's argument that caste was religious (hence his demand to annihilate Hinduism). D. R. Nagaraj, *The Flaming Feet and*

Other Essays: The Dalit Movement in India (London: Seagull Books, 2011). Faisal Devji suggests that "disagreement" is, in some ways, an insufficient term for thinking the differences between Gandhi and Ambedkar. See Faisal Devji, "Gandhi and Ambedkar, a False Debate," *The Hindu*, February 22, 2016.

56. Ambedkar is the first to offer an analysis of Gandhi's political act in *What Congress and Gandhi Have Done for the Untouchables* (in CWBRA, vol. 9).

57. CWMG, vol. 61, p. 38.

58. See Nagaraj, *The Flaming Feet and Other Essays*, 53.

59. From *Harijan*, quoted in Nagaraj, *The Flaming Feet and Other Essays*, 53

60. Nagaraj, *The Flaming Feet and Other Essays*, 55.

61. Desai misses, of course, the other things that the Dalit boy's absence might prove in a Dalit (non-Gandhian) idiom: the assertion of self-reliance, skepticism of the idea that caste could be solved by working with caste-Hindus, and the creativity to lie in ways that would satisfy caste-Hindus' piety without endangering himself.

62. *Harijan*, June 10, 1933, quoted in Nagaraj, *The Flaming Feet and Other Essays*, 55.

63. Burton and Hofmeyr, eds., *Ten Books That Shaped the British Empire*.

64. This collective of Indian anticolonial agitators in London centered around Shyamji Krishnavarma and Madame Cama in Highgate, and collectively produced an influential periodical, *Indian Sociologist*, featuring articles and essays by Lala Har Dayal and V. D. Savarkar.

65. Vinay Lal's comprehensive essay remains one of the best accounts of this transnational circuit. Lal, "Gandhi's West, the West's Gandhi," *New Literary History* 40, no. 2 (2009): 281–313. See also Parel, *Gandhi's Philosophy and the Quest for Harmony*; as well as essays in Brandon M. Terry and Tommie Shelby, eds., *To Shape a New World: Essays on the Political Philosophy of Martin Luther King, Jr.* (Cambridge: Harvard University Press, 2018) and Jack Turner, *A Political Companion to Henry David Thoreau* (Lexington: University Press of Kentucky, 2009).

66. It seems difficult to square the demand for empirical proof of Gandhi's sources (or limit them to only the texts that appear on this list) with Gandhi's interest in "experimenting" with truth.

67. This works the other way around as well. It is the anti-teleological anti-authoritarianism of Gandhi's project that makes sense of the Ruskin and Carpenter entries in "Some Authorities." Ruskin and Carpenter (and Oscar Wilde) were interested less in the assertion of their own authority, and instead were more interested in practices of hermeneutics and criticism that marked a queer *fin de siècle* politics of non-recognition and liberal self-assertion. See Gandhi, *Affective Communities*.

68. Skaria, "Relinquishing Republican Democracy," 226.

69. Gandhi, *Hind Swaraj*, 10.

70. Gandhi, *Hind Swaraj*. Skaria's translation from the Gujarati version renders this even more provocative: "I understand your thoughts on civilization. I will have to think over them. You must not assume that I can take them in all at once. You must not even keep such hopes." Skaria, "Relinquishing Republican Democracy," 222.

71. Gandhi, *Hind Swaraj*, 40.

72. Gandhi, *Hind Swaraj*, 74.

73. Parel, in Gandhi, *Hind Swaraj*, 46.

74. Simona Sawhney, *The Modernity of Sanskrit* (Minneapolis: University of Minnesota Press, 2009).

75. John J. McAleer, *Ralph Waldo Emerson: Days of Encounter* (Boston: Little, Brown and Company, 1984).

76. Gandhi, *Affective Communities*, 183.

4. Bhagat Singh's Jail Notebook

1. Bhagat Singh, "'Hunger Strikers' Demands (June 24, 1929)," in K. C. Yadav, ed., *Fragrance of Freedom* (Gurgaon: Hope India, 2006), 265–66.

2. Kama Maclean, *A Revolutionary History of Interwar India: Violence, Image, Voice and Text* (New York: Oxford University Press, 2015).

3. Kama Maclean, "Revolution and Revelation, or, When Is History Too Soon?," *South Asia: Journal of South Asia Studies* 39, no. 3 (July 2, 2016): 678–94.

4. See J. Daniel Elam, "The 'Arch Priestess of Anarchy' Visits Lahore," in *Postcolonial Studies* 16, no. 2 (2013): 151. I do not find it useful to single out particular scholars for individual indictment (besides, of course, myself); instead, I am more interested in the rhetorical tics that show up across much of the scholarship on Bhagat Singh as a whole. Readers interested in a bibliography of such work on Bhagat Singh will find a reasonably robust selection scattered—perhaps "commonplaced," or anthologized, in other words—throughout this chapter.

5. In a closely related vein, David Scott examines the relationship between colonial authority (archives, state formations) and postcolonial writing, which has, in the wake of Edward Said and Michel Foucault, asserted a relationship between power and knowledge. How might anticolonial writing, when re-examined, reveal a different logic of power and knowledge with a commitment to egalitarianism and unknowing? See David Scott, *Refashioning Futures* (Princeton, N.J.: Princeton University Press, 1999).

6. Bhagat Singh's philosophical genealogy actually prefigures the now-established canon of democratic theory. In his jail notebook and throughout his writings, he cites the democratic revolutionary theories of Jean-Jacques Rousseau and Thomas Paine, as well as the radical utopian writings of Henry David Thoreau and Friedrich Engels. Singh's writings therefore suggest this academic intellectual canon, so often credited to post-war political theory departments in the United States, had many roots, some of which are more global—not to say more revolutionary—than we tend to imagine.

7. Some pages might have been destroyed by the jail guards or might have been smuggled out for illicit circulation. Pages appear to have been prenumbered in the notebook.

8. S. Irfan Habib, *To Make the Deaf Hear* (Delhi: Three Essays Collective, 2007).

9. Holmes corresponded with Nehru, Gandhi, and Dhan Gopal Mukerji, and published regularly in the Calcutta-based *Modern Review*.

10. Upton Sinclair published several editions of *The Cry for Justice*: 1915, 1921, 1963, and 1964. A 1996 version is also available. (Unlike the 1915 edition, the subsequent editions were published by various leftist publishing organizations in Philadelphia, Boston, and New York. The 1915 edition was self-published from Pasadena, California.) The content differs considerably between the four editions published during Sinclair's lifetime. Bhagat Singh's jail notebook page numbers correspond to the 1915 edition only, not the 1921 edition.

11. Upton Sinclair, *The Cry for Justice: An Anthology of the Literature of Social Protest* (self-published, Pasadena, California, 1915).

12. In 1930, Upton Sinclair sent M. K. Gandhi a signed copy of *The Cry for Justice*. Sinclair to Gandhi, November 26, 1930, Pyarelal Files Misc. #19, Nehru Memorial Museum and Library, New Delhi (hereafter referred to as NMML). He sent other books and pamphlets throughout the 1930s.

13. Sinclair, *Cry for Justice*, 3.
14. Sinclair, *Cry for Justice*, cover.
15. Sinclair, *Cry for Justice*, 18.
16. Sinclair, *Cry for Justice*.
17. Sinclair, *Cry for Justice*, 5.
18. Sinclair, *Cry for Justice*, 21.
19. See Bhagat Singh, "Anarchism," in Yadav, *Fragrance of Freedom*. I have written about this in *Postcolonial Studies* (2013).

20. This account is likely based on Kumari Lajjawati's oral history transcript at NMML.

21. See Chris Moffat's *India's Revolutionary Inheritance* for an additional discussion of the circulation of Bhagat Singh's writings.

22. L. V. Mitrokhin, *Lenin in India* (Delhi: Allied, 1981); Bhupendra Hooja, ed., *A Martyr's Notebook* (Delhi: Sanghar Vidya Sabha Trust, 1994); and Chaman Lal, ed., *The Jail Notebook and Other Writings* (Delhi: LeftWord Books, 2007).

23. Isabel Hofmeyr, *Gandhi's Printing Press* (Cambridge: Harvard University Press, 2014), especially 6–7.

24. Leah Price, *The Anthology and the Rise of the Novel* (Cambridge: Cambridge University Press, 2000).

25. This is not to suggest that commonplaces are never associated with authority and mastery, but the corroboration of this is necessarily other single-author books produced as a result. As I discuss shortly, Bhagat Singh's "other books" are nonexistent despite our historiographical desire to find them.

26. A commonplace book might thus be contrasted with an anthology, especially in Leah Price's outstanding work. *Cry for Justice*'s insistence on radical egalitarianism stands in direct contrast with the didacticism of the editor's notes in the anthologies Price analyzes.

27. David Arnold, "The Self and the Cell: Indian Prison Narratives as Life Histories," in David Arnold and Stuart Blackburn, eds., *Telling Lives in India: Biography, Autobiography, and Life History* (Bloomington: Indiana University Press, 2004), 31. See also Sunil Khilnani, "Gandhi and Nehru," in Arvind Krishna Mehrotra ed., *A Concise History of Indian Literature in English* (Delhi: Permanent Black, 2008), 151–76.

28. Gramsci's complete notebooks give a much better sense of how Gramsci thought, which was more circuitous and tentative than the most common English translation would suggest. The complete notebooks are available in English: Antonio Gramsci, *Prison Notebooks*, ed. Joseph A. Buttigieg and Antonio Callari (New York: Columbia University Press, 2011). The first English translation influenced a substantial amount of work in postcolonial studies, cultural studies, and critical race theory, and therefore remains an important document: Antonio Gramsci, *Selections from the Prison Notebooks of Antonio Gramsci*, ed. Quintin Hoare and Geoffrey Nowell-Smith (New York: International Publishers, 1999). Scholars have foregrounded the importance of philology in Gramsci's writings (and especially his indebtedness to Vico). See especially: Edward W. Said, *The World, the Text, and the Critic* (Cambridge:

Harvard University Press, 1983); Timothy Brennan, "Edward Said as a Lukácsian Critic: Modernism and Empire," *College Literature* 40, no. 4 (2013): 14; Joseph W. Childers, "Of Prison Notebooks and the Restoration of an Archive," *Rethinking Marxism* 18, no. 1 (January 1, 2006): 9–14.

29. See Simona Sawhney, "Death in Three Scenes of Recitation," *Postcolonial Studies* 16, no. 2 (2013): pp. 202–15; and Simona Sawhney, "Bhagat Singh: A Politics of Death and Hope," in Anshu Malhotra and Farina Mir, eds., *Punjab Reconsidered* (Delhi: Oxford University Press, 2012), 377–408. See also Kama Maclean and J. Daniel Elam, eds., *Revolutionary Lives in South Asia: Acts and Afterlives of Anticolonial Political Action* (London: Routledge, 2014).

30. Kama Maclean, "The Portrait's Journey: The Image, Social Communication, and Martyr-Making in Colonial India," in *Journal of Asian Studies* 70, no. 4 (2011): 1051–82.

31. Bipan Chandra, *Nationalism and Colonialism in Modern India* (Delhi: Orient Longman, 1997), 232.

32. It includes scholarship and popular writings in Hindi, Urdu, Punjabi, and English, as well as in Tamil, Telegu, and Kannada.

33. See Leela Gandhi, "The Pauper's Gift," *Public Culture* 23, no. 1 (2011): 27–38.

34. For a fine historical account that nevertheless replicates this masculinist, action-focused philosophy, see Maia Ramnath, *Haj to Utopia* (Berkeley: University of California Press, 2012). I discuss this more extensively in Chapter 1 in my consideration of Lala Har Dayal.

35. Or, perhaps, *actively* "destructive."

36. See the letter from Bhagat Singh to Jaidev Gupta, July 24, 1930, in the appendix of the Gupta Oral History Transcript, NMML.

37. K. C. Yadav and Babar Singh, eds., *Bhagat Singh: The Making of a Revolutionary* (Gurgaon: Hope Press, 2006), 108.

38. Gupta Oral History Transcript, 77, NMML.

39. Yadav and Singh, eds., *Bhagat Singh: The Making of a Revolutionary*, 115.

40. In his oral history transcript at NMML, Durga Das Khanna reports: "At this Bhagat Singh enquired if I had read Gandhiji's speeches. I replied in the affirmative and added that I had been reading the *Young India* regularly for some time and had also read his book the *Hind Swaraj*. This pleased both Bhagat Singh and Sukhdev. They said, 'Well, we are glad that you have the reading habit. This will go a long way to help you in life whether you agree with us or not.'" Durga Das Khanna, interviewed by S. L. Manchanda, Oral History Transcript, May 16, 1976, OHT 294, 6, NMML. Thank you to Kama Maclean for drawing my attention to this.

41. Yadav and Singh, eds., *Bhagat Singh: The Making of a Revolutionary*, 109.

42. Nikhil Govind has written about Bhagat Singh and *Anandamath*. See Nikhil Govind, *Between Love and Freedom* (Delhi: Routledge, 2014).

43. Yadav and Singh, eds., *Bhagat Singh: The Making of a Revolutionary*, 149.

44. Chaman Lal, Introduction in *The Jail Notebook and Other Writings* (Delhi: LeftWord Books, 2007), 23.

45. Kuldip Nayar, *The Martyr: Bhagat Singh—Experiments in Revolution* (Delhi: Har-Anand Publications, 2000).

46. Lal, Introduction, 21–22.

47. According to Shiv Verma, "They were: (1) The Ideal of Socialism, (2) Autobiography, (3) History of Revolutionary Movement in India, (4) At the door of Death." Quoted in Yadav, *Fragrance of Freedom*, 3.

48. Habib, *To Make the Deaf Hear*, 112.

49. There were and remain politically pragmatic reasons for insisting on Bhagat Singh's mastery. These include countering the colonial allegations that his politics were untheorized or irrational commitments to "terrorism." See Kama Maclean, "The History of a Legend: Accounting for Popular Histories of Revolutionary Nationalism in India," in *Modern Asia Studies* 46, no. 6 (November 2012): 1540–71.

50. Chris Moffat, "Experiments in Political Truth," in *Postcolonial Studies* 16, no. 2, 185; see also Chris Moffat, *India's Revolutionary Inheritance: Politics and the Promise of Bhagat Singh* (Cambridge: Cambridge University Press, 2019).51. Shiv Varma, quoted in Lal, Introduction, 22.

52. This is a curious but fairly common historiographical move. Bipan Chandra's essay, "The Revolutionary Terrorists," is a prime example. Throughout the essay, Chandra repeatedly uses the reading lists of the HSRA and Bhagat Singh to "corroborate" the future rewards such reading would accomplish, including an "Indian Revolution." See Bipan Chandra, "The Revolutionary Terrorists," in *Nationalism and Colonialism in Modern India* (Delhi: Orient Longman, 1997), 228–56. I think this is also in line with Anjali Arondekar's analysis of the "missing chapter" of Richard Burton's writings. See Anjali Arondekar, *For the Record:On Sexuality and the Colonial Archive in India* (Durham, N.C.: Duke University Press, 2009).

53. On "ethics" versus "politics," see Leela Gandhi, "The Pauper's Gift." "Semi-public" also refers to studies of print culture more broadly, where print circulation marked both private and public spheres. In my use, "semi-public" may align, in some ways, with Michael Warner's "counterpublic" as a mode of analysis rather than an empirical object. See Michael Warner, *Publics and Counterpublics* (Cambridge: MIT Press, 2001).

54. For a discussion of this point, see Maclean, *A Revolutionary History of Interwar India*, 36. Bhagat Singh's letters from jail signal performatively his willingness to, and even interest in, death.

55. See, for example, "Joint Statement at Court," in Yadav, *Fragrance of Freedom*, 247–54, and Bhagat Singh, "Introduction to *Dreamland*," in Chaman Lal, ed., *The Jail Notebook and Other Writings* (Delhi: LeftWord Books, 2007), 151–56.

56. Isabel Hofmeyr describes M. K. Gandhi's reading practices as "slow," in that they are pitted against "fast" methods of transportation and communication that Gandhi famously disavowed. Bhagat Singh's reading practices might have been more urgent—and therefore "faster"—than Gandhi's. At the same time, I would argue that the opposite of Gandhi's "slow reading" is not "fast reading," but rather "reading towards mastery." In this sense, both Gandhi and Bhagat Singh are theorists of reading as a nonteleological act—even when (or especially when) one reads in the face of imminent death.

57. Leela Gandhi, *Common Cause* (Chicago: University of Chicago Press, 2014), 133.

58. Bipan Chandra, *Nationalism and Colonialism in Modern India*, 249.

59. Bhagat Singh, "Introduction to *Dreamland*," 156. Ram Saran Das was convicted in the 1915 Lahore Conspiracy Case and wrote *Dreamland* while in jail. After his release, he was affiliated with the HSRA, but wavered in his support of revolutionary action. In his essay, Bhagat Singh writes that he strongly disagreed with Ram Saran Das's view of revolutionary action, which is exactly why he was keen to write a supportive Introduction. In other words, reading for Bhagat Singh is not a passive project, but rather an active one that features critiquing and disagreeing with texts.

60. To complete de Certeau's thought: "*Who* reads, in fact? Is it I, or some part of me?" See Michel de Certeau, *The Practice of Everyday Life* (Berkeley: University of California Press, 1984), 173.

61. See Said, *Humanism and Democratic Criticism*.

62. Gandhi, *Common Cause*, 128.

63. Gandhi, *Common Cause*, 145–46. This is a citation from Homi Bhabha, who is, in turn, citing Salman Rushdie, *The Satantic Verses* (New York: Penguin, 1988). In other words, the most vibrant strains of postcolonial theory are indebted in part to anticolonial reading and nonauthorial citation.

64. It seems very possible that Bhagat Singh's "Why I am an Atheist" was inspired by Bertrand Russell's "Why I am not a Christian," a lecture Russell delivered in March 1927 that was subsequently published by Watts & Co. later the same year. Watts & Co. books were distributed in British India—they would later publish former Ghadr Party Leader Lala Har Dayal's books—and it seems likely that Bhagat Singh would have read "Why I am not a Christian" in some form. On the other hand, the connection between these two texts relies primarily on the similarity of their titles. Bhagat Singh had access to other writings on Christianity and Christian agnosticism by Bertrand Russell, most notably Russell's 1927 pamphlet, "Has Religion Made Useful Contributions to Civilization?," the first paragraph of which appears in Bhagat Singh's jail notebook. The other reference, which Bhagat Singh cites directly in his essay, is Mikhail Bakunin's 1872 posthumous and unfinished manuscript, "God and the State." In 1916, Emma Goldman published an English translation of the essay in her publication *Mother Earth*, issues of which Bhagat Singh received through radical Punjabi circuits between San Francisco and Lahore. For more on these circuits of transnational anarchism, see my essay in *Postcolonial Studies, History Workshop Journal*, and the phenomenal analysis in Clare Hemmings, *Considering Emma Goldman* (Durham, N.C., Duke University Press, 2018).

65. Bhagat Singh, "Why I am an Atheist," in Yadav, *Fragrance of Freedom*, 25–28.

66. Edmund Husserl, *The Crisis of the European Sciences and Transcendental Philosophy* (Evanston, Ill.: Northwestern University Press, 1970 [1935]).

67. Emma Goldman, *Living My Life* (New York: Penguin, 2006 [1931]); Randolph Bourne, *War and the Intellectuals: Collected Essays, 1915–1919* (New York: Hackett, 1999); E. M. Forster, *Two Cheers for Democracy* (New York: Harvest, 1962 [1951]); Simona Sawhney, "Bhagat Singh: A Politics of Death and Hope," in *Punjab Reconsidered*, ed. Anshu Malhotra and Farina Mir (London: Oxford University Press, 2012); John Dewey, *Freedom and Culture* (New York: Prometheus, 1989 [1939]); William James, *Pragmatism* (New York: American Library, 1987 [1907]).

68. Stathis Gourgouris, *Lessons in Secular Criticism* (New York: Fordham University Press, 2013), 69. Gourgouris amusingly but concisely makes the distinction between credo-atheism and secularism: "I am not even a secularist. I am an atheist" (65).

69. Gourgouris, *Lessons in Secular Criticism*, 22–24.

70. Edward Said, "Traveling Theory," in *The World, the Text, and the Critic* (Cambridge: Harvard University Press, 1983), 241–71. Quoted in Seth Lerer, "Auerbach's Shakespeare," *Philological Quarterly* 90, no. 1 (2011), 24.

72. Auerbach's dramatic claim that there were no libraries in Istanbul has been the subject of academic debate, which I have partially discussed in the Introduction and

will return to, in a different vein, in the Epilogue. For our purposes here, we may say simply that the validity of this claim is both nonexistent and irrelevant.

73. See Seth Lerer, *Error and the Academic Self: The Scholarly Imagination, Medieval to Modern* (New York: Columbia University Press, 2002), 241.

74. Moffat, *India's Revolutionary Inheritance*.

75. See Erich Auerbach's Afterword to *Mimesis*.

76. Auerbach, *Mimesis*, 574.

77. Sawhney, "Bhagat Singh: A Politics of Love and Death."

78. Mulk Raj Anand, "The Terrorist," *Selected Short Stories* (Delhi: Penguin, 2006), 91.

79. Anand, "The Terrorist," 91–98.

80. Anand, "The Terrorist," 101.

81. To be clear, it was Batukeshwar Dutt who accompanied Bhagat Singh to the Legislative Assembly; Sukhdev was an active member of the HSRA and was hanged alongside Bhagat Singh, but he was not actually present at the bombing.

82. "The Terrorist," then, signals a fundamental rift in the PWA even as early as a year after its founding. For a discussion of Agyeya's work, see Snehal Shingavi, "Agyeya's Unfinished Revolution: Sexual and Social Freedom in Shekhar: Ek Jivani," *South Asia: Journal of South Asian Studies* 39, no. 3 (July 2016): 577–91.

83. For a detailed discussion on this point, see Maclean, *A Revolutionary History of Interwar India*, 119–46.

84. M. K. Gandhi, "The Cult of the Bomb," February 1, 1930, in CWMG, vol. 361.

85. Gandhi, "The Cult of the Bomb."

86. Gandhi's philosophy is too often flattened for philosophical and political exigency, but for a fuller discussion of Gandhi's thought along these lines, see Chapter 3. Here, I am referring only to the particular iteration of the philosophy that appears in "Cult of the Bomb." For a more detailed discussion of the relationship between Gandhi's "non-violence" and HSRA's "violence," see Maclean, *A Revolutionary History of Interwar India*.

87. Gandhi, "The Cult of the Bomb." This replicates, in many ways, the colonial discourse about Bhagat Singh. See Maclean, "The History of a Legend."

88. Ghadar Party, "*Shabash!*," South Asians in North America Collection, no. 342, Bancroft Library, University of California, Berkeley, CA.

89. Again, to be clear, Gandhi describes how his own political/ethical plan should avoid this as well; I discuss this in greater depth in Chapter 3.

90. HRSA, "The Philosophy of the Bomb," Indian Proscribed Tracts, South Asia Microform Project (University of Chicago), Reel 3, item 28, npg.

91. Elam, "The 'Arch Priestess of Anarchy' Visits Lahore."

92. Yadav, *Fragrance of Freedom*, 32.

93. This is made even more complicated by Gandhi's productively promiscuous translations of *satya* (see Chapter 3), with which Bhagat Singh was frustratedly familiar; Gandhi's *satya* could also mean "God" as well as "soul" and "being."

94. As I mentioned in Chapter 3, Bhagat Singh seems to be Gandhi's only adversary who understood Gandhi's desire for irrelevance.

95. Anand, "The Terrorist," 99. The selection here retains the original punctuation used in the short story in order to show the typographical errors that underwrite the alternative reading I am suggesting.

Epilogue: Stopping and Leaving

1. Frantz Fanon, *The Wretched of the Earth* (New York: Grove Press, 2004), 235.
2. See Edward W. Said, *Beginnings: Intention and Method* (New York: Basic Books, 1975).
3. Nanak Chand Rattu, *Reminiscences and Rememberances [Sic] of Dr. B. R. Ambedkar* (New Delhi: Falcon Books, 1995); Gail Omvedt, *Seeking Begumpura: The Social Vision of Anticaste Intellectuals* (New Delhi: Navayana, 2008).
4. Patchen Markell, *Bound by Recognition* (Princeton, N.J.: Princeton University Press, 2003). See also Elizabeth Povinelli, *The Cunning of Recognition* (Durham, N.C.: Duke University Press, 2002); Glen Sean Coulthard, *Red Skin, White Masks: Rejecting the Colonial Politics of Recognition* (Minneapolis: University of Minnesota Press, 2014).
5. J. Daniel Elam, "The Martyr, the Moviegoer: Bhagat Singh at the Cinema," *BioScope: South Asian Screen Studies* 8, no. 2 (December 1, 2017): 181–203.
6. Anne-Lise François, *Open Secrets: The Literature of Uncounted Experience* (Stanford, Calif.: Stanford University Press, 2008).
7. To be sure, "colour-caste" was an important intellectual and political project that preceded them, as well as the concern of many of their contemporaries.
8. Anupama Rao, *The Caste Question: Dalits and the Politics of Modern India* (Berkeley: University of California Press, 2009), 129.
9. D. S. Marriott, *Whither Fanon?: Studies in the Blackness of Being* (Stanford, Calif.: Stanford University Press, 2018), xv.
10. See Marriott, *Whither Fanon?*, 245–46.
11. Rao, *Caste Question*, 167.
12. Kama Maclean, *A Revolutionary History of Interwar India: Violence, Image, Voice and Text* (New York: Oxford University Press, 2015).
13. This is a counterintuitive claim only if we consider European colonial rule across the world to have been "a rupture." On closer inspection, we find that no colonial project has operated this way. In India, for example, Queen Victoria became the Empress of the Raj and the logical successor to the Mughal Empire. John Stuart Mill's famous defense of British rule in India was that its natives were children that needed British help to "mature" into civilized adults (nonage). Imperial rule secures itself in between world history and the future it promises to engender. See also Fanon's chapter on "National Culture" in *The Wretched of the Earth*.
14. Frantz Fanon, *The Wretched of the Earth* (New York: Grove Press, 2004), 150, 135, 236.
15. Fanon, *Wretched of the Earth*, 101.
16. Fanon, *Wretched of the Earth*, 21. See also page 33.
17. Fanon, *Wretched of the Earth*, 54.
18. Fanon, *Wretched of the Earth*, 109, 22.
19. Marriott, *Whither Fanon?*, 36.
20. Marriott, *Whither Fanon?*, 28–29.
21. Fanon, *Wretched of the Earth*, 22.
22. Fanon, *Wretched of the Earth*, 66–67.
23. Marriott, *Whither Fanon?*, 36.
24. Fanon, *Wretched of the Earth*, 83; Marriott, *Whither Fanon?*, 36, 20.
25. Fanon, *Wretched of the Earth*, xlv.

26. Aniket Jaaware, *Practicing Caste: On Touching and Not Touching* (New York: Fordham University Press, 2019), 4; Kandice Chuh, *The Difference Aesthetics Makes: On the Humanities "after Man"* (Durham, N.C.: Duke University Press, 2019); Alexis Shotwell, *Against Purity* (Minneapolis: University of Minnesota Press, 2012), 19.

27. See Marc Crépon, *Murderous Consent* (New York: Fordham University Press, 2019).

28. Jaaware, *Practicing Caste*, 195–96.

29. Quoted in Anupama Rao, *The Caste Question* (Berkeley: University of California Press, 2009), 66

30. Indeed, Gandhi does tell sex-workers to "stop" in his articles on temple prostitution. See Ajay Skaria, "Only One Word, Properly Altered: Gandhi and the Question of the Prostitute," *Postcolonial Studies* 10, no. 2 (June 2007): 219–37.

31. I discuss this scene in Chapter 2 as well; for an exhaustive and outstanding account, see Anand Teltumbde, *Mahad: The Making of the First Dalit Revolt* (Delhi: Aakar Books, 2016).

32. Quoted in Teltumbde, *Mahad*, 123.

33. Ambedkar, *Thoughts on Pakistan*; in B. R. Ambedkar, *Collected Works of B. R. Ambedkar*, vol. 8, p. 353 (hereafter referred to as CWBRA).

34. As Shruti Kapila and Jésus Chàirez-Garza have recently written, Ambedkar's defense of Pakistan relied primarily on Ambedkar's peculiar conceptualization of "sovereignty" as separate from, though parasitical to, "society." See Shruti Kapila, "Ambedkar's Agonism, Sovereign Violence and Pakistan as Peace," *Comparative Studies in South Asia, Africa, and the Middle East* 39, no 1 (2019): 184–95; Jesús Cháirez-Garza, "B. R. Ambedkar, Partition and the Internationalisation of Untouchability, 1939–47," *South Asia: Journal of South Asian Studies* 42, no. 1 (January 2019): 80–96; Jesús Cháirez-Garza, "'Bound Hand and Foot and Handed over to the Caste Hindus': Ambedkar, Untouchability and the Politics of Partition," *The Indian Economic and Social History Review* 55, no. 1 (January 2018): 1–28.

35. The best accounts of this debate can be found in Gauri Viswanathan, *Outside the Fold: Conversion, Modernity, and Belief* (Princeton, N.J.: Princeton University Press, 1998), and Ajay Skaria, "Ambedkar, Marx and the Buddhist Question," *South Asia: The Journal of South Asian Studies*. 38, no. 3 (July 2015): 450–65.

36. Rao, Foreword to Jaaware, *Practicing Caste*, ix.

37. To recall our earlier conversation in Chapter 2, Ambedkar relies heavily on Bergson's *Two Sources of Religion and Morality* in his texts on conversion. His interest here is in "habit" and custom as the practices of Hinduism, over and above law. This is why religious conversion is necessary in addition to (or perhaps instead of) legal reform by the end of Ambedkar's life.

38. Gail Omvedt, *Ambedkar: Towards an Enlightened India* (Delhi: Penguin, 2004).

39. CWBRA, vol. 5, pp. 411–16.

40. Skaria, "Ambedkar, Marx, and the Buddhist Question," and Skaria, "'Can the Dalit Articulate a Universal Position?': The Intellectual, the Social, and the Writing of History," *Social History* 39, no. 3 (2014): 340–58.

41. Christophe Jaffrelot, *Dr. Ambedkar and Untouchability: Fighting the Indian Caste System* (New York: Columbia University Press, 2005), 163. Scott Stroud argues that Ambedkar places "supreme value on individual autonomy" in conversion to Buddhism, a conclusion so illogical that it can only be reached by willfully misreading

Ambedkar's work. See Scott Stroud, "The Rhetoric of Conversion as Emancipatory Strategy in India: Bhimrao Ambedkar, Pragmatism, and the Turn to Buddhism," *Rhetorica* 35, no. 3, 314–45.

42. Leela Gandhi, *Postcolonial Theory: A Critical Introduction*, second edition. (New York: Columbia University Press, 2019), 201.

43. Jaaware, *Practicing Caste*, 6. His claim here is inspired by Ambedkar if not necessarily Ambedkar's Buddhism.

44. Ambedkar, *Buddha and His Dhamma* (in CWBRA, vol. 11, pp. 126–28).

45. Ambedkar uses this phrase, which is indebted to John Dewey's particular use of "reconstruction," throughout his writings on Buddhism. See also Gail Omvedt, *Ambedkar: Towards an Enlightened India* (Delhi: Penguin 2004), 149–50.

46. Jennet Kirkpatrick, *The Virtues of Exit* (Chapel Hill: University of North Carolina Press, 2017), 119–20.

47. Alexander Livingston, "Book Review: The Virtues of Exit: On Resistance and Quitting Politics, by Jennet Kirkpatrick," *Political Theory* 47, no. 4 (August 2019): 612–16.

48. See Richard Wright, *The Color Curtain: A Report on the Bandung Conference* (Oxford: University Press of Mississippi, 1995); James Baldwin, interviewed by Jordan Elgrably, "James Baldwin, The Art of Fiction No. 78," *The Paris Review* 91 (Spring 1984).

49. Juliet Hooker, "'A Black Sister to Massachusetts': Latin America and the Fugitive Democratic Ethos of Frederick Douglass," *The American Political Science Review; Washington* 109, no. 4 (November 2015): 690–702, 692. See also Juliet Hooker, *Theorizing Race in the Americas: Douglass, Sarmiento, Du Bois, and Vasconcelos* (New York: Oxford University Press, 2017) and, though their use of the term is different in significant ways, Stefano Harney and Fred Moten, *The Undercommons: Fugitive Planning & Black Study* (New York: Minor Compositions, 2013).

50. Rao, *The Caste Question*, 159.

51. François, *Open Secrets*; Roland Barthes, Introduction, Renaud Camus, *Tricks: 25 Encounters* (New York: St. Martin's Press, 1981), vii.

52. Erich Auerbach, "Philology of *Weltliteratur*," in James I. Porter and Jane O. Newman, eds., *Time, History, and Literature: Selected Essays of Erich Auerbach* (Princeton, N.J.: Princeton University Press, 2014).

53. Jaaware, *Practicing Caste*, 195.

54. Didier Eribon, *Une morale du minoritaire: variations sur un thème de Jean Genet* (Paris: Fayard, 2001). The translation is mine.

55. Auerbach, *Mimesis*, 559, translation modified. See also page 556.

56. Auerbach, *Mimesis*, 574.

57. In Chapter 1, Auerbach makes a very clear but often overlooked comment on National Socialism, German literary tradition, and the urgency of his project. See James I. Porter, "Erich Auerbach and the Judaizing of Philology," *Critical Inquiry* 35, no. 1 (2008): 115–47.

58. For an excellent critique of this position, see Gloria Fisk, *Orhan Pamuk and the Good of World Literature* (New York: Columbia University Press, 2018).

59. Aamir R. Mufti, "Auerbach in Istanbul: Edward Said, Secular Criticism, and the Question of Minority Culture," *Critical Inquiry* 25, no. 1 (October 1998).

60. See Emily Apter, "Global Translation: The 'Invention' of Comparative Literature, Istanbul, 1933," *Critical Inquiry* 29, no. 2 (2003): 253–81; Fisk, *Orhan Pamuk and the*

Good of World Literature; Mufti, "Auerbach in Istanbul"; and Kader Konuk, *East-West Mimesis: Auerbach in Turkey* (Stanford, Calif.: Stanford University Press, 2010).

61. Konuk, *East-West Mimesis*.
62. Auerbach, "Philology of *Weltliteratur*." Ellipses in the original.
63. Auerbach, "Philology of *Weltliteratur*."
64. Auerbach, "Philology of *Weltliteratur*." For arguments that lean in favor of cosmopolitanism (for good reasons, though ways that do not align with the project I am suggesting here), see Timothy Brennan, *At Home in the World: Cosmopolitanism Now* (Cambridge: Harvard University Press, 1997); Pheng Cheah, Bruce Robbins, et. al., *Cosmopolitics: Thinking and Feeling Beyond the Nation* (Minneapolis: University of Minnesota Press, 1998); and multiple essays in Edward Said, *Reflections on Exile and Other Essays* (Cambridge: Harvard University Press, 2000); and Edward Said, *The World, the Text, and the Critic* (Cambridge: Harvard University Press, 1984).
65. These words appear (seemingly interchangeably) in Auerbach's essay as: *Ansatzpunkt, Ausgangspunkt, Ansatzphänomen*. See Erich Auerbach, "Philogie der Weltliteratur" in Walter Muschg, *Weltliteratur; Festgabe für Fritz Strich zum 70. Geburtstag* (Bern: Francke, 1952), 39–50.
66. Auerbach, *Mimesis*, 536.
67. Fanon, *Wretched of the Earth*, 66–67.
68. Seth Lerer, *Error and the Academic Self: The Scholarly Imagination, Medieval to Modern* (New York: Columbia University Press, 2002), 227.
69. Auerbach, *Mimesis*, 531. For a longer discussion of this, see Erich Auerbach, "On the Serious Imitation of the Everyday," in Gustave Flaubert, *Madame Bovary*, ed. Margaret Cohen (New York: Norton, 2004), 423–29.
70. Woolf, quoted in *Mimesis*, 525.
71. This is the epitaph to *Mimesis*; it is the first line of Andrew Marvell's "To His Coy Mistress" (published in 1681). It is, at first glance, a compelling manifesto for a book that self-consciously attempts a perpetually partial study of "western literature," in the face of what looks like the end of the (western) world. On the other hand, the poem's anti-Semitism is notable ("And you should, if you please, refuse / Till the conversion of the Jews"), and troubles a straightforward reading of this epitaph. Lerer and Porter have both written about this in more depth. We might say, alternatively, that Auerbach is writing at the moment when this "conversion" has become a deathly reality; in other words, we have neither world enough nor time.
72. Lerer, *Error and the Academic Self*, 226, 190; James I. Porter, "Old Testament Realism in the Writings of Erich Auerbach," in Shai Ginsburg, Martin Land, and Jonathan Boyarin, eds., *Jews and the Ends of Theory* (New York: Fordham University Press, 2019), 195, 207. Reviews of *Mimesis* in the 1950s, as Lerer has shown (*Error and the Academic Self*), were keen to emphasize the continuities—"the unbroken flow of learning"—of the book's place in the history of philological comparativism, omitting the "fissures of exile" and its internal "discontinuities of style" in order to make it appropriate for academic reception.
73. Auerbach, *Mimesis*, 10, 532.
74. James I. Porter, "Disfigurations: Erich Auerbach's Theory of Figura," *Critical Inquiry* 44 (Autumn 2017): 80–113, 103. *Wirklichkeitsauffassung* is in Auerbach, *Mimesis* [German edition], 16.
75. Auerbach, *Mimesis*, 552; translation modified.

76. Auerbach, *Mimesis*, 546–47.
77. Auerbach, *Mimesis*, 549.
78. Auerbach, *Mimesis*, 552.
79. Auerbach, *Mimesis*, 557.
80. This is Lerer's provocative suggestion, aligning Auerbach with Dante (*mi ritrovai per una selva oscura*). Additionally, in the same vein, we could suggest Auerbach finding himself in Proust, from his earlier selection in "The Brown Stocking": "*je me retrouvai seul avec maman*" (543).
81. Auerbach, *Mimesis*, 557, translation modified.
82. Auerbach, "Philology of *Weltliteratur*," 260.

Bibliography

Primary and Secondary Sources

Adorno, Theodor. *Minima Moralia: Reflections on a Damaged Life*. London: Verso, 2005.
Adorno, Theodor, and Fredric Jameson, et. al. *Aesthetics and Politics*. London: Verso, 2007.
Agnani, Sunil M. *Hating Empire Properly: The Two Indies and the Limits of Enlightenment Anticolonialism*. New York: Fordham University Press, 2013.
Ahmad, Aijaz. *In Theory*. London: Verso, 2007.
———. "'Show Me the Zulu Proust': Some Thoughts on World Literature." *Revista Brasileira de Literatura Comparada* 17 (2017): 11–45.
Ahmad, Dohra. *Landscapes of Hope: Anti-Colonial Utopianism in America*. Oxford: Oxford University Press, 2009.
Ahmed, Siraj. *Archaeology of Babel: The Colonial Foundation of the Humanities*. Stanford, Calif.: Stanford University Press, 2018.
———. "Notes from Babel: Toward a Colonial History of Comparative Literature." *Critical Inquiry* 39, no. 2 (Winter 2013): 296–326.
Alessandrini, Anthony. *Frantz Fanon and the Future of Cultural Politics: Finding Something Different*. Lanham, Md.: Lexington Books, 2014.
———, ed. *Frantz Fanon: Critical Perspectives*. New York: Routledge, 1999.
Allan, Michael. *In the Shadow of World Literature: Sites of Reading in Colonial Egypt*. Princeton, N.J.: Princeton University Press, 2016.
Alter, Joseph S. *Gandhi's Body: Sex, Diet, and the Politics of Nationalism*. Philadelphia: University of Pennsylvania Press, 2000.
Ambedkar, B. R. *Ambedkar: Autobiographical Notes*. Pondicherry: Navayana, 2003.

———. *Collected Writings of B. R. Ambedkar*. Bombay: Education Department, Government. of Maharashtra, 1979.
Anand, Mulk Raj. *Selected Short Stories*. Delhi: Penguin, 2006.
Anderson, Amanda, and Joseph. Valente, eds. *Disciplinarity at the Fin de Siècle*. Princeton, N.J.: Princeton University Press, 2002.
Anderson, Benedict. *Imagined Communities: Reflections on the Origin and Spread of Nationalism*. Rev. ed. London: Verso, 2006.
Andrews, C. F. *Mahatma Gandhi's Ideas (1929): Including Selections from His Writings*. London: Routledge, 2016.
Anker, Elizabeth S., and Rita Felski, eds. *Critique and Postcritique*. Durham, N.C.: Duke University Press, 2017.
Appadurai, Arjun. "Our Gandhi, Our Times." *Public Culture* 23, no. 2 (May 1, 2011): 263–64.
Appadurai, Arjun, et al. "Mission Statement Responses." *Comparative Studies of South Asia, Africa and the Middle East* 33, no. 2 (August 28, 2013): 137–39.
Apter, Emily. *Against World Literature: On the Politics of Untranslatability*. London: Verso, 2013.
———. "Global Translation: The 'Invention' of Comparative Literature, Istanbul, 1933." *Critical Inquiry* 29, no. 2 (2003): 253–81.
———. *The Translation Zone: A New Comparative Literature*. Princeton, N.J.: Princeton University Press, 2006.
Arendt, Hannah. *Between Past and Future*. New York: Viking, 1961.
———. *Crises of the Republic*. New York: Harcourt Brace, 1972.
———. *The Human Condition*. Chicago: University of Chicago Press, 1998.
———. *Origins of Totalitarianism*. New York: Schocken Books, 1951.
Arnold, David, and Stuart Blackburn, eds. *Telling Lives in India: Biography, Autobiography, and Life History*. Bloomington: Indiana University Press, 2004.
Arnold, Sir Edwin. *The Light of Asia: Or, The Great Renunciation*. London: Kegan Paul, Trench, Trübner, 1892.
Arondekar, Anjali R. *For the Record: On Sexuality and the Colonial Archive in India*. Durham, N.C.: Duke University Press, 2009.
Arthur, Paige. *Unfinished Projects: Decolonization and the Philosophy of Jean-Paul Sartre*. London: Verso, 2010.
Asad, Talal. "Conscripts of Western Modernity" in Christine Gailey, ed. *Dialectical Anthropology: Essays in Honor of Stanley Diamond: Civilization in Crisis*. Gainesville: University Press of Florida, 1992, 333–51.
———. *Is Critique Secular?: Blasphemy, Injury, and Free Speech*. Berkeley: Townsend Center for the Humanities, University of California, 2009.
Auerbach, Erich. *Dante: Poet of the Secular World*. New York: NYRB Classics, 2007.
———. *Mimesis: Dargestellte Wirklichkeit in Der Abendländischen Literatur*. Bern: A. Francke A. G. Verlag, 1946.
———. *Mimesis: The Representation of Reality in Western Literature*. Princeton, N.J.: Princeton University Press, 2013.

———. "Philologie der Weltliteratur." In *Weltliteratur; Festgabe für Fritz Strich zum 70. Geburtstag*, edited by Walter Muschg, 39–52. Bern: Francke, 1952.
———. "Philology and Weltliteratur." Translated by Edward Said and Marie Said. *Centennial Review* 13 (1969).
Bandyopadhyaya, Sibaji. *Three Essays on the Mahabharata: Exercises in Literary Hermeneutics*. New Delhi: Orient BlackSwan, 2016.
Barthes, Roland. *The Pleasure of the Text*. New York: Hill and Wang, 1975.
Baucom, Ian. *Specters of the Atlantic: Finance Capital, Slavery, and the Philosophy of History*. Durham, N.C.: Duke University Press, 2005.
Baxter, Matthew H. "The Jewish Gandhi Question, or, Ich and Swa: Martin Buber and the Five Minute Mahatma." In Daniel Kapust and Helen Kinsella, eds. *Comparative Political Theory in Time and Place: Theory's Landscapes*. London: Palgrave, 2016.
Beecroft, Alexander. *An Ecology of World Literature: From Antiquity to the Present Day*. Brooklyn, N.Y.: Verso, 2015.
Benjamin, Walter. *Berliner Kindheit um neunzehnhundert*. Berlin: Suhrkamp Verlag, 2013.
———. *Illuminations: Essays and Reflections*. New York: Schocken Books, 1968.
———. *Reflections: Essays, Aphorisms, Autobiographical Writings*. New York: Schocken Books, 1968.
———. *Walter Benjamin: Selected Writings*. Edited by Howard Eiland and Gary Smith. Cambridge: Harvard University Press, 1996.
Bergson, Henri. *Creative Evolution*. New York: H. Holt, 1913.
———. *Key Writings*. Edited by Keith Ansell. London: Bloomsbury, 2002.
———. *The Two Sources of Morality and Religion*. New York: H. Holt, 1935.
Berman, Marshall. *All That Is Solid Melts into Air: The Experience of Modernity*. New York: Simon and Schuster, 1981.
Beverley, John. *Against Literature*. Minneapolis: University of Minnesota Press, 1993.
Bhabha, Homi K. *The Location of Culture*. London: Routledge, 1994.
Bipan Chandra. *Nationalism and Colonialism in Modern India*. Delhi: Orient Longman, 1979.
Birla, Ritu. "Might as Well Face It, We're Addicted to Gandhi." *Public Culture* 23, no. 2 (May 2011): 471–80.
Birla, Ritu, and Faisal Devji. "Guest Editors' Letter: Itineraries of Self-Rule." *Public Culture* 23, no. 2 (May 2011): 265–68.
Bloch, Ernst. *The Spirit of Utopia*. Stanford, Calif.: Stanford University Press, 2002.
Borges, Jorge Luis. *Collected Fictions*. New York: Penguin Books, 1999.
Bourne, Randolph. *War and the Intellectuals: Collected Essays, 1915–1919*. New York: Hackett, 1999.
Brennan, Timothy. *At Home in the World: Cosmopolitanism Now*. Cambridge: Harvard University Press, 1997.
———. *Borrowed Light*. Stanford, Calif.: Stanford University Press, 2014.

———. "Edward Said as a Lukácsian Critic: Modernism and Empire." *College Literature* 40, no. 4 (2013).
———. "Fanon for the Present." *College Literature* 45, no. 1 (2018).
———. "Joining the Party." *Postcolonial Studies* 16, no. 1 (2013): 68–78.
Brown, Emily C. *Har Dayal, Hindu Revolutionary and Rationalist*. Tucson: University of Arizona Press, 1975.
Brueck, Laura. *Writing Resistance: The Rhetorical Imagination of Hindi Dalit Literature*. New York: Columbia University Press, 2014.
Burton, Antoinette M., and Isabel Hofmeyr. *Ten Books That Shaped the British Empire: Creating an Imperial Commons*. Durham, N.C.: Duke University Press, 2014.
Camus, Renaud. *Tricks: 25 Encounters*. New York: St. Martin's Press, 1981.
Capps, John M., and Donald Capps, eds. *James and Dewey on Belief and Experience*. Urbana: University of Illinois Press, 2005.
Carter, Mia., and Barbara Harlow, eds. *Archives of Empire*. Durham, N.C.: Duke University Press, 2003.
Casanova, Pascale. *The World Republic of Letters*. Cambridge: Harvard University Press, 2004.
Cassin, Barbara. *Sophistical Practice: Toward a Consistent Relativism*. New York: Fordham University Press, 2014.
Cassin, Barbara, Steven Rendall, and Emily S. Apter, eds. *Dictionary of Untranslatables: A Philosophical Lexicon*. Princeton, N.J.: Princeton University Press, 2014.
Chairez-Garza, J. F. "'Bound Hand and Foot and Handed over to the Caste Hindus': Ambedkar, Untouchability and the Politics of Partition." *The Indian Economic and Social History Review* 55, no. 1 (January 2018): 1–28.
———. "B. R. Ambedkar, Franz Boas and the Rejection of Racial Theories of Untouchability." *South Asia: Journal of South Asian Studies* 41, no. 2 (2018): 281–96.
———. "B. R. Ambedkar, Partition and the Internationalisation of Untouchability, 1939–47." *South Asia: Journal of South Asian Studies* 42, no. 1 (January 2, 2019): 80–96.
———. "Touching Space: Ambedkar on the Spatial Features of Untouchability." *Contemporary South Asia* 22, no. 1 (January 2, 2014): 37–50.
Chakrabarty, Dipesh. *Provincializing Europe: Postcolonial Thought and Historical Difference*. Princeton, N.J.: Princeton University Press, 2008.
Chakravorty, Swapan, and Abhijit Gupta. *Print Areas: Book History in India*. Orient Blackswan, 2004.
Chatterjee, Partha. *Nation and Its Fragments: Colonial and Postcolonial Histories*. London: Oxford University Press, 1997.
———. *Nationalist Thought and the Colonial World: A Derivative Discourse?* London: Zed Books, 1986.
———. *The Politics of the Governed: Reflections on Popular Politics in Most of the World*. New York: Columbia University Press, 2004.

Cheah, Pheng. *What Is a World?: On Postcolonial Literature as World Literature.* Durham, N.C.: Duke University Press, 2016.
Cheah, Pheng, and Bruce Robbins, eds., *Cosmopolitics: Thinking and Feeling Beyond the Nation.* Minneapolis: University of Minnesota Press, 1998.
Cherki, Alice. *Frantz Fanon: A Portrait.* Ithaca, N.Y.: Cornell University Press, 2006.
———. *Frantz Fanon: portrait.* Paris: Seuil, 2000.
Chernyshevsky, Nikolay Gavrilovich. *What Is to Be Done?* Ithaca, N.Y.: Cornell University Press, 1989.
Childers, Joseph W. "Of Prison Notebooks and the Restoration of an Archive." *Rethinking Marxism* 18, no. 1 (January 2006): 9–14.
Chuh, Kandice. *The Difference Aesthetics Makes: On the Humanities "after Man."* Durham, N.C.: Duke University Press, 2019.
Ciccariello-Maher, George. *Decolonizing Dialectics.* Durham, N.C.: Duke University Press, 2017.
Colón, Gabriel Alejandro Torres, and Charles A. Hobbs. "The Intertwining of Culture and Nature: Franz Boas, John Dewey, and Deweyan Strands of American Anthropology." *Journal of the History of Ideas* 76, no. 1 (2015): 139–62.
Cotkin, George. *William James, Public Philosopher.* Baltimore: Johns Hopkins University Press, 1990.
Coulthard, Glen Sean. *Red Skin, White Masks: Rejecting the Colonial Politics of Recognition.* Minneapolis: University of Minnesota Press, 2014.
Crépon, Marc. *Murderous Consent.* New York: Fordham University Press, 2019.
Damrosch, David. *What Is World Literature?* Princeton, N.J.: Princeton University Press, 2003.
Darnton, Robert. "Literary Surveillance in the British Raj: The Contradictions of Liberal Imperialism." *Book History* 4, no. 1 (2001): 133–76.
Dasgupta, Uma, ed. *Friendships of "Largeness and Freedom": Andrews, Tagore, and Gandhi: An Epistolary Account, 1912–1940.* New Delhi: Oxford University Press, 2018.
Davids, Caroline, and A. F. Rhys. *Buddhism: A Study of the Buddhist Norm.* New York: H. Holt, 1912.
de Certeau, Michel. *The Practice of Everyday Life.* Berkeley: University of California Press, 1988.
Deleuze, Gilles. *Kafka: Toward a Minor Literature.* Minneapolis: University of Minnesota Press, 1986.
Derrida, Jacques. *Monolingualism of the Other, or, The Prosthesis of Origin.* Stanford, Calif.: Stanford University Press, 1998.
———. *Politics of Friendship.* London: Verso, 1997.
Detienne, Marcel. *Comparing the Incomparable.* Stanford, Calif.: Stanford University Press, 2008.
Devji, Faisal. "Gandhi and Ambedkar, a False Debate." *The Hindu*, February 22, 2016.

———. *The Impossible Indian: Gandhi and the Temptation of Violence*. Cambridge: Harvard University Press, 2012.
———. *Muslim Zion: Pakistan as a Political Idea*. Cambridge: Harvard University Press, 2013.
Dewey, John. *Democracy and Education: An Introduction to the Philosophy of Education*. New York: Macmillan, 1916.
———. *Freedom and Culture*. New York: Prometheus, 1989.
———. *The Later Works: 1925–1953*. Carbondale: Southern Illinois University Press, 1988.
Dharmavira. *Lala Har Dayal and Revolutionary Movements of His Times*. New Delhi: India Book Co, 1970.
Diagne, Souleymane Bachir. *Postcolonial Bergson*. New York: Fordham University Press, 2019.
Dirks, Nicholas B. *Castes of Mind: Colonialism and the Making of Modern India*. Princeton, N.J.: Princeton University Press, 2001.
Dirlik, Arif. "Chinese History and the Question of Orientalism." *History and Theory* 35, no. 4 (December 1996): 96–118.
Doniger, Wendy, ed. *The Laws of Manu*. New York: Penguin Books, 1991.
Dreyfus, Hubert L. *Michel Foucault, beyond Structuralism and Hermeneutics*. 2nd ed. Chicago: University of Chicago Press, 1983.
Du Bois, W. E. B. "Sociology Hesitant." *boundary 2* 27, no. 3 (2000): 37–44.
Dubreuil, Laurent. *The Refusal of Politics*. Edinburgh: Edinburgh University Press, 2016.
Dussel, Enrique. *Philosophy of Liberation*. Eugene, Ore.: Wipf and Stock Publishers, 2003.
Edelman, Lee. *No Future: Queer Theory and the Death Drive*. Durham, N.C.: Duke University Press, 2004.
Elam, J. Daniel. "The Anticolonial Ethics of Lala Har Dayal's Hints for Self Culture." *Nehru Memorial Museum and Library Occasional Lectures*, no. 11. New Delhi: Nehru Memorial Museum and Library, 2013.
———. "An Anticolonial Theory of Reading." *PMLA* 134, no. 1 (January 2019): 172–77.
———. "Bhagat Singh's Atheism." *History Workshop Journal* (2020): 1–13.
———. "Echoes of Ghadr." *Comparative Studies of South Asia, Africa and the Middle East* 34, no. 1 (2014): 9–23.
———. "The Martyr, the Moviegoer: Bhagat Singh at the Cinema." *Bioscope-South Asian Screen Studies* 8, no. 2 (December 2017): 181–203.
———. Review of *Unconditional Equality: Gandhi's Religion of Resistance*, by Ajay Skaria. *Political Theory* 46, no. 3 (June 2018): 493–98.
Elam, J. Daniel, and Chris Moffat. "On the Form, Politics and Effects of Writing Revolution." *South Asia: Journal of South Asian Studies* 39, no. 3 (July 2016): 513–24.
Elgrably, Jordan. "James Baldwin, The Art of Fiction No. 78." *The Paris Review* (1984).

Eribon, Didier. *Une morale du minoritaire: variations sur un thème de Jean Genet*. Paris: Fayard, 2001.
Erikson, Erik H. *Gandhi's Truth on the Origins of Militant Nonviolence*. New York: Norton, 1969.
Fanon, Frantz. *Black Skin, White Masks*. New York: Grove Press, 2008.
———. *Les damnés de la terre*. Paris: Découverte/Poche, 2002.
———. *A Dying Colonialism*. Boston: Grove/Atlantic, 1994.
———. *Freedom and Alienation*. Edited by Robert J. C. Young and Jean Khalfa. London: Bloomsbury, 2018.
———. *Peau noire, masques blancs*. Paris: Éditions du Seuil, 1952.
———. *Pour la révolution africaine: écrits politiques*. Paris: F. Maspero, 1964.
———. *The Wretched of the Earth*. New York: Grove Press, 2004.
Felski, Rita. *The Limits of Critique*. Chicago: University of Chicago Press, 2015.
———. *Uses of Literature*. London: Blackwell, 2008.
Ferguson, Kennan. "La Philosophie Americaine: James, Bergson, and the Century of Intercontinental Pluralism." *Theory & Event* 9, no. 1 (March 2006).
Figueira, Dorothy M. *Aryans, Jews, Brahmins: Theorizing Authority through Myths of Identity*. Albany: SUNY Press, 2002.
Fischer, Sibylle. *Modernity Disavowed: Haiti and the Cultures of Slavery in the Age of Revolution*. Durham, N.C.: Duke University Press, 2004.
Fischer-Tiné, Harald. *Shyamji Krishnavarma*. Delhi: Routledge, 2014.
Fisk, Gloria. *Orhan Pamuk and the Good of World Literature*. New York: Columbia University Press, 2018.
Flores, Ruben. *Backroads Pragmatists: Mexico's Melting Pot and Civil Rights in the United States*. Philadelphia: University of Pennsylvania Press, 2014.
Forster, E. M. *Commonplace Book*. Edited by Philip Gardner. Stanford, Calif.: Stanford University Press, 1985.
———. *Howards End*. New York: Norton, 1998.
———. *Two Cheers for Democracy*. New York: Harvest, 1962.
Foucault, Michel. *The Order of Things: An Archaeology of the Human Sciences*. New York: Vintage Books, 1973.
François, Anne-Lise. *Open Secrets: The Literature of Uncounted Experience*. Stanford, Calif.: Stanford University Press, 2008.
Gajarawala, Toral Jatin. *Untouchable Fictions: Literary Realism and the Crisis of Caste*. New York: Fordham University Press, 2013.
Gandhi, Leela. *Affective Communities: Anticolonial Thought, Fin-De-Siècle Radicalism, and the Politics of Friendship*. Durham, N.C.: Duke University Press, 2006.
———. "After Virtue: Notes On Early-Twentieth-Century Socialist Antimaterialism." *ELH* 77, no. 2 (2010): 413–46.
———. *The Common Cause: Postcolonial Ethics and the Practice of Democracy, 1900–1955*. Chicago: University of Chicago Press, 2014.
———. "The Pauper's Gift: Postcolonial Theory and the New Democratic Dispensation." *Public Culture* 23, no. 1 (January 2011): 27–38.

———. *Postcolonial Theory: A Critical Introduction*. Second edition. New York: Columbia University Press, 2019.

———. "Postcolonial Theory and the Crisis of European Man." *Postcolonial Studies* 10, no. 1 (March 2007): 93–110.

Gandhi, M. K., and Haridas Muzumdar. *Sermon on the Sea*. Chicago: Universal Publishing, 1924.

Gandhi, M. K., and John Ruskin. *Ruskin: Unto His Last; a Paraphrase*. Ahmedabad: Navajivan, 1951.

Gandhi, M. K., and Rabindranath Tagore. *The Mahatma and the Poet: Letters and Debates between Gandhi and Tagore, 1915–1941*. Edited by Sabyasachi Bhattacharya. New Delhi: National Book Trust, India, 1997.

Gandhi, Mohandas Karamchand. *An Autobiography: Or, The Story of My Experiments with Truth*. Ahmedabad: Navajivan Publishing House, 1948.

———. *The Collected Works of Mahatma Gandhi*. New Delhi: Publications Division, Ministry of Information and Broadcasting, Govt. of India, 1958.

———. *Hind Swaraj and Other Writings*. Edited by Anthony Parel. Cambridge: Cambridge University Press, 2009.

Ganguly, Debjani. *This Thing Called the World: The Contemporary Novel as Global Form*. Durham, N.C.: Duke University Press, 2016.

Gaonkar, Dilip Parameshwar, ed. *Alternative Modernities*. Durham, N.C.: Duke University Press, 2001.

———. "On Cultures of Democracy." *Public Culture* 19, no. 1 (January 2007): 1–22.

Gaonkar, Dilip Parameshwar, and Elizabeth A. Povinelli. "Technologies of Public Forms: Circulation, Transfiguration, Recognition." *Public Culture* 15, no. 3 (October 2003): 385–97.

Geetha, V. "Unpacking a Library: Babasaheb Ambedkar and His World of Books." https://thewire.in/caste/unpacking-library-babasaheb-ambedkar-world-books.

Geroulanos, Stefanos. *An Atheism That Is Not Humanist Emerges in French Thought*. Stanford, Calif.: Stanford University Press, 2010.

Getachew, Adom. *Worldmaking after Empire: The Rise and Fall of Self-Determination*. Princeton, N.J.: Princeton University Press, 2019.

Ginsburg, Shai, and Jonathan Boyarin, eds. *Jews and the Ends of Theory*. New York: Fordham University Press, 2019.

Giri, Ananta Kumar. "Gandhi, Tagore, and a New Ethics of Argumentation." Journal of Human Values 7, no. 1 (2001), 43–63.

Glissant, Édouard. *Caribbean Discourse: Selected Essays*. Charlottesville: University Press of Virginia, 1989.

———. *Poetics of Relation*. Ann Arbor: University of Michigan Press, 1997.

———. *Traité du tout-monde*. Paris: Gallimard, 1997.

Goldman, Emma. *Living My Life*. New York: Penguin, 2006.

Gordon, Avery. *Ghostly Matters: Haunting and the Sociological Imagination*. Minneapolis: University of Minnesota Press, 2008.

———. *The Hawthorn Archive: Letters from the Utopian Margins.* New York: Fordham University Press, 2018.
Goswami, Manu. "'Provincializing' Sociology: The Case of a Premature Postcolonial Sociologist." In *Political Power and Social Theory 24.* Bingley, UK: Emerald Group, 2013.
Gourgouris, Stathis. *Lessons in Secular Criticism.* New York: Fordham University Press, 2013.
Govind, Nikhil. *Between Love and Freedom.* Delhi: Routledge, 2014.
Gramsci, Antonio. *Prison Notebooks.* Edited by Joseph A. Buttigieg and Antonio. Callari. New York: Columbia University Press, 2011.
———. *Selections from the Prison Notebooks of Antonio Gramsci.* Edited by Quintin Hoare and Geoffrey. Nowell-Smith. New York: International Publishers, 1999.
Grewal, P. M. S. *Bhagat Singh, Liberation's Blazing Star.* New Delhi: LeftWord, 2007.
Guillén, Claudio. *The Challenge of Comparative Literature.* Cambridge: Harvard University Press, 1993.
Guillory, John. *Cultural Capital: The Problem of Literary Canon Formation.* Chicago: University of Chicago Press, 1993.
Gupta, Pamila. "Gandhi and the Goa Question." *Public Culture* 23, no. 2 (May 2011): 321–30.
Guru, Gopal. *The Cracked Mirror: An Indian Debate on Experience and Theory.* New Delhi: Oxford, 2012.
Habib, S. Irfan. *To Make the Deaf Hear: Ideology and Programme of Bhagat Singh and His Comrades.* Gurgaon: Three Essays Collective, 2007.
Halberstam, Jack. *The Queer Art of Failure.* Durham, N.C.: Duke University Press, 2011.
Hale, H. W. *Political Trouble in India 1917–1937.* Allahabad: Chugh Publications, 1973.
Hall, Stuart, David Morley, and Kuan-Hsing Chen, eds. *Stuart Hall: Critical Dialogues in Cultural Studies.* London: Routledge, 1996.
Hamacher, Werner. *Minima Philologica.* New York: Fordham University Press, 2015.
Har Dayal. *The Bodhisattva Doctrine in Buddhist Sanskrit Literature.* Delhi: Motilal Banarsidass, 1970.
———. *Forty-Four Months in Germany and Turkey, February 1915 to October 1918.* London: P. S. King & Son, 1920.
———. *Hints for Self-Culture.* Delhi: Rajkamal Publications, 1948.
———. *Letters of Lala Har Dayal.* Edited by Dharmavira. Ambala Cantt.: Indian Book Agency, 1970.
———. "The Social Conquest of the Hindu Race." *Modern Review* VI, no. 3 (September 1909): 239–48.
———. *Thoughts on Education: Reprint of Articles Originally Published in 1908.* New Delhi: Vivek Swadhyaya Mandal, 1969.

Har Dayal, et. al. *Marx Comes to India*. Delhi: Manohar Book Service, 1975.
Harney, Stefano, and Fred Moten. *The Undercommons: Fugitive Planning & Black Study*. New York: Minor Compositions, 2013.
Harris, Henry. *The Birth of the Cell*. New Haven: Yale University Press, 1999.
Hartman, Saidiya. *Wayward Lives, Beautiful Experiments: Intimate Histories of Social Upheaval*. New York: Norton, 2019.
Hayot, Eric. *On Literary Worlds*. New York: Oxford University Press, 2016.
Hemmings, Clare. *Considering Emma Goldman: Feminist Political Ambivalence & the Imaginative Archive*. Durham, N.C.: Duke University Press, 2018.
Herbert, Christopher. *Victorian Relativity: Radical Thought and Scientific Discovery*. Chicago: University of Chicago Press, 2001.
Hofmeyr, Isabel. *Gandhi's Printing Press: Experiments in Slow Reading*. Cambridge: Harvard University Press, 2013.
———. "Violent Texts, Vulnerable Readers: Hind Swaraj and Its South African Audiences." *Public Culture* 23, no. 2 (May 2011): 285–97.
Hohendahl, Peter Uwe. *The Institution of Criticism*. Ithaca, N.Y.: Cornell University Press, 1982.
Hooja, Bhupendra, ed., *A Martyr's Notebook*. Delhi: Sanghar Vidya Sabha Trust, 1994.
Hooker, Juliet. "'A Black Sister to Massachusetts': Latin America and the Fugitive Democratic Ethos of Frederick Douglass." *The American Political Science Review; Washington* 109, no. 4 (November 2015): 690–702.
———. *Theorizing Race in the Americas: Douglass, Sarmiento, Du Bois, and Vasconcelos*. New York: Oxford University Press, 2017.
Horkheimer, Max, and Theodor Adorno. *Dialectic of Enlightenment: Philosophical Fragments*. Stanford, Calif.: Stanford University Press, 2002.
Howe, Lawrence Westerby. "The Process of Endosmosis in the Bergsonian Critique," *The Modern Schoolman*, LXV, November 1987, 29–45.
Husserl, Edmund. *The Crisis of the European Sciences and Transcendental Philosophy*. Evanston, Ill.: Northwestern University Press, 1970.
Iskandar, Adel, and Hakem Rustom, eds. *Edward Said: A Legacy of Emancipation and Representation*. Berkeley: University of California Press, 2010.
Jaaware, Aniket. *Practicing Caste: On Touching and Not Touching*. New York: Fordham University Press, 2019.
Jaffrelot, Christophe. *Dr. Ambedkar and Untouchability: Fighting the Indian Caste System*. New York: Columbia University Press, 2005.
Jain, Harish, ed. *Bhagat Singh's "Jail Note Book": Its Context and Relevance*. Chandigarh, India: Unistar, 2016.
James, Henry. *The Figure in the Carpet and Other Stories*. Penguin UK, 2007.
James, William. *Essays in Psychical Research*. Cambridge: Harvard University Press, 1986.
———. *A Pluralistic Universe*. Cambridge: Harvard University Press, 1977.
———. *Pragmatism*. Cambridge: Harvard University Press, 1975.

———. *The Varieties of Religious Experience*. Cambridge: Harvard University Press, 1985.
———. *William James: Selected Unpublished Correspondence, 1885–1910*. Edited by Frederick J. Down Scott. Columbus: Ohio State University Press, 1986.
———. *Writings, 1902–1910*. New York: Library of America, 1987.
Jargose, Anna-Marie. *Inconsequence*. Ithaca, N.Y.: Cornell University Press, 2002.
Jayawardena, Kumari. *The White Woman's Other Burden: Western Women and South Asia during British Colonial Rule*. London: Routledge, 1995.
Jogdand, P. G., and Ramesh Kamble. "The Sociological Traditions and Their Margins: The Bombay School of Sociology and Dalits." *Sociological Bulletin* 62, no. 2 (2013): 324–45.
Jondhale, Surendra, and Johannes Beltz, eds. *Reconstructing the World: B. R. Ambedkar and Buddhism in India*. New Delhi: Oxford University Press, 2004.
Joshi, Priya. *In Another Country: Colonialism, Culture, and the English Novel in India*. New York: Columbia University Press, 2002.
Kadam, K. N. *The Meaning of the Ambedkarite Conversion to Buddhism and Other Essays*. Mumbai: Popular Prakashan, 1997.
Kapila, Shruti. "Ambedkar's Agonism, Sovereign Violence and Pakistan as Peace," *Comparative Studies in South Asia, Africa, and the Middle East* 39, no. 1 (2019): 184–95.
———. "Gandhi before Mahatma: The Foundations of Political Truth." *Public Culture* 23, no. 2 (2011): 431–48.
———. "A History of Violence." *Modern Intellectual History* 7, no. 2 (August 2010): 437–57.
———. "Self, Spencer and Swaraj: Nationalist Thought and Critiques of Liberalism, 1890–1920." *Modern Intellectual History* 4 (2007): 109–27.
Kapila, Shruti, and C. A. Bayly, eds. *An Intellectual History for India*. London: Cambridge University Press, 2010.
Kapila, Shruti, and Faisal Devji, eds. *Political Thought in Action: The Bhagavad Gita and Modern India*. Cambridge: Cambridge University Press, 2013.
Keer, Dhananjay. *Dr. Ambedkar: Life and Mission*. Bombay: A.V. Keer, 1954.
Kirkpatrick, Jennet. *The Virtues of Exit: On Resistance and Quitting Politics*. Chapel Hill: University of North Carolina Press, 2017.
Kishwar, Madhu. "Gandhi on Women." *Economic and Political Weekly* 20, no. 40 (1985): 1691–702.
Konuk, Kader. *East-West Mimesis: Auerbach in Turkey*. Stanford, Calif.: Stanford University Press, 2010.
Kumar, Aishwary. *Radical Equality: Ambedkar, Gandhi, and the Risk of Democracy*. Stanford, Calif.: Stanford University Press, 2015.
Lal, Chaman, ed., *The Jail Notebook and Other Writings*. Delhi: LeftWord Books, 2007.

Lal, Vinay. "The Gandhi Everyone Loves to Hate." *Economic and Political Weekly* 43, no. 40 (October 2008): 55–64.

———. "Gandhi's West, the West's Gandhi." *New Literary History* 40, no. 2 (2009): 281–313.

Latour, Bruno. "Why Has Critique Run out of Steam? From Matters of Fact to Matters of Concern." *Critical Inquiry* 30, no. 2 (2004): 225–48.

Lear, Jonathan. *Radical Hope: Ethics in the Face of Cultural Devastation*. Cambridge: Harvard University Press, 2009.

Lefebvre, Alexandre. *Human Rights and the Care of the Self*. Durham, N.C.: Duke University Press, 2018.

———. *Human Rights as a Way of Life: On Bergson's Political Philosophy*. Stanford, Calif.: Stanford University Press, 2013.

Lefebvre, Alexandre, and Melanie Allison White, eds. *Bergson, Politics, and Religion*. Durham, N.C.: Duke University Press, 2012.

Lerer, Seth. "Auerbach's Shakespeare." *Philological Quarterly* 90, no. 1 (2011).

———. *Error and the Academic Self: The Scholarly Imagination, Medieval to Modern*. New York: Columbia University Press, 2002.

———, ed. *Literary History and the Challenge of Philology*. Stanford, Calif.: Stanford University Press, 1996.

Levine, Alan, and Daniel S. Malachuk, eds. *A Political Companion to Ralph Waldo Emerson*. Lexington: University Press of Kentucky, 2011.

Levine, Caroline, and B. Venkat Mani. "What Counts as World Literature?" *Modern Language Quarterly: A Journal of Literary History* 74, no. 2 (2013).

Levin, Harry. *Grounds for Comparison*. Cambridge: Harvard University Press, 1972.

Lih, Lars T. *Lenin Rediscovered: A Commentary and New Translation of What Is to Be Done?* Boston: Brill, 2006.

Livingston, Alexander. "Book Review: *The Virtues of Exit: On Resistance and Quitting Politics*, by Jennet Kirkpatrick." *Political Theory* 47, no. 4 (August 2019): 612–16.

———. *Damn Great Empires!: William James and the Politics of Pragmatism*. New York: Oxford University Press, 2016.

London, Jack. *The Little Lady of the Big House*. New York: Macmillan, 1916.

Long, David, and Peter Wilson, eds. *Thinkers of the Twenty Years' Crisis*. London: Oxford University Press, 1996.

Loomba, Ania. *Revolutionary Desires*. London: Routledge, 2018.

Louro, Michele L. *Comrades against Imperialism: Nehru, India, and Interwar Internationalism*. Cambridge: Cambridge University Press, 2018.

Lowe, Lisa. *The Intimacies of Four Continents*. Durham, N.C.: Duke University Press, 2015.

Lynch, Deidre. *Loving Literature: A Cultural History*. Chicago: University of Chicago Press, 2015.

Macey, David. *Frantz Fanon: A Biography*. London: Verso, 2012.

Maclean, Kama. "The History of a Legend: Accounting for Popular Histories of Revolutionary Nationalism in India." *Modern Asia Studies* 46, no. 6 (November 2012): 1540–71.

———. "The Portrait's Journey: The Image, Social Communication and Martyr-Making in Colonial India." *The Journal of Asian Studies* 70, no. 4 (November 2011): 1051.

———. "Revolution and Revelation, or, When Is History Too Soon?" *South Asia: Journal of South Asia Studies* 39, no. 3 (July 2, 2016): 678–94.

———. *A Revolutionary History of Interwar India: Violence, Image, Voice and Text*. New York: Oxford University Press, 2015.

Maclean, Kama, and J. Daniel Elam. "Who Is a Revolutionary?" *Postcolonial Studies* 16, no. 2 (2013): 113–23.

Maitra, Keya. "Ambedkar and the Constitution of India: A Deweyan Experiment." *Contemporary Pragmatism* 9, no. 2 (December 2012): 301–20.

Majeed, Javed. *Autobiography, Travel and Postnational Identity: Gandhi, Nehru and Iqbal*. London: Palgrave Macmillan, 2007.

Malhotra, Anshu, and Farina Mir, eds. *Punjab Reconsidered: History, Culture, and Practice*. New Delhi: Oxford University Press, 2012.

Mani, B. Venkat. *Recoding World Literature: Libraries, Print Culture, and Germany's Pact with Books*. New York: Fordham University Press, 2017.

Mantena, Karuna. *Alibis of Empire: Henry Maine and the Ends of Liberal Imperialism*. Princeton, N.J.: Princeton University Press, 2010.

Markell, Patchen. *Bound by Recognition*. Princeton, N.J.: Princeton University Press, 2003.

Marriott, David S. *Whither Fanon?: Studies in the Blackness of Being*. Stanford, Calif.: Stanford University Press, 2018.

Marx, Karl. *The First Indian War of Independence: 1857–1859*. London: Lawrence and Wishart, 1980.

Masuzawa, Tomoko. *The Invention of World Religions, or, How European Universalism Was Preserved in the Language of Pluralism*. Chicago: University of Chicago Press, 2005.

Mawani, Renisa. *Across Oceans of Law: The Komagata Maru and Jurisdiction in the Time of Empire*. Durham, N.C.: Duke University Press, 2018.

McAleer, John J. *Ralph Waldo Emerson: Days of Encounter*. Boston: Little, Brown, 1984.

Mehrotra, Arvind Krishna, ed., *A Concise History of Indian Literature in English*. Delhi: Permanent Black, 2008.

Mehta, Uday S. *Liberalism and Empire: A Study in Nineteenth-Century British Liberal Thought*. Chicago: University of Chicago Press, 1999.

———. "Patience, Inwardness, and Self-Knowledge in Gandhi's Hind Swaraj." *Public Culture* 23, no. 2 (May 2011): 417–29.

Melas, Natalie. "Afterlives of Comparison: Literature, Equivalence, Value," in Rónán McDonald, ed. *The Values of Literary Studies: Critical Institu-

tions, Scholarly Agendas. Cambridge: Cambridge University Press, 2015, 172–87.

——. *All the Difference in the World: Postcoloniality and the Ends of Comparison*. Stanford, Calif.: Stanford University Press, 2007.

——. "Comparison and Postcoloniality." In Steven Tötösy de Zepetnek and Tutun Mukherjee, eds., *Companion to Comparative Literature, World Literatures, and Comparative Cultural Studies*. Delhi: Cambridge University Press, 2014.

——. "Merely Comparative." *PMLA* 128, no. 3 (2013).

Mignolo, Walter D., and Catherine E. Walsh. *On Decoloniality: Concepts, Analytics, Praxis*. Durham, N.C.: Duke University Press, 2018.

Mill, John Stuart. *"On Liberty" and Other Writings*. London: Cambridge University Press, 1989.

Miller, D. A. *The Novel and The Police*. Berkeley: University of California Press, 1988.

Mills, C. Wright. *The Sociological Imagination*. New York: Oxford University Press, 1959.

Mitrokhin, L. V. *Lenin in India*. Delhi: Allied, 1981.

Moffat, Chris. "Bhagat Singh's Corpse." *South Asia: Journal of South Asian Studies* 39, no. 3 (July 2016): 644–61.

——. "Experiments in Political Truth." *Postcolonial Studies* 16, no. 2 (2013): 185–201.

——. *India's Revolutionary Inheritance: Politics and the Promise of Bhagat Singh*. London: Cambridge University Press, 2019.

——. "Politics and the Work of the Dead in Modern India." *Comparative Studies in Society and History* 60, no. 1 (2018).

Mufti, Aamir. "Auerbach in Istanbul: Edward Said, Secular Criticism, and the Question of Minority Culture." *Critical Inquiry* 25, no. 1 (October 1998).

——. *Forget English!: Orientalisms and World Literatures*. Cambridge: Harvard University Press, 2016.

——. "Global Comparativism." *Critical Inquiry* 31, no. 2 (2005): 472–89.

Mukherjee, Arun. "B. R. Ambedkar, John Dewey, and the Meaning of Democracy," *New Literary History* 40, no. 2 (2009): 345–70.

Nagaraj, D. R. *The Flaming Feet and Other Essays: The Dalit Movement in India*. Calcutta: Seagull Books, 2011.

Nayar, Kuldip. *The Martyr: Bhagat Singh—Experiments in Revolution*. Delhi: Har-Anand Publications, 2000.

Newton, Adam Zachary. *Jewish Studies As Counterlife: A Report to the Academy*. New York: Fordham University Press, 2019.

——. *To Make the Hands Impure: Art, Ethical Adventure, the Difficult and the Holy*. New York: Fordham University Press, 2016.

Nietzsche, Friedrich. *The Anti-Christ, Ecce Homo, Twilight of the Idols: And Other Writings*. Edited by Aaron Ridley. New York: Cambridge University Press, 2005.

Olivelle, Patrick, and Suman Olivelle, eds. *Manu's Code of Law: A Critical Edition and Translation of the Manava-Dharmasastra*. New York: Oxford University Press, 2005.
Omissi, David E. *Indian Voices of the Great War: Soldiers' Letters, 1914–18*. London: Palgrave Macmillan Press, 1999.
Omvedt, Gail. *Ambedkar: Towards an Enlightened India*. New Delhi: Penguin, 2004.
———. *Dalits and the Democratic Revolution: Dr. Ambedkar and the Dalit Movement in Colonial India*. New Delhi: Sage Publications, 1994.
———. *Seeking Begumpura: The Social Vision of Anticaste Intellectuals*. New Delhi: Navayana, 2008.
———. *Understanding Caste: From Buddha to Ambedkar and Beyond*. New Delhi: Orient Blackswan, 2011.
Orsini, Francesca. *The Hindi Public Sphere 1920–1940: Language and Literature in the Age of Nationalism*. London: Oxford University Press, 2009.
———. *Print and Pleasure: Popular Literature and Entertaining Fictions in Colonial North India*. New Delhi: Permanent Black, 2017.
Pappas, Gregory Fernando, ed. *Pragmatism in the Americas*. New York: Fordham University Press, 2011.
Paranjape, Makarand R. "'Natural Supernaturalism?' The Tagore–Gandhi Debate on the Bihar Earthquake." *The Journal of Hindu Studies* 4, no. 2 (July 2011): 176–204.
Parel, Anthony. *Gandhi's Philosophy and the Quest for Harmony*. Cambridge: Cambridge University Press, 2006.
Paul, E. Jaiwant. *Lala Har Dayal*. Delhi: Roli Books, 2008.
Pollock, Sheldon. "Future Philology? The Fate of a Soft Science in a Hard World." *Critical Inquiry* 35, no. 4 (2009).
———. "Liberating Philology." *Verge: Studies in Global Asias* 1, no. 1 (April 2015): 16–21.
———. "Philology in Three Dimensions." *Postmedieval* 5, no. 4 (January 2014).
Porter, James I. "Disfigurations: Erich Auerbach's Theory of Figura." *Critical Inquiry* 44, no. 1 (September 2017): 80–113.
———. "Erich Auerbach and the Judaizing of Philology." *Critical Inquiry* 35, no. 1 (2008): 115–47.
———. "Erich Auerbach's Earthly (Counter-)Philology." *Digital Philology: A Journal of Medieval Cultures* 2, no. 2 (2013).
———. *Nietzsche and the Philology of the Future*. Stanford, Calif.: Stanford University Press, 2000.
Porter, James I., and Jane O. Newman, eds. *Time, History, and Literature: Selected Essays of Erich Auerbach*. Princeton, N.J.: Princeton University Press, 2014.
Povinelli, Elizabeth A. *The Cunning of Recognition: Indigenous Alterities and the Making of Australian Multiculturalism*. Durham, N.C.: Duke University Press, 2002.

Price, Leah. *The Anthology and the Rise of the Novel*. Cambridge: Cambridge University Press, 2000.
Proust, Marcel. *Against Sainte-Beuve and Other Essays*. New York: Penguin, 1994.
Ramnath, Maia. *Haj to Utopia: How the Ghadar Movement Charted Global Radicalism and Attempted to Overthrow the British Empire*. Berkeley: University of California Press, 2011.
Ranganathan, S. R. *The Five Laws of Library Science*. Madras: Madras Library Association, 1931.
Rao, Anupama. *The Caste Question: Dalits and the Politics of Modern India*. Berkeley: University of California Press, 2009.
———. "Introduction: Insurgent Thought," *Comparative Studies in South Asia, Africa, and the Middle East* 34, no. 1 (Spring 2014): 2–8.
Rattu, Nanak Chand. *Reminiscences and Rememberances [Sic] of Dr. B. R. Ambedkar*. New Delhi: Falcon Books, 1995.
Rinehart, Robin. "From Bhagat Singh, Atheist, To Agnostic Khushwant: Mapping Sikh Irreligiosity." *Sikh Formations: Religion, Culture, Theory* 11, no. 1–2 (May 2015): 160–73.
Robbins, Bruce. "Secularism, Elitism, Progress, and Other Transgressions: On Edward Said's 'Voyage in.'" *Social Text*, no. 40 (Autumn 1994), 25–37.
Rubin, Andrew. *Archives of Authority: Empire, Culture, and the Cold War*. Princeton, N.J.: Princeton University Press, 2012.
Sadana, Rashmi. *English Heart, Hindi Heartland: The Political Life of Literature in India*. Berkeley: University of California Press, 2012.
Said, Edward W. *Beginnings: Intention and Method*. New York: Basic Books, 1975.
———. *Culture and Imperialism*. New York: Vintage Books, 1994.
———. *Humanism and Democratic Criticism*. New York: Columbia University Press, 2004.
———. *On Late Style: Music and Literature against the Grain*. New York: Pantheon Books, 2006.
———. *Orientalism*. 25th Anniversary ed. New York: Vintage Books, 2003.
———. *Reflections on Exile and Other Essays*. Cambridge: Harvard University Press, 2000.
———. *The World, the Text, and the Critic*. Cambridge: Harvard University Press, 1983.
Sanger, Margaret. "Does Mr. Gandhi Know Women? What He Told Me At Wardha," *The Illustrated Weekly of India*, January 19, 1936.
Sawhney, Simona. "Death in Three Scenes of Recitation." *Postcolonial Studies* 16, no. 2 (2013).
———. *The Modernity of Sanskrit*. Minneapolis: University of Minnesota Press, 2009.
Saxena, Akshya. "A Worldly Anglophony: Empire and Englishes." *Interventions* 20, no. 3 (April 2018): 317–24.

Scott, David. *Conscripts of Modernity: The Tragedy of Colonial Enlightenment.* Durham, N.C.: Duke University Press, 2004.

———. *Refashioning Futures: Criticism after Postcoloniality.* Princeton, N.J.: Princeton University Press, 1999.

Scott, J. Barton. *Spiritual Despots: Modern Hinduism and the Genealogies of Self-Rule.* Chicago: University of Chicago Press, 2016.

Sedgwick, Eve Kosofsky. *Epistemology of the Closet.* Berkeley: University of California Press, 1990.

Seth, Sanjay. *Subject Lessons: The Western Education of Colonial India.* Durham, N.C.: Duke University Press, 2007.

Shatz, Adam. "Where Life Is Seized." *London Review of Books*, January 19, 2017.

Shelby, Tommie, and Brandon M. Terry, eds. *To Shape a New World: Essays on the Political Philosophy of Martin Luther King, Jr.* Cambridge: Harvard University Press, 2018.

Shingavi, Snehal. "Agyeya's Unfinished Revolution: Sexual and Social Freedom in Shekhar: Ek Jivani." *South Asia: Journal of South Asian Studies* 39, no. 3 (July 2016): 577–91.

Shotwell, Alexis. *Against Purity.* Minneapolis: University of Minnesota Press, 2012.

Shotwell, James. *The Faith of an Historian and Other Essays.* New York: Walker and Company, 1964.

Sinclair, Upton. *The Cry for Justice.* Pasadena, Calif.: self-published, 1915.

Singh, Bhagat. *Select Speeches & Writings.* Edited by D. N. Gupta. New Delhi: National Book Trust, 2007.

Singh, Julietta. *No Archive Will Restore You.* Santa Barbara, Calif.: punctum books, 2018.

———. *Unthinking Mastery: Dehumanism and Decolonial Entanglements.* Durham, N.C.: Duke University Press, 2018.

Sinha, Mrinalini. *Specters of Mother India: The Global Restructuring of an Empire.* Durham, N.C.: Duke University Press, 2006.

Skaria, A. "Ambedkar, Marx and the Buddhist Question." *South Asia: Journal of South Asian Studies* 38, no. 3 (July 2015): 450–65.

———. "'Can the Dalit Articulate a Universal Position?': The Intellectual, the Social, and the Writing of History." *Social History* 39, no. 3 (2014): 340–58.

———. "Only One Word, Properly Altered: Gandhi and the Question of the Prostitute." *Postcolonial Studies* 10, no. 2 (June 2007): 219–37.

———. "The Opening and Obscuring of Nonwilling Freedom." *Contemporary South Asia* 25, no. 4 (October 2, 2017): 439–50.

———. "Relinquishing Republican Democracy: Gandhi's Ramarajya." *Postcolonial Studies* 14, no. 2 (2011): 203–29.

———. *Unconditional Equality: Gandhi's Religion of Resistance.* Minneapolis: University of Minnesota Press, 2016.

Skinner, Quentin. *Visions of Politics*. London: Cambridge University Press, 2002.
Slate, Nico. *Colored Cosmopolitanism: The Shared Struggle for Freedom in the United States and India*. Cambridge: Harvard University Press, 2017.
Smith, Gary, ed. *On Walter Benjamin: Critical Essays and Recollections*. Cambridge: MIT Press, 1991.
Sohi, Seema. *Echoes of Mutiny: Race, Surveillance, and Indian Anticolonialism in North America*. New York: Oxford University Press, 2014.
———. "Sites of 'Sedition,' Sites of Liberation: Gurudwaras, the Ghadr Party, and Anticolonial Mobilization," *Sikh Formations* 10, no. 1 (2014), 5–22.
Spencer, Herbert. *The Principles of Sociology*. New York: D. Appleton and Company, 1898.
———. *Social Statics*. London: Williams and Norgate, 1892.
———. *The Study of Sociology*. New York: D. Appleton and Company, 1906.
Spivak, Gayatri Chakravorty. *A Critique of Postcolonial Reason: Toward a History of the Vanishing Present*. Cambridge: Harvard University Press, 1999.
———. *Death of a Discipline*. New York: Columbia University Press, 2003.
Sprinker, Michael, ed. *Edward Said: A Critical Reader*. London: Blackwell, 1992.
Srinivasan, Ragini Tharoor. "Divisions of Labor: Between Cheah's Worlds." *Qui Parle: Critical Humanities and Social Sciences* 25, no. 1 (2016): 243–61.
———. "South Asia from Postcolonial to World Anglophone." *Interventions* 20, no. 3 (April 2018): 309–16.
Steinmetz, George ed. *Sociology and Empire*. Durham, N.C.: Duke University Press, 2013.
Stroud, Scott. "Creative Democracy, Communication, and the Uncharted Sources of Bhimrao Ambedkar's Deweyan Pragmatism." *Education and Culture* 34, no. 1 (2018).
———. "The Rhetoric of Conversion as Emancipatory Strategy in India: Bhimrao Ambedkar, Pragmatism, and the Turn to Buddhism." *Rhetorica: A Journal of the History of Rhetoric* 35, no. 3 (2017): 314–45.
Suhrud, Tridip, ed. *An Autobiography, or, The Story of My Experiments with Truth: A Table of Concordance*. New Delhi: Routledge, 2010.
Tarde, Gabriel. *Les lois sociales*. Paris: Les empêcheurs de penser en rond, 1999.
———. *On Communication and Social Influence: Selected Papers*. Chicago: University of Chicago Press, 2011.
Teltumbde, Anand. *Dalits: Past, Present and Future*. London: Routledge, 2017.
———. *Mahad: The Making of the First Dalit Revolt*. Delhi: Aakar Books, 2016.
Turner, Jack, ed. *A Political Companion to Henry David Thoreau*. Lexington: University Press of Kentucky, 2009.
Turner, James. *Philology: The Forgotten Origins of the Modern Humanities*. Princeton, N.J.: Princeton University Press, 2014.
Viswanathan, Gauri. *Masks of Conquest: Literary Study and British Rule in India*. New York: Columbia University Press, 1989.

———. *Outside the Fold: Conversion, Modernity, and Belief.* Princeton, N.J.: Princeton University Press, 1998.
Waraich, Malvinderjit Singh, ed., *Revolutionaries in Dialogue.* Chandigarh: Unistar Press, 2007.
Weber, Max. *The Religion of India: The Sociology of Hinduism and Buddhism.* New York: Free Press, 1958.
Weber, Thomas. *Going Native: Gandhi's Relationship with Western Women.* New Delhi: Lotus Collection, 2011.
Weinstein, Philip M. *Unknowing: The Work of Modernist Fiction.* Ithaca, N.Y.: Cornell University Press, 2005.
Wellek, René. *A History of Modern Criticism: 1750–1950.* New Haven: Yale University Press, 1955.
———. *Theory of Literature.* New York: Harcourt, Brace & World, 1956.
Wilder, Gary. *Freedom Time: Negritude, Decolonization, and the Future of the World.* Durham, N.C.: Duke University Press, 2015.
Woolf, Virginia. *The Common Reader.* New York: Houghton Mifflin Harcourt, 1986.
———. *The Second Common Reader.* New York: Houghton Mifflin Harcourt, 1986.
Wright, Richard. *The Color Curtain: A Report on the Bandung Conference.* Oxford: University Press of Mississippi, 1995.
Yadav, K. C., ed. *Bhagat Singh: Fragrance of Freedom.* Gurgaon: Hope India, 2006.
———, ed. *Bhagat Singh: Making of a Revolutionary: Contemporaries' Portrayals.* Gurgaon: Hope India, 2006.
Yengde, Suraj, and Anand Teltumbde, eds. *The Radical in Ambedkar: Critical Reflections.* Delhi: Penguin Random House, 2018.
Young, Robert. *Postcolonialism: An Historical Introduction.* London: Wiley Blackwell, 2001.
———. *White Mythologies: Writing History and the West.* London: Routledge, 1990.
Yusufji, Salim, ed. *Ambedkar: The Attendant Details.* New Delhi: Navayana, 2017.
Zelliot, Eleanor. *Dr. Babasaheb Ambedkar and the Untouchable Movement.* New Delhi: Blumoon Books, 2004.
———. *From Untouchable to Dalit: Essays on the Ambedkar Movement.* New Delhi: Manohar Publications, 1992.
Ziolkowski, Jan, ed. *On Philology.* University Park: Pennsylvania State University Press, 1990.

Archival Sources

Home Political Files. National Archives of India (NAI). New Delhi.
Krüger, Horst. Papers. Zentrum der Moderner Orient (ZMO). Berlin.
India Office Files. African & Asian Collection. British Library, London.

Manuscript Collection. Nehru Memorial Museum and Library (NMML). New Delhi.
Neutrality Case Files (1913–1920). National Archives at San Francisco. San Bruno, Calif.
South Asians in North America Collection. Bancroft Library. University of California, Berkeley.

Index

Adorno, Theodor W., 10, 68
ahimsa, 72, 73, 74–75
Ahmad, Dohra, 140n50
Algeria, 1, 10, 114
Ambedkar, B. R., 7, 14, 16, 30; antiauthoritarian critique and, 45–47, 49, 52–54, 56, 58, 59, 62–65, 116–17; Buddhism and, 45, 46, 63–64, 65, 121–24; at Columbia, 44–45, 55; Dewey's influence on, 55–57; endosmosis and, 56–59, 61, 65; Gandhi viewed by, 82, 84; Hinduism viewed by, 48, 54, 60–61, 122; Indian Constitution and, 45, 114, 121, 122; on inter-caste marriage, 61–62; as legal activist, 59; *Manusmriti* and, 53–54, 120; Nietzsche and, 51–52; philology and, 50, 52–53; sociology and, 8, 45, 46, 48, 49, 59, 63; sociophilia and, 63–66; as theorist of reading, 47–48, 54
Anand, Mulk Raj, 108–9, 110–11
Annihilation of Caste (Ambedkar), 45, 53, 57, 59–61, 123
anticolonialism: anonymity and, 8–9, 125; as antiauthoritarianism, xiii, 2, 4, 72, 110, 117, 125; as critique, 4, 6–9, 18, 21, 28, 30, 36, 37, 40, 41, 43, 47, 69, 107; imagined futures of, 3–4, 7–8, 116; impatience of, 117; in interwar writings, 20–21; liberalism and, 14; philology and, 5, 16–18, 113, 126; reading as, ix–x, xii–xiii, 21, 22, 25, 28, 30, 37, 42, 47, 85–86, 94, 98, 104, 113; as refusal, 114, 120, 125; unknowing and, 2, 4, 106, 113; utopianism of, 3, 14, 16, 21–23, 38, 115, 140n50
aparigraha, 73, 74, 76
Arendt, Hannah, 2, 68
Arya Samaj, 53, 60
asceticism, 8, 9, 15–16, 37, 46, 64, 75, 85, 93, 127
Auerbach, Erich, 6, 10–11, 16–18, 49, 107, 126–29, 140n57
Azad, Chandrashekhar, 20

Bakunin, Mikhail, 100, 162n64
Baldwin, James, 124–25
Bandung Conference (1955), 55, 125
baraabari de arth ("The Meaning of Equality"; pamphlet), 19–21, 25, 27, 34, 39, 42
Barthes, Roland, 11, 166n51
Benjamin, Walter, 9–10, 11, 16
Bentham, Jeremy, 71, 137n17
Bergson, Henri, 34, 44, 58–59, 61, 149n18
Bhagat Singh, viii, xiii, 7, 14, 16; atheism and, 105–7, 110; death of, 93, 114; fictional treatment of, 108; hagiography of, 99; Har Dayal and, 19–21, 22, 39; inconsequential demands of, 94, 99, 103–5; in prison, 92–93; prison notebook of, 94–95, 97–99, 101–3, 107, 115; reading theory and practices of, 100–4; theories of revolution and, 8, 20, 25, 93–95, 99–100, 102–5, 110, 115

190 / INDEX

Bhagavad Gita, 70, 72, 89, 154n12
Black Skin, White Masks (Fanon), 1, 2, 65–66
Boas, Franz, 44–45
Bourne, Randolph, 106
Brecht, Bertolt, 10
Brennan, Timothy, 42, 138n18, 141n61, 146n40, 160n28, 167n64
British Empire: censorship and, 23, 25; liberalism and, x, xiii, 90, 115, 141n68; resistance to, 15; self-mastery and independence linked by, 2, 5, 14, 90
Brooks, Van Wyck, 43
Brown, Emily, 146n55
The Buddha and His Dhamma (Ambedkar), 63, 122, 123
Buddha or Karl Marx (Ambedkar), 54, 122
Buddhism, 30, 45, 63–64, 65, 121–24, 146n55, 165n41
Burton, Antoinette, 85

Carpenter, Edward, 87, 157n67
Casanova, Pascale, 11, 69, 143n85
caste system, 7, 8, 24, 45, 51–54, 60–62, 64, 83–84, 120–24, 125
Certeau, Michel de, 11, 90, 105
Chaírez-Garza, Jesús Francisco, 45, 165n34
Cherki, Alice, 2, 136n1
Chuh, Kandice, 9, 139n33, 142n81, 165n26
comparative literature, 5, 12–14, 49
The Cry for Justice (Sinclair), 95–97, 98

Dalits (Untouchables), 53, 60; Ambedkar and, 7, 45, 64, 120–24, 125; Gandhi and, 83–84; Har Dayal and, 24
Desai, Mahadev, 72, 77, 78–79, 83
Devji, Faisal, 74, 138n30, 153n6, 154n21, 155n30, 157n55
Dewey, John, 44–45, 55–58, 61–62, 106, 166n45
Detienne, Marcel, 13
Dharmavira, 29
Douglass, Frederick, 125
Du Bois, W. E. B., 55
Durkheim, Emile, 34, 149n30

egalitarianism, vii, ix–xii, xiv; anticolonialism linked to, 2, 14, 22, 114–15; critique as, 13, 14, 64, 114; in interwar writings, 6; obligatationary, 74, 84; origins of, 3; reading as, 16–17
Emerson, Ralph Waldo, 75, 77, 90
endosmosis, 56–59, 61, 65
Engels, Friedrich, 94, 158n6

Eribon, Didier, 18, 126
Etiemble, René, 140n57

Fanon, Frantz, 16, 125, 137n18; on Algeria, 10; Blackness and, 116; *Black Skin, White Masks*, 1, 2, 65–66; on Europe, 113–14, 117–18; on national independence, 118–20; on "new man," 6; on violence, 1–2, 10, 117; *The Wretched of the Earth*, 1–3, 6, 113, 117, 119
Fanon, Josie, 1
fascism, xii, xiii, 4, 5, 6, 12, 32, 126, 129
Fischer-Tiné, Harald, 34
Fisk, Gloria, 142n72, 143n85, 166n58
The Five Laws of Library Science (Ranganathan), vii–x
Forster, E. M., 106, 162n67
Forty-Four Months in Germany and Turkey (Har Dayal), 31
François, Anna-Lise, 140n49, 143n91, 164n6, 166n51

Gandhi, Leela: on inconsequence, 94, 104–5; 137n17; on postcolonial theory, 23, 161n53; on utopian practices, 8, 37, 64, 87, 90, 123
Gandhi, Mohandas K., xiii, 7, 14, 21, 53, 68, 98, 109–10, 114; Ambedkar vs., 45, 46, 57, 120; apologies by, 75–77, 85; asceticism of, 37, 75; on *brahmacharya*, 73, 79, 80; failures of, 69–70, 74, 77–82, 83–84, 125; fasting by, 70, 74, 77, 82–83, 84; McAleer and, 67–68; revolutionaries' impatience with, 20; Sanger's debates with, 75–81; Sanskrit and, 70, 72, 74; "some authorities" and, 86–88; theories of reading and, 85–86, 89–90; theories of renunciation and, 8, 69, 71–77, 79, 81, 82, 89; unknowingness and, 90–91; as vegetarian, 16, 70, 71
Ghadr di Gunj (poetry collection), 26, 27, 33
Ghadr Party, 7, 25, 35, 42–43, 95; Bhagat Singh and, 19–21, 97, 109, 162n64; masculinist views in, 28–29; publications of, 26–27, 109
Glissant, Édouard, 140n53, 141n66, 142n80
Goethe, Johann Wolfgang von, 9–10
Goldman, Emma, 97, 106, 162n64
Gramsci, Antonio, 99, 159n28
Guru, Gopal, 48

Habib, S. Irfan, 95, 101
Har Dayal, 7, 8, 14, 109; autodidacticism and, 35–36; censorship and, 23; ethical

practice and, 36–37; in fiction, 40; on generosity and self-sacrifice, 31–32; on history and revolution, 27–28, 32–33, 39; reading practices of, 22, 29–30, 41–43; refusing authorial position and, 24; Spencer's influence on, 34, 35, 41; "world-state" and, 16, 22, 25, 32–33, 35–39, 41, 115

Harijan (newspaper), 69, 74, 77, 78–80, 83

heterogeneity: in comparative literature, 12, 16, 126; as heteronomous, x, 12, 117, 126, 119; social collectivity and, 5, 46, 55, 56, 63, 117, 119, 124

Hind Swaraj (Gandhi), 69, 70, 72–73, 77, 85–90

Hindustan Ghadr (newspaper), 19, 26

Hindustan Socialist Republican Army (HSRA), 7, 20, 39, 92–93, 100, 108–10, 138n23

Hints for Self Culture (Har Dayal), 22–23, 25–27, 30–32, 35–37, 43

Hofmeyr, Isabel, 21, 85, 86, 89, 98

Hooker, Juliet, 125

Hugh of St. Victor, 127

Husserl, Edmund, 6, 48, 106

impossibility: critique and, 10–11, 14, 126–29; as political theory, 3, 18, 25, 54, 65, 105, 114–15

inconsequence: as political theory, 5, 8, 103–5, 115, 137n17; reading and, ix, xii, 94, 103–5, 126

"India and the Prerequisites of Communism" (Ambedkar), 54, 56–57

Indian independence, xiii, 45, 114

Indian Mutiny (1857), 19, 20, 26, 27–28, 33, 42

Indian Opinion (periodical), 85, 86

"The Indian Peasant" (Har Dayal), 24, 27, 41

Indian Sociologist (periodical), 34

Irish Republican Army, 20, 96

Islam, 26, 121, 149n22

Jaaware, Aniket, 46, 48–49, 65, 120, 123, 152n79, 165n26

Jaffrelot, Christopher, 123

Jallianwala Bagh Massacre (1919), 20

James, Henry, 11

James, William, 24, 34, 55, 58, 106

Jat-Pat Todak Mandal, 59–60

Johnson, Barbara, 16

Jones, William, 50, 62, 148n18, 149n28, 154n12

Konuk, Kader, 127

Kapila, Shruti, 34, 87, 165n34

Kartar Singh Sarabha, 19–20, 47, 109

King, Martin Luther, Jr., 87

Krishnavarma, Shyamji, 34, 157n64

Lahore Resolution (1940), 121

Lajpat Rai, Lala, 20, 93, 95

Lal, Chaman, 97, 98, 101

The Laws of Manu. See *Manusmriti*

Lenin, Vladimir, 95, 101

Lerer, Seth, 128, 143n87, 163n73, 168n80

liberalism, 9, 14, 53, 56, 59, 68, 137n17, 139n33; British Empire and, x, xiii, 90, 115, 141n68; self-culture books on, xii, 32, 41; as subject, 46, 63, 73–74, 118, 149n47, 157n67

London, Jack, 39–40, 95, 96

Macaulay, T. B., ix, x, xiii

Maclean, Kama, 6, 93, 99, 117

Mahad Protest (1927), 45, 53, 120–21

Majeed, Javed, 70

Mani, B. Venkat, 17, 135n15

Manusmriti (*The Laws of Manu*), 50–54, 61–62, 120

Marriott, David, 119, 136n8, 138n25, 153n97, 164nn9-10,19–20,23

Martinique, 1, 114

Marx, Karl, 9–10, 55, 94, 95, 100, 101, 145n21, 149n18

Marxism, 20, 37, 39, 101, 103, 122

Masuzawa, Tomoko, 49, 50

Mazzini, Giuseppe, xi, 32, 87, 111

McAleer, John, 67, 90

Melas, Natalie, 140nn53–55, 149n20

Mill, John Stuart, 95, 137n17, 164n13

Mimesis (Auerbach), 10–11, 18, 107, 126–29, 140n57

Modern Review, 21, 30

Moffat, Chris, 102, 107, 159n21

Morris, William, 22, 25, 38, 149n18

Mukherjee, Arun, 48, 55, 56, 57

Müller, Max, 50, 148n18, 149n23

Nagaraj, D. R., 82, 84

Nazism, 10, 12, 52, 75, 125, 129

negritude, 139n32

Nehru, Jawaharlal, 93, 109, 114

Newton, Adam Zachary, 11, 138n24

Nietzsche, Friedrich, 51–52

Olivelle, Patrick, 149n28

Omvedt, Gail, 122, 148, 162n45

192 / INDEX

Pakistan, xiii, 118, 121
Parel, Anthony, 86, 87, 157n65
philology, 4–5, 6, 8, 12, 167n72; Ambedkar's use of, 46, 50, 52–53; anticolonialism linked to, 13–14, 16, 18, 36, 113, 140n52, 143n85; categorization and hierarchy in, 49–50; disciplinary history of, 48–49
"The Philosophy of the Bomb," 109–10
Poona Pact (1932), 45, 82–83, 122
Porter, James, 128, 142n77, 143n87, 150n38, 167nn72–73
postcolonialism: anticolonial thought and, 3, 5, 23, 25, 93–94, 103, 162n63; decoloniality vs., 137–38n18; as national independence, xiii; as utopianism, 2, 3, 21, 116
Progressive Writers' Association (PWA), 108
Proust, Marcel, 11
Public Libraries Act (India, 1948), xiii–xiv

Ranganathan, S. R., vii–x; critique of Macaulay by, x–xi; in library system formation, xiii; readers given primacy by, x, xi; utopianism of, xi–xii, xiv
Rao, Anupama, 48, 116, 121, 122, 146n43
reading: 4–5, 11–12; Ambedkar's theory of, 47–48, 54; as anticolonialism, ix–x, xii–xiii, 16–17, 21, 22, 85–86, 102–4, 113; Bhagat Singh's theory and practice of, 100–4; Gandhi and, 85–86, 89–90; Har Dayal's practice of, 22, 29–30, 41–43
revolution: Bhagat Singh and, 8, 20, 25, 93–95, 99–100, 102–5, 110, 115; Bolshevik, 8, 101, 106; French, 45, 53; Har Dayal and, 27–28, 32–33, 39; inconsequentiality and, xii, 94, 104; *inquilab zindabad*, 20, 25, 93; in perpetuity, 25; as philosophy, 19, 33; reading as, 97, 99, 105, 117; as recognizably political, 26–27, 100, 103, 110
Robbins, Bruce, 142n71, 167n64
Rousseau, Jean-Jacques, 95, 158n6
Ruskin, John, 87, 157n67
Russell, Bertrand, 95, 101, 162n64

Said, Edward, 11, 13, 49, 106–7, 126–27, 137n15, 141n61, 144n9

Sanger, Margaret, 69–70, 77–81
Sartre, Jean-Paul, 1–2, 119
satyagraha, 72–79, 86–90, 110, 150n42
Savarkar, V. D., 28, 157n64
Sawhney, Simona, 89, 99, 107
Schlegel, Friedrich, 9–10
Scott, David, 3, 158n5
Sinclair, Upton, 95–97, 98, 101
Singh, Bhagat. *See* Bhagat Singh
Skaria, Ajay, 71, 74, 75, 76, 83, 88, 123, 138n30, 150n8
sociology, 22, 95, 147n70; Ambedkar and, 8, 44–46, 59, 63, 148–49n18; disciplinary history of, 48–52, 55
Spencer, Herbert, xii, 22, 25, 33–35, 38, 41, 69, 87
Sukhdev, 100, 108
Swaraj, 72–74, 108, 109, 114. *See also Hind Swaraj* (Gandhi)

Tagore, Rabindranath, 69–70, 75, 77, 81–82, 95, 97
Tarde, Gabriel, 63, 149n30
Teltumbde, Anand, 53, 151n60
Theosophy, 16, 70, 72, 97
Thoreau, Henry David, 87, 124, 158n6
Trotsky, Leon, 95, 106

Untouchables. *See* Dalits

vitalism, 55, 57, 64, 68

Wellek, René, 107, 140n57
Whitman, Walt, 24, 95
"Why I Am an Atheist" (Bhagat Singh), 105, 110
Wilde, Oscar, 100, 157n67
Woolf, Virginia, 11, 127–28, 129
world literature, 11, 16, 17, 36, 68, 126, 141n61, 142n69, 143n85, 150n30
The Wretched of the Earth (Fanon), 1–3, 6, 113, 117, 119
Wright, Richard, 124–25

Yashpal, 100, 108–9

J. Daniel Elam is Assistant Professor of Comparative Literature at the University of Hong Kong.

www.ingramcontent.com/pod-product-compliance
Lightning Source LLC
Chambersburg PA
CBHW020109020526
44112CB00033B/1115